Kermit Culture

Kermit Culture

Critical Perspectives on Jim Henson's Muppets

Edited by JENNIFER C. GARLEN
and ANISSA M. GRAHAM

McFarland & Company, Inc., Publishers
Jefferson, North Carolina, and London

For the lovers, the dreamers
and everyone who helped
make this book happen

LIBRARY OF CONGRESS CATALOGUING-IN-PUBLICATION DATA

Kermit culture : critical perspectives on Jim Henson's Muppets /
  edited by Jennifer C. Garlen and Anissa M. Graham.
       p.   cm.
  Includes bibliographical references and index.

  ISBN 978-0-7864-4259-1
  softcover : 50# alkaline paper

  1. Muppet show (Television program)   I. Garlen, Jennifer C.,
1972–   II. Graham, Anissa M., 1973–
PN1992.77.M853K48   2009
791.45'72 — dc22   2009011916

British Library cataloguing data are available

©2009 Jennifer C. Garlen and Anissa M. Graham.
All rights reserved

*No part of this book may be reproduced or transmitted in any form
or by any means, electronic or mechanical, including photocopying
or recording, or by any information storage and retrieval system,
without permission in writing from the publisher.*

Cover images ©2009 Shutterstock

Manufactured in the United States of America

McFarland & Company, Inc., Publishers
  Box 611, Jefferson, North Carolina 28640
  www.mcfarlandpub.com

Table of Contents

Preface   1

Part One : Audience Participation

How to Become a Muppet; or, The Great Muppet Paper
BEN UNDERWOOD   9

The Muppets as a Metaphor for the Self
GIDEON HABERKORN   25

Stuffed Suits and Hog-Wild Desire
LYNNE D. SCHNEIDER   40

The Muppet Show Re-Forms the Fringe
ANISSA M. GRAHAM   54

Part Two : Adaptation and Performance

From Muppetry to Puppetry
JENNIFER STOESSNER   71

The Muppets and Shakespeare
HUGH H. DAVIS   81

"Starring Kermit the Frog as Bob Cratchit": Muppets as Actors
GINGER STELLE   92

A Rainbow for the 21st Century: *The Muppets' Wizard of Oz* and the Reimagination of the American Myth
ALISSA BURGER   103

Gonzo, (the Great) Cultural Critic
JENNIFER C. GARLEN   116

Part Three : Theories and Strategies

The American Journey Narrative in the Muppets Movies
TARA K. PARMITER   129

It's Time to Get Together for Some Sex and Violence on *The Muppet Show*?
    KATHLEEN E. KENNEDY   142

"British to a Fang, British to a Whisker": Reconsidering *The Muppet Show*'s National Identity
    RAYNA DENISON   154

The Muppet Show as Educational Critique
    JULIE G. MAUDLIN   170

The Uniquely Strong but Feminine Miss Piggy
    MARYANNE FISHER and ANTHONY COX   181

Muppets and Money
    ANDREW LEAL   202

Appendix: The Muppet Show   217
About the Contributors   223
Index   227

Preface

"This is a narrative of very heavy-duty proportions."
Dr. Teeth, *The Muppet Movie*

Television viewers in the late 1970s found a landscape filled with comedy. Thinking comedies, like *All in the Family*, *Maude*, *M*A*S*H*, and *The Jeffersons*, asked their audiences to consider major social issues, like race relations and sexual equality. Then there were the more standard comedies, like *Three's Company* and *Laverne and Shirley*, with their reliance on broad slapstick to get a laugh. In many ways, the decade of the 1970s was the age of the sitcom. Added into this cauldron of hilarity in 1976 was *The Muppet Show*. Most comedies in the 1970s involved a fixed cast of characters who had weekly adventures to which the audience played voyeur. *The Muppet Show*, while it involved a fixed cast, departed from the sitcom formula with its incorporation of the variety show format so popular in the early days of television. Perhaps the most obvious difference between *The Muppet Show* and its competition was its cast. The types (a harried organizer, a bossy woman, a bumbling sidekick) were common on all sitcoms, but the actors on *The Muppet Show* were startlingly different because they were puppets! Still, these puppets held their own against live actors both within the confines of the series and without in the ratings.

A brief history of *The Muppet Show* offers some insight into the elements that made it unique among television comedy programs. Jim Henson and his core group of puppeteers had already been working with Muppets for years when they first created *The Muppet Show*. Early versions of the Muppets had appeared on television commercials, *The Ed Sullivan Show*, *The Jimmy Dean Show* and *Sam and Friends*. Muppet characters like Big Bird and Bert and Ernie had become well-known to American children after *Sesame Street* first hit the airwaves in 1969, but Henson and his performers wanted to do more with the art form and push the envelope for puppetry, and this meant that they needed to create their own venue in which to pursue those goals. Thus the concept for *The Muppet Show* was born. When the half-hour syndicated program aired in the United States, it appeared in the adult-oriented prime time slot, indicating the scope of its intended viewing audience and differentiating it from other televised puppet shows. Each episode was built around the appearance of a guest star with numerous sketches by regular Muppet characters. The show's writers, including Henson, Jack Burns and Jerry Juhl, among others, worked with the puppeteers to create a wide range of sketches, from the tastefully classical to the truly strange. The chief puppeteers over the course of the show included Henson, Frank Oz, Dave Goelz, Richard Hunt, Steve Whitmire, Jerry Nelson, Louise Gold, Kathy Mullen, Eren Ozker and John Lovelady. Each puppeteer had particular Muppet characters to perform but also worked large numbers of Muppets for chorus lines and crowd scenes, which allowed the puppeteers to develop minor Muppet characters into major ones over time and to upstage one another with scene-stealing performances by ostensibly "background" characters. The dynamic nature of the show meant that viewers never knew what to expect from one episode to the next. The fact that no human actors formed part of the regular cast might have accounted for some of the difficulty that *The Muppet Show* faced in attracting guest stars during the program's first season, but the appearance of Rudolf Nureyev in the second season proved a turning point, and for the rest of its career the show drew from a wide range of celebrities, from Liberace and Julie Andrews to Johnny Cash and Roger Moore.

By the end of their five year run on television, the Muppets had transcended their original medium to become true multi-media celebrities. They appeared in books like *The Muppet Show Book* in 1978, their first movie, *The Muppet Movie*, was released in 1979, and they became familiar icons in the world of personal accessories from clothing to jewelry. Today, Muppets are everywhere. We see them on billboards and buttons, on television commercials and talk shows. Nobody has to explain who they are; consumers recognize Kermit and Miss Piggy the way they recognize Marilyn Monroe and Mickey Mouse. Recently, the release of the series on DVD has helped the Muppets' presence to expand again with new lines of products and a sizable presence on the Internet, including their very own Wiki (http://muppet.wikia.com/wiki/Main_Page), an online encyclopedia written by devotees of the show. The Muppets' popularity today is as great as it was at the height of the original show's run, thanks in part to savvy marketing by their various parent organizations over the years, including the Walt Disney Company. In fact, Disney's work to perpetuate the Muppets' appeal predates its official acquisition of the characters in 2004; Disney integrated an entire theme park attraction featuring the Muppets into its Hollywood Studios park in 1991 and California Adventure park in 2001, thus ensuring that millions of children and adults from around the world would continue to be exposed to the Muppets in all their zany glory.

Good marketing certainly accounts for some of the Muppets' continued success, but other elements played a significant part in forging their original appeal. To begin with, the innovative puppetry that formed the core of the program attracted adult audiences as well as children. There had been successful television programs featuring puppets before: *The Howdy Doody Show*, *Kukla, Fran and Ollie*, *Captain Kangaroo* and *H.R. Pufnstuf* all used puppets to great effect, but they were simpler shows, more focused on entertaining children than their parents. *The Muppet Show* merged many different types of puppetry, including traditional hand puppets, marionettes, rod puppets and full body puppets, into a single show, which set it apart from other puppet programs; furthermore, the sheer artistry that the Muppet puppeteers demonstrated — in tap dancing numbers, motorcycle rides, and intricate puppet performances of all kinds—fascinated adult viewers. Many of the programs featuring puppets before and after the Muppets incorporated a strong didactic element, as well, using the puppet characters to teach children moral lessons about sharing or rudimentary ideas about reading and math. *The Muppet Show*, however, eschewed such overtly didactic concerns in favor of a variety show format that took its cues from vaudeville and popular adult programs like *The Ed Sullivan Show*, *The Tonight Show* and *Rowan & Martin's Laugh-In*. The Muppets' connection to this kind of programming ran deep; many of the characters and sketches that eventually appeared on *The Muppet Show* had originally debuted on *The Ed Sullivan Show*. Additional influences came from the show's production in Britain, where *Monty Python's Flying Circus* and *The Goon Show* popularized the kind of absurdist comedy that *The Muppet Show* frequently embraced. Each episode of the original series featured a sketch intended solely for British audiences; these sketches were cut for commercial time on American television. These exclusive British segments, and many segments that aired in the United States, as well, evoked London music hall culture and featured traditional tunes that British audiences would have recognized immediately, although American viewers ignorant of their origin might have found them odd choices, even for *The Muppet Show*.

The Muppet characters reflect these diverse influences and ideals in their personalities; sophisticated, nuanced and highly individuated, they nonetheless embody the conventional character types of classic situational comedy. Kermit, the harassed manager of the show, functions as its voice of reason and acts as straight man to many of the jokes and gags. He also performs the role of host and interviews guest stars in traditional talk show style. Miss Piggy, the resident diva, evolves from first season chorus girl to fully fledged star over the course of the series; she takes her star status seriously, domineering her co-stars, guest stars and especially her beloved frog. Fozzie, the bumbling bear comedian, peddles his vaudevillian shtick to a tough audience, but his insecurity and genuine sweetness make him lovable even when his jokes are terrible. Fozzie also often works as Kermit's sidekick, the Costello to Kermit's Abbot. The relationships between these three major characters clearly connect *The Muppet Show* to the situational comedy; they persist over time but develop and fluctuate as the characters interact with one another.

The backstage scenes draw mainly from this sitcom tradition, and many of the show's "on stage" sketches take their cues from musical variety programs, but *The Muppet Show* also manages to run the gamut of television genres, particularly those that were most popular during the era when the program was originally on the air. The recurring sketches that make up some of *The Muppet Show's* most memorable bits function as parodies of these genres. "Pigs in Space" is a hilarious mixture of *Star Trek*, Flash Gordon and Buck Rogers, with some *Dr. Strangelove* allusions thrown in for good measure. "Veterinarian's Hospital" mocks the medical drama and soap opera simultaneously, taking its inspiration from the long-running *General Hospital* but also nodding to shows like *Marcus Welby, MD*, and *M*A*S*H*. "Bear on Patrol" skewers the cop show, "Muppet News Flash" parodies the newscast, and "Muppet Sports" takes on Howard Cosell and ABC's *Wide World of Sports*. Additional characters add even more layers and genres to the sketches that make up the show: Gonzo epitomizes the obscure performance *artiste*, Bunsen Honeydew and Beaker mock scientific methods in "Muppet Labs," Statler and Waldorf function as equal parts peanut gallery and Greek chorus, and the Electric Mayhem both parody and perpetuate the myth of the rock band.

Given this complexity and the enduring appeal of *The Muppet Show* and its cast, it is surprising that so few scholars have thus far offered critical readings of them. Only a handful of articles and essays have been published (although *Sesame Street* has, of course, drawn considerable attention over the years because of its role as an educational program). In the work that has been published, the Muppets tend to appear as examples or means to the ends of the authors' other arguments: they themselves are not the actual subjects of the discussions. The release of the original show on DVD should allow for some correction to this critical oversight. The maturation of Generation X scholars, who literally grew up with the show, also means that more work is likely to be done, especially considering the rising recognition of the importance of popular culture studies as a whole.

This collection of essays seeks to begin to fill this gap. *Kermit Culture* represents the work and ideas of a global community of scholars and Muppet enthusiasts. Although we recognize the appeal and importance of the larger Muppet universe, including *Sesame Street, Fraggle Rock, The Dark Crystal, Jim Henson's The Storyteller, Farscape* and the many additional creations of The Jim Henson Company and Jim Henson's Creature Shop, our efforts here focus on the core group of Muppets from *The Muppet Show* and the other films and productions that feature them. The essays presented in this volume approach different elements of *The Muppet Show* and different Muppet characters and themes using a wide variety of critical perspectives and academic disciplines.

The first part, "Audience Participation," presents essays that focus on the Muppets' relationships with their audiences, both real and imaginary. Ben Underwood's "How to Become a Muppet; or, The Great Muppet Paper" focuses attention on the ways in which shared aspirations unite the Muppets and make viewers become part of the Muppet community. Gideon Haberkorn investigates the discourse and content of the show as a means of examining personal identity in "The Muppets as a Metaphor for the Self." In "Stuffed Suits and Hog-Wild Desire," Lynne D. Schneider evaluates the roles and significance of Statler and Waldorf, the Muppet Theater's resident hecklers. In "*The Muppet Show* Re-Forms the Fringe," Anissa M. Graham contends that the series realigns viewers' notions of normal and fringe culture through its characters and guest stars.

Part Two, "Adaptation and Performance," collects essays that offer interpretations of the Muppets as performed characters, actors and adaptors of cultural material. In "From Muppetry to Puppetry," Jennifer Stoessner delves into Henson's career as a puppeteer and *The Muppet Show's* relationship to and promotion of puppetry as an innovative art form. Hugh H. Davis explores the Muppets' use of Shakespearean texts and influences in "The Muppets and Shakespeare." Ginger Stelle's essay, "'Starring Kermit the Frog as Bob Cratchit': Muppets as Actors," considers the complex duality of the Muppets as fictional characters and performers. Alissa Burger critiques the Muppets' revision of L. Frank Baum's classic novel in "A Rainbow for the 21st Century: *The Muppets' Wizard of Oz* and the Reimagination of American Myth." Jennifer C. Garlen offers a reading of Gonzo as *The Muppet Show's* chief agitator for art and culture in "Gonzo, (the Great) Cultural Critic."

Part Three, "Theories and Strategies," offers essays that view the Muppet characters, programs and films through various critical lenses. Tara K. Parmiter discusses the Muppets' use of travel as a metaphor in "The American Journey Narrative in the Muppets Movies." Kathleen E. Kennedy investigates the changing roles of sexuality and violence over the course of the television series in "It's Time to Get Together for Some Sex and Violence on *The Muppet Show*?" In "'British to a Fang, British to a Whisker': Reconsidering *The Muppet Show's* National Identity," Rayna Denison argues that the show's largely American cast and team of writers do not prevent it from being a quintessentially British creation. Julie G. Maudlin analyzes the relationship between *The Muppet Show* and the state of American education in the late 1970s in "*The Muppet Show* as Educational Critique." In "The Uniquely Strong but Feminine Miss Piggy," Maryanne Fisher and Anthony Cox evaluate Miss Piggy's use of traditionally masculine and feminine behaviors, making the claim that Miss Piggy's duality allows her to have universal appeal. Andrew Leal rounds out the section with his examination of the theme of consumerism and commercialism in "Muppets and Money."

This volume, intended for both scholarly and general audiences, serves merely as an introduction to the wealth of ideas and readings that *The Muppet Show* and its characters can inspire. Our goals are to demonstrate the breadth and scope of the Muppets as cultural icons and to offer some understanding of why they hold so much meaning for so many viewers around the world. We hope, too, that this collection of essays will inspire future critical readings that explore the wider world of the Muppets and Jim Henson's creations, so that we can eventually gain a fuller, clearer picture of the impact one imaginative man and a handful of felt has had on the world we live in today.

Part One

Audience Participation

How to Become a Muppet; or, The Great Muppet Paper[1]
Ben Underwood

> "All my life I've wanted to own a thousand frog leg restaurants, and you're the key, Greenie."
> Doc Hopper, *The Muppet Movie*

Doc Hopper proclaims his ambition as a restaurateur to explain why he's been harassing Kermit the Frog for the preceding hour of *The Muppet Movie*. Hopper believes Kermit must become the official television spokes frog of Doc Hopper's French Fried Frog Legs in order for the restaurant chain to expand. Kermit has earlier refused Hopper's business proposition in no uncertain terms: "All I can see are millions of frogs on tiny crutches." While the confrontation between Kermit and Hopper seems quite unusual given our expectations for a Hollywood feature film, perhaps the strangest part of all is that, in the midst of a pseudo–Western man-to-frog showdown, Hopper professes his life-long aspiration: "to own a thousand frog leg restaurants." Kermit recognizes Hopper's explanation as a confession of ambition, and responds, "I've got a dream, too, but it's about singing and dancing and making people happy. That's the kind of dream that gets better the more people you share it with, and, well, I've found a whole bunch of friends, who have the same dream, and it kind of makes us like a family." In essence, Kermit counters Hopper's dream with a more inviting alternative. Rather than success in the restaurant business, he and his friends want to become famous entertainers.

Showdowns are not typical narrative sites for contemplating characters' most tender hopes. Such scenes more commonly settle plots: one character wins, another loses. This sequence contains such resolution when Animal, thanks to Dr. Bunsen Honeydew's Insta-Grow Pills, enlarges to the size of a parade balloon and scares away Hopper and his minions. Yet even with Animal literally looming over the scene at his "sadly temporary" enormous size, Kermit and Hopper's debate casts a larger shadow over the film than the Animal-induced denouement. In fact, although dreams don't usually fit into showdowns, the film has been building to this particular clash of dreams all along. The dream confrontation is essential to understanding not only this scene, or *The Muppet Movie*, but also the entire body of Muppet work. From plots to production choices, dreams drive the Muppets.[2]

The point of this scene, and of many Muppet productions, is that it's better to have "the kind of dream that gets better the more people you share it with" than a hermetic one like Hopper's. This is not to say that one should try to be an entertainer rather than a restaurateur. For the Muppets, sharing your dream counts. What you dream of doing, or the content of your dream, matters little, if at all. The imperative to share drives the Muppets to cultivate their dream not only among themselves, but also to incorporate the audience, and this inclusion functions in both the Muppet films and *The Muppet Show*. The Muppets' *modus operandi* is to invite viewers to share the dream, and in effect, to become Muppets, to Muppetize. Not to put too fine a point on it, to watch the Muppets is to be a Muppet. What the audience's incorporation into the Muppet cadre means is that what is most endearing about the Muppets — that the fan feels like one of them — is simultaneously what is most insidious about them — the fan can't help but feel like one of them. The viewer's extra-consensual incorporation into the Muppet fold bolsters audience affection for the characters by drawing the audience into the same identity group with the Muppets. This move, along with the emphasis on dreams, aligns the Muppets with two intimately related and deeply entrenched American ideologies: emphasizing identity over ideas and the pursuit of happiness.

Many viewers likely regard the contrasting contents of Hopper's and Kermit's dreams as the essence of their conflict, and it's easy to see the appeal of this interpretation. Who wouldn't want to be a movie star, especially if the alternative is running frog leg restaurants? Despite the difference in job title, however, Kermit and Hopper have a great deal in common. Their plans both involve financial success. Hopper is a self-proclaimed businessman, seeking to build his chain-restaurant empire, and Kermit, while he wants to sing and dance and make people happy, sets out for Hollywood in response to World Wide Studios' open casting call for "frogs wishing to become rich and famous." That Kermit and Hopper both seek financial success makes it virtually impossible to read a critique of capitalism into the Muppets. We might prefer Kermit's method of accumulating wealth to Hopper's, but they are both working within the logic of capital. This complicity with capitalism makes a great deal of sense given the Muppets' emphasis on identity and dreams, both of which are important ideological supports of American capitalism. Along with the *Onion*'s fictitious op-ed author Larry Groznic, we may wish to find significance in the fact that, in rejecting Hopper's business proposition, "Kermit refuse[s] to Judas his race to a corrupt corporation, even though it mean[s] giving up his dream of stardom," but we should recognize that Kermit chooses among various capitalist alternatives. He does not interrogate the terms of those choices. By raising this point, I'm not suggesting that the Muppets should (or even that they could, given their station in commercial television) critique capitalism. This economic perspective suggests a frontier of the seemingly boundless idealism that runs through the Muppets: The Muppets are a product of commercial television. This parameter is also useful in understanding other facets of Jim Henson's career. For instance, he stopped making commercials with his characters once they began appearing on *Sesame Street* in 1969 because he saw a conflict between using his creations to educate and using them to sell (Morrow 72). Such a move resists unfettered capitalism, as does Kermit's refusal to become Hopper's spokesfrog, but not capitalism itself. The same could be said of Henson's approach to Muppet merchandise: "There's a [...] difference between a kid seeing a character on the screen and really wanting a Fozzie Bear that you make available to him — and selling a toy and turning out a television show based on that" (qtd. in Durrett 86). So while Henson and Kermit are uneasy about certain money-making techniques, they are both, like Hopper, consummate capitalists.

A related commonality between Kermit and Hopper is that they both take for granted that dreams rationalize actions. The Horatio-Alger-style rags-to-riches myth that undergirds capitalism depends on the pursuit of dreams. Kermit leaves the swamp to follow his dream, and Hopper chases him to follow his own. The phrase "following your dream," Walter Benn Michaels argues, "at this moment in American history appears to have almost talismanic power" (194). Michaels's point is that one can justify any action, no matter how implausible, by claiming that you're "following your dream." Michaels claims of *American Idol*, "What the show presents is both a vision of the world in which the truly talented will succeed (the American dream!) and a vision of the high level of self-deception — I'm talented! I will succeed! — required to live happily in that world (the American delusion)" (194–95). While Michaels's point has far-reaching political and social implications, to understand how "following your dream" can shift from valiant to delusional, think of any of the throngs of the talentless who are convinced they will win the show's competition. The pursuit of one's dreams at the cost of one's grip on the external world has been a topic of Western cultural products as least as far back as Don Quixote's attack on windmills. *The Muppet Movie* takes the importance of following one's dreams, even when they are delusional, as a fundamental premise. As different as the protagonist and antagonist are, their common belief in the explanatory power of dreams unites them. Dreams, in the movie, rationalize any action, from flying in an expert frog killer, to forming a showbiz partnership with a congenitally unfunny bear-comedian. The utility and commonality of dreams also put everyone on the same playing field; from chicken-obsessed plumbers to Miss Bogen County, everyone has a dream.

When it comes to the Muppets, one can't place much emphasis on dream content because it's difficult, beyond a few generalities, to draw from the film (or anywhere else) precisely what the Muppets' dreams consist of. The Muppet identity takes precedence over Muppet ideas. Other than some relatively uncontroversial statements about positivity and world peace, Henson never explicitly spelled out the motivations behind his creations. This observation is not a denigration of Henson or his work. He was not, after all, attempting to articulate a coherent philosophical position, but I would contend that he was channeling distinctly American traditions and ideologies. Henson's vagueness is significant given that so many fans regard the Muppets as embodying an important message. Most of these fans would be hard pressed, however, to explain what that message is. Some examples of Henson's admirable yet hazy explanations of his dreams follow: Sidney I. Dobrin has, quite correctly, as Henson's notes attest (Finch, *The Works* 200), emphasized the ecological messages in Henson's work. Additionally, Henson told the team developing *Fraggle Rock* that their "task was to create a series that was going to stop war in the world" (Kenworthy qtd. in Finch, *The Works* 202). In notes toward a reflective essay on his career, Henson wrote, "I believe that we can use television and film to be an influence for good; that we can help to shape the thoughts of children and adults in a positive way. [...] When I was young, my ambition was to be one of the people who made a difference in this world. My hope still is to leave the world a little bit better for having been here" (qtd. in Finch, *The Works* 241). Whatever the message Henson intended for any given project, the idea that dreams justify actions was important to him throughout his career; indeed, he uses the idea to justify his own actions.

Even though the difference in the contents of Hopper's and Kermit's dreams doesn't amount to a substantial disparity, their aspirations contrast in another way, which proves to be the soul of the showdown. What matters is not what you dream of, but whom you dream with. Kermit asks Hopper, "Once you get all those restaurants, who're you going to share it [sic] with? Who are your friends, Doc?" In Kermit's own assessment, the meaningful difference between himself and Hopper is that he shares his dream with his friends, while Hopper hasn't invited anyone to join him in his franchised (ad)venture. Hopper recognizes the force of Kermit's question. He replies, "I got [sic] lots of friends," and turns to his assistant Max as an example. When Max responds by shaking his head, Hopper loses the showdown of dreams even before Animal becomes enormous. If Max, and Hopper's other associates, had said, 'We're with you, Doc. Let's follow our dream of building a frog-leg-restaurant empire together,' then the terms and resolution of the conflict would be drastically altered. In this hypothetical case, Animal's arbitrary intervention would have been solely responsible for Kermit and friends winning the day, and the issue of sharing dreams would not be central, as it is in the actual film. The point of the showdown, then, isn't that you should sing and dance instead of frying frog legs, but rather that you should find friends who share your dream.

The arguments I make about how Kermit the Frog and company share their dream, and Muppetize their audience, account, at least partially, for the success of these characters. As is often cited, at the height of its popularity, *The Muppet Show* was broadcast in 100 countries and watched by 235 million viewers (Dobrin 236, among others). James Robert Parish observes that during *The Muppet Show*'s run, "the Muppets became the most commercially successful puppets in world history," and claims that "[t]he show continues to delight new viewers in constant reruns" (3), not to mention the recent and planned DVD releases. The Staff of Henson Associates writes that the Muppets "are probably the most widely recognized puppets in history, and their two leading players, Kermit the Frog and Miss Piggy, are lurking on the threshold of that pantheon once reserved for the likes of Tracy and Hepburn, Garbo and Gilbert, Bogart and Bacall" (34). Indeed, in 2002 Kermit verifiably crossed into the Hollywood pantheon when he was awarded a star on the walk of fame. (Henson and Big Bird already had stars.) When asked, while *The Muppet Show* was in production, to explain its popularity, Lord Lew Grade, the financial backer of this and many other Henson projects, made reference to the talent of the performers, but ultimately concluded, "There's no accounting for this kind of success. It's a phenomenon, and that's all you can really say about it" (qtd. in Finch, *Of Muppets* 25). If anyone could have illuminated the Muppets' success, it should have been Lord Grade. He was the one who saw the potential of the show when every major U.S. network turned it down. We might expect an answer about the show's broad demographic appeal, which is the argument Henson himself makes in the pitch reel he assembled to sell the show to CBS (*Season One*). Instead, the television mogul asserts the impossibility of explanation. Despite Lord Grade's demurring, I would, in anticipation of an argument I articulate below, attribute the popularity of the Muppets to the fact that when you watch the Muppets, you become a Muppet.

The Muppet Movie, I have argued, advocates teaming up with people who have the same dream as you, and *The Muppets Take Manhattan* follows suit.[3] The frame story of *The Muppet Movie*—the Muppets are watching a screening of their own film—emphasizes the importance of the troupe's assemblage, and the narrative dramatizes it. In the screening room, Robin asks, "Uncle Kermit, is this about how the Muppets really got started?" Kermit tells him, "Well, it's sort of approximately how it happened." *The Muppets Take Manhattan* offers an alternative history of the group's genesis and expansion. Unlike the first movie, in *The Muppets Take Manhattan*, the core crew is assembled from the beginning. Kermit, however, is convinced that their dream of performing their musical, *Manhattan Melodies*, on Broadway won't come true because "there's still something missing" from the show. The climax of the film comes when Kermit figures out what the something is: "That's it! That's what's been missing from the show! That's what we need! More frogs and dogs and bears and chickens and whatever!" He tells the Muppets' new friends, "You're not gonna watch the show! You're gonna be in the show!" As in *The Muppet Movie*, the real purpose of the dream is finding people who share it.

The point of these films is that you should share your dreams because the people (or puppets) who share them with you become "like a family," as Kermit puts it. The movies establish a group identity based on the common dream and demonstrate how new members join the family. The idea of the dream family also accounts for the Muppets' method of recruiting their audience for *The Muppet Show*. In short, watching the show amounts to trying out at an open casting call for potential Muppets "wishing to become rich and famous." As with the like-minded collaborators Kermit accumulates on his way to Hollywood (in *The Muppet Movie*), and the friends the Muppets make at their temp jobs (in *The Muppets Take Manhattan*), the viewers of *The Muppet Show* become part of the troupe. They become Muppets.

It's possible to join the Muppets because they're not a closed clique. On the show, you often can't tell who is a part of the Muppet cast and who isn't. The boundary between performer and stage crew, or between performer and audience, is indiscernible. I'm not making a pseudo-deconstructive claim that these categories are indeterminate; rather, my point is that, on *The Muppet Show*, these groups are not sharply defined or mutually exclusive. This purposeful ambiguity makes the Muppet ensemble permeable. The permeability of the Muppet troupe is why Kermit says the shared dream "kind of makes us like a family," instead of saying that it 'makes us a family.' The traditional Western definition of *family* is a group of people related by blood or legally binding marriages. The Muppets, in contrast, are the kind of family you can join just by sharing a dream. Since it's hard to pin down what the dream consists of, it's not as if you can be Muppetized simply by saying or thinking that you share the dream. You can't coherently profess to share a dream that you can't articulate. The Muppets, then, don't find recruits by offering an appealing ideological or philosophical program in their dream; instead, the Muppets treat their viewers as if they already share the dream and are thus already part of the group.

The trans-categorical status of many characters on the show blurs the boundary between performer and crew. Characters like Hilda the Seamstress, George the Janitor, Beau Regarde, and Scooter belong to the backstage crew, yet they make regular appearances on stage. Scooter's willingness to exploit the fact that his uncle owns the theater may account for his ability to break into performing, but it's more difficult to understand how George can be ordered to clean up the stage on which he will later perform. Equally inexplicably, Hilda is simultaneously in charge of altering costumes, bantering with guest stars, and introducing sketches. Kermit himself blurs standard theater responsibilities, operating as stage manager, master of ceremonies, and performer.

The uncertainty of roles results from complex play with numerous genres. Although it's not necessary to map out the show's rugged generic terrain in order to enjoy it, considering the logic of the show's negotiation of genre offers an entry point into understanding the Muppetization of the audience. The show itself is aware of its slippery generic status. At the beginning of the Rich Little episode (*Season Two*), Kermit welcomes viewers to "another half hour of whatever this is," and in the Jaye P. Morgan episode (*Season Two*), to "another one of those things entitled *The Muppet Show*." Christopher Finch suggests a wide variety of genre categories, all of which are appropriate: a backstage drama, a variety show, or a docu-drama about a mental institution (*Of Muppets* 28). As Finch's ingenious catalog attests, the show's generic possibilities are as madcap as its antics. Rather than concocting a single sufficiently complex description, or list of descriptions, I will parse out the show's negotiation of various sets of organizing conventions. Tracing this multi-generic trajectory will provide a handle on how the status of the audience shifts, depending on the generic conventions in play. To put the point another way, tracking the show's generic hybridity will reveal how it Muppetizes its fans.

Because it so obviously and pervasively permeates *The Muppet Show*, vaudeville offers a point of generic departure. Within this model, the Muppets put on a live performance in their theater before an in-house audience. What makes the already strange premise of anthropomorphic felt-and-fur animals putting on a stage show even more interesting is who occupies the theater seats — or rather, what. Reaction shots of an applauding audience recur in numerous episodes, and the reaction shots reveal that the staged performances are by Muppets, for Muppets. Though not exclusively, the action on stage is often filmed from the perspective of the theater audience. After the first season, the show's theme-song sequence emphasizes this perspective. As the Muppets take the stage and the orchestra begins to play, the television viewer can see the backs of other theater goers' heads at the bottom of the screen, in the foreground of the shot. If, as this perspective makes unavoidable, the television viewer imagines that she is watching from the audience of the Muppet theater, and the audience is composed of Muppets, then the television viewer must also imagine that she herself is a Muppet. Perhaps a syllogism will clarify my point: All theater audience members are Muppets. The television viewer's perspective makes her part of the theater audience. Therefore, the television viewer is a Muppet. Before you can check to see if you're sprouting blue fur, the situation becomes more complex.

As I've argued, it's often impossible to ascertain whether characters are members of the crew or the cast, and the composition of the Muppet theater audience makes the line between performer and audience equally difficult to adjudicate. The viewer watches the Muppets on television, while Muppets are watching Muppets in the theater. Some Muppets perform and others watch, but the viewer observes both groups. Moving from the vaudeville premise to thinking of *The Muppet Show* as, in some sense, what it is—a television puppet show—might seem to resolve the confusion of audience and performer. After all, human puppeteers operate both the performer-Muppets and the audience-Muppets, and the television viewer watches the performance of these real people. The puppet show paradigm might lead us to think that performer and audience are mutually exclusive, but the blurring of these roles is not so easily pushed aside. Dave Goelz, who performs the Great Gonzo among others, said of the Muppeteers, "We are the only performers in the world that [sic] are our audience at the same time!"[4] The Muppeteers were often highly appreciative of their own work. In his introduction to the Steve Martin episode, Brian Henson reveals that this particular episode didn't employ a laugh track. The cackling you hear is coming from the performers and crew who were unable to contain their reactions as they were filming (*Best of*).

This imbrication of puppet performer and audience results from the method of television puppetry that Henson began developing on his first show, *Sam and Friends*, in the mid-fifties. Finch elucidates one of Henson's innovative techniques of television puppetry: "Producers of earlier puppet programs on television had simply placed a camera in front of a traditional puppet theater and shown the proceedings from the viewpoint of someone sitting in the audience. Jim quickly realized that his real theater was the television set in the viewer's home" (*The Works* 18). Finch contends that Henson brings the Muppets' theater into the viewer's home. (I would add, as I've been arguing, that Henson also does the reverse: he brings the viewer into the imaginary theater.) In Henson's technique, the frame established by the camera replaces the traditional puppet theater. Rather than hiding behind a wall, the Muppeteers stay out of the shot. While they would sometimes conceal themselves behind a part of the set, they would often hold the Muppets above their heads. The camera would shoot only the action taking place six or more feet off the floor, leaving the Muppeteers completely out of the shot.

For this innovation in puppetry to function, the Muppeteers must keep their bodies entirely out of the frame. In order to do so and to be able to see what he was doing, Henson began performing while watching a monitor that showed him exactly what the television viewer saw. *Sam and Friends* was, like all early television, a live broadcast, and there was no difference between what Henson watched on his monitor as he was performing and what appeared on televisions in homes throughout the Washington D.C./Baltimore area during the five-minute broadcasts. The monitor system was also essential for *The Muppet Show*, which, although not live, still required the performers to be their own audience, as Goelz observes. If anyone could be said to be a Muppet, it would be the Muppeteers. They *are* the Muppets, if for no other reason than they bring the otherwise inert puppets to life. Yet even the Muppeteers are part of the audience.

If thinking of the program as vaudeville requires us to realize that *The Muppet Show* is by Muppets, for Muppets, then simultaneously, within the television-puppet-show framework, the show is by Muppeteers, for Muppeteers. The audience joins the performers, and the reciprocal also occurs: the performers join the audience. It might, at this point, seem that I'm implying that the show confuses the viewer with regard to the roles of various characters, or about her own status as a member of the audience or as a performer. In fact, the viewer unconsciously processes all the complications I've been discussing, and it is only when one pauses to parse out the logic of the show that these ambiguities of audience and performer emerge. While Kermit occupies an unusual mix of roles in the theater, to enjoy the show, the viewer never need worry that he's a performer, the emcee, and the stage manager. Yet this is not to say that I'm projecting complication. The Muppets rely on various logics, structures, and technologies that the viewer doesn't necessarily take into account. Of the technical devices that the Muppets employ, Henson explains, "Every time we use mechanics, we try to keep them very 'unmechanical.' As soon as the audience starts thinking about the cleverness of it all, it stops thinking about the performance. When the Muppets are on screen, I want the audience to believe in the moment" (qtd. in Staff 18–19). What Henson says here about the literal hidden machinery of *The Muppet Show* also applies to the figurative hidden machinery of the show's generic structure. You don't consider everything behind the scenes as you're enjoying the show, but without these machinations, there wouldn't be a show. In addition, the show personifies its self-consciousness of the blurring of the roles of spectator and performer in a three-headed Muppet who appears in the Vincent Price episode (*Season One*). The creature explains that one head is the straight man, another the comedian, and the third is the audience: "No matter how bad we are, we'll always love us." This character demonstrates that the show is invested in precisely the issues I've been discussing, and that one advantage of fusing performer and audience is that doing so facilitates empathy and appreciation. You are much more likely to love a show that you're a part of, in one sense or another.

Even after all of these complications of the audience and performer roles, we still haven't considered the implications of the fact that *The Muppet Show* is also a "backstage drama," as Finch correctly suggests. This dimension of the show furthers the performer/audience merger, and thus the viewer's Muppetization. Imagining yourself sitting in the Muppet theater makes you an audience-Muppet, and the backstage scenes continue your transformation by making you a performer-Muppet. This behind-the-scenes dimension was a facet of the show from its inception, including the even more generically thorny "Sex and Violence" pilot, and it gained momentum as the show developed. After the initial episodes of the first season, more of the show began taking place backstage, with guest stars appearing in as many or more backstage sequences as on-stage performances. For almost all of the first season, episodes begin, after the theme song, with Kermit in front of the red stage curtain introducing the first act. Later in the series, the show more typically employs a cold open that occurs backstage with Scooter calling out, "fifteen seconds to curtain, [insert guest star's name]!" followed by a quick gag set in the guest star's dressing room. With the backstage migration of the show, not only do the placement and frequency of sketches taking place off stage change, but also the content as well. Through much of the first season, "backstage drama" would aptly describe the vignettes that take place off stage. They deal mostly with backstage issues: problems with actors, scenes, costumes, etc. These sketches create a fairly simple dichotomy between the vaudeville show on the one hand, and the backstage drama on the other. As early as the end of the first season, however, one of Valerie Harper's biggest numbers takes place backstage. At this point — when the guest stars are performing backstage — the generic logic of the vaudeville/backstage-drama duality breaks down. Within the world of the show, which is to say, not thinking of it as a television puppet show, whom could Harper be performing for?

Fortunately, the show provides an answer. Before the song, Harper asks Kermit if she can audition for the opening number. When the song is over, we hear an applause track, as if, impossibly, Harper has been performing for the audience in the Muppet theater from backstage. The camera then pulls back to reveal a small crowd of the Muppet ensemble cheering Harper. The television viewer is privy to what is ostensibly a backstage audition watched only by the Muppets themselves. (Of course, the song constitutes the actual opening number of the television episode.) Apart from the fact that the viewer has to draw on several sets of conventions at once to make sense of this scene, seeing Harper's so-called audition creates a sense of being a Muppet insider. Not even the Muppet theater audience sees this performance, after all. The same points also apply to Ethel Merman's performance of "There's No Business Like Show Business" (*Season One*), and Merman's performance adds yet another generic wrinkle. She begins singing backstage to comfort Fozzie Bear, who is despairing over the state of his career. Mid-song, however, she transitions to the stage and continues with the next verse. With her movement from singing to a friend in a relatively private setting to a staged performance, all pretense of maintaining the vaudeville/backstage-drama dual-genre disintegrates. Most sketches, even Harper's song, fit under the heading of one of the genres, but Merman's is not simply a song sung backstage. Her performance crosses the border between vaudeville and backstage drama, and there is no way to account for her number using either one. In effect, at this point, the show emphasizes its status as a television puppet show by kicking the props from under the generic conventions it plays with. In subsequent seasons, the generically incomprehensible backstage number becomes a staple of the show. Milton Berle, Rudolf Nureyev, Elton John, Julie Andrews, and Dudley Moore, among others, all perform at least part of a song backstage (*Season Two* and *Best of*).

Rather than weakening the Muppets' call to join them, such revelations of the show's generic conventions strengthen the audience's Muppetization. Finch has argued of Henson's work, "It is typical of Jim's approach to puppetry, as well as to film and television, that he starts by telling the audience, 'This is an illusion you're watching.' Paradoxically, this has the effect of making it easier to accept the illusion, perhaps because members of the audience have been let in on the secret and thus can enjoy the role of co-conspirator" (*The Works* 122). Finch's point is that even when the Muppets are at their most meta, so to speak, lampooning conventions and spotlighting illusions, Muppet productions are inclusive. They pull in the viewer by making her complicit in the show's illusions. Part of Muppetization is willing suspension of disbelief, to borrow Samuel Taylor Coleridge's famous phrase: "The audience is convinced that it has seen things happen that could not be; because the viewers' own imaginations are involved they willingly fill in gaps for themselves" (Staff 18). My point is not simply that the show relies on the viewers' imaginations. When Merman marches onto the stage and continues her song, by watching and playing along as the generic conventions crumble, the viewer's imagination is less important than her ability to seamlessly negotiate the demands of multiple genres. Generic dexterity makes the viewer a co-conspirator in the show's play with conventions, and thereby, in yet another sense, a Muppet. This inclusivity, as we've seen, also functions in *The Muppet Movie*. Not only is the narrative of the film an account of the Muppets' accumulation of characters, but the film's frame story — the Muppets are watching their own film — blurs the line between performer and audience, in much the same way as *The Muppet Show*. Muppets watch Muppets. The film revels in its status as film, and the viewer shares the film's illusions with the Muppets as they watch together. While both *The Muppet Movie* and *The Muppet Show* highlight their own fictionality, in the film, the pretense of the characters' reality is jealously guarded. The movie, to put the point a different way, suggests that it is only a movie, but it never admits that the characters are only puppets. In fact, the film goes to great lengths, with its technically innovative full-body shots of Kermit riding a bicycle or dancing on stage with Fozzie, to make the puppets seem like living entities moving about in the real world.

Admissions of the puppetry medium do occur in *The Muppet Show*, however. In the Juliet Prowse episode, for instance, Kermit drinks a glass of milk through a straw (*Season One*). Between sips, he looks into the camera to say, "Think about this, friends." This bit invites the viewer to become a co-conspirator, as Finch says, by recognizing that Kermit is a puppet. Puppets can't drink milk, or anything else, so in order to get Kermit's joke, you must consider the medium of puppetry. Unless you do, drinking milk is hardly a feat worthy of televising. In this metatextual moment, Kermit also uses one of the staple tropes of *The Muppet Show*. He directly addresses the camera. In a show that employs a plethora of comedic tropes (sight gags, puns, sarcasm, etc.) perhaps the most prominent is the delivery of a punch line while looking straight into the camera, which is to say, directly addressing the television viewer. Direct address in the on-stage sequences is incredibly prominent, but fairly straightforward and comprehensible under the vaudeville genre. The performers are talking to the theater audience. Backstage, however, direct address has a more complex and pivotal status, and it furthers the viewer's Muppetization. While direct address has a specific significance on *The Muppet Show*, a variety of television programming employs this technique. To elucidate the practice, Robert C. Allen distinguishes between the "cinematic mode" and the "rhetorical mode" (116). In the cinematic mode, actors maintain the fourth wall. They converse and interact with one another, never looking at the camera, so that the viewer watches like a proverbial fly. In contrast, "Rather than pretending the viewer isn't there, the rhetorical mode simulates the face-to-face encounter by directly addressing the viewer and, what is more important, acknowledging both the performer's role as addresser and the viewer's role as addressee" (Allen 117–18). When Kermit drinks the milk, the addresser (Kermit, the performer) and the addressee (you, the television viewer) enter into a simulated face-to-face encounter. The rhetorical mode stands out in the backstage sequences because the cinematic mode would work just as well if *The Muppet Show* were a standard backstage drama. The Muppets use the rhetorical mode to recast the backstage segments as opportunities to Muppetize the viewer. In nearly every episode, characters directly address the viewer from backstage, often multiple times in the same sketch. One example among many occurs in the Jim Nabors episode, when Scooter fails to get one of Fozzie's perennially bad jokes (*Season One*). Fozzie: "Let me tell you about my nearsighted cousin. He's so rich his automobile is fitted with a prescription windshield." Scooter: "Okay, tell me about him." After a comedic pause, Fozzie comments to the camera, "Lucky his uncle owns this place." This instance captures the standard function of the rhetorical mode on the show. It's as if Fozzie says to the viewer, 'You get it because you're one of us.' Direct address pulls the viewer deeper into the Muppet cadre than the backstage sequences would if they employed the cinematic mode exclusively. Again, as with the performer/audience ambiguity, the rhetorical mode is a structural principle of the show, and the viewer never needs to register its occurrence or significance to be Muppetized.

Two characters in particular embody many of the generic and tropological issues central to Muppetization. Statler and Waldorf blur the boundary between performer and audience, and they are agents of co-conspiracy par excellence. Within the fictional vaudeville show, they are part of the audience. The two curmudgeonly hecklers are, through the lens of the television puppet show, cast members. Their insults and banter are part of the television program, and they are, after all, puppets. Even more explicitly than with anyone else, Statler and Waldorf are concurrently audience members and performers. They dramatize this fact, and the show's generic hybridity, in the Zero Mostel episode (*Season Two*), when, bored with the show on stage, they pull out a television and inadvertently tune in to *The Muppet Show* where they watch themselves watching the vaudeville Muppet show. Statler: "What is that?" Waldorf: "It looks like two ancient old guys sitting in a theatre box watching television." Statler: "That's crazy! No one would watch junk like that." On occasion, they move beyond even such blatant commentary to actively participate in the show via occasional appearances back or on stage. In the Beverly Sills episode (*Best of*), Statler objects during Kermit's opening monologue, "Oh no, I can't take any more of your opening numbers." Kermit responds, "Listen, guys, I'm tired of all this criticism. What would you do for an opening number?" They reply by singing a song from their customary theater box. After the first chorus, the old men are suddenly backstage. Suit jackets removed, they hustle around and bark orders at stagehands, sidelining Kermit and taking over as stage managers. After a musical interlude, the curtain rises on the number that the two old gentlemen have supposedly just improvised. Chorus girls continue the song that began in the box. When Statler and Waldorf enter stage left, dressed in classic vaudevillian suits, to tell a few jokes, Fozzie appears in their box to heckle them and get some much-deserved revenge. He shouts, "No good! Not funny! Bring on the bear!"[5] When the song concludes, we see a reaction shot of the audience in which the entire theater full of Muppets applauds, and then we cut back to the opera box, where Statler and Waldorf have resumed their usual station.

Back in their seats, they cheer their own just-concluded efforts. Waldorf rhetorically asks Statler, "Now why can't they do numbers like that?" and Kermit answers, "We just did." Once they realize Kermit is right, Waldorf concedes, "So you did." They immediately reverse their assessment, making their usual harsh judgments. Statler observes that the number "wasn't very good after all," and they begin booing. In this scene, all the elements of the show's personnel are mixed up: audience members are backstage and then on stage, the stage manager is displaced, and the show's staple comedian is in the audience. This sequence demonstrates that to watch the Muppets is to be a Muppet. To watch *The Muppet Show* is to be one of the audience-Muppets, and as Statler and Waldorf demonstrate, the road from audience-Muppet to performer-Muppet isn't a rocky one. In fact, on this show, it seems much more difficult to remain in a single category than to shift among roles.

With all this position switching and the various means of audience Muppetization, when Kermit tells the hecklers, "We just did," the *we* includes not only the performer-Muppets, the stagehand-Muppets, the audience-Muppets, and the Muppeteers and production crew who make the television show, but also the television viewer. Everyone is part of the show. Dreams don't get as much attention on the show as in *The Muppet Movie*, but the same logic of inclusivity applies in both. In the movie, to share the dream is to join the troupe; in the show, to watch the show is to be in the show. Whether it's going to Hollywood, making it on Broadway, staging a vaudeville performance, or opening frog leg restaurants, what's important is that you find people who share your dream.

In their films, the Muppets convey this message via the stories of how they assembled, while the generic logic of the show allows the Muppets to practice what they preach, so to speak, by including the viewer. The final lines of *The Muppet Movie*, aimed directly at the viewer, are from Kenny Ascher and Paul Williams's song "Finale: The Magic Store" and are sung by a crowd of Muppets so large that it requires a crane shot.

The thanks offered in the song isn't just the usual appreciation performers express to their audience — thanks for your financial support — though it's certainly that, too. However, with the permeability of the troupe and the various methods of Muppetizing the viewer, *you* are thanked not just for watching or buying movie tickets, but for sharing the dream, for being a Muppet. Thanks.

Notes

1. "The Great Muppet Paper" is also the title of an unrealized short-film script I coauthored with Misty Herrin and Robert Higgs.
2. I use the term *Muppet* to refer to the characters featured in *The Muppet Show* and

the first three Muppet films: *The Muppet Movie, The Great Muppet Caper,* and *The Muppets Take Manhattan*. My restriction of *Muppet* is not standard. In an interview with Judy Harris, Henson reserves the term for the brightly colored, cartoonish figures of *The Muppet Show* and *Sesame Street*, and rules out the more realistic puppets of *The Dark Crystal*. This clarification doesn't settle the definition, however. The puppets featured in the first season of *Saturday Night Live* were billed as Muppets, yet they employ an odd mixture of the cuddly cute and the realistically grotesque. Regardless of how we define *Muppet*, the conclusions I reach here apply to many of Henson's projects that I do not have the space to consider at present. Martha Kinder lends credence to this conjecture. While she has many other theoretical fish to fry, she picks up on some of the features of the Muppets that I examine here, particularly the significance of characters directly addressing the television audience in *Jim Henson's Muppet Babies* (62–71). Also, in his essay on the best of the latter-day Muppet films, *The Muppet Christmas Carol*, Hugh H. Davis's mentions the Muppets' penchant for direct address, play with generic conventions, and the conflation of audience and performer (101).

3. The other early Muppet film, *The Great Muppet Caper*, also depicts the assemblage of the Muppets when Kermit, Fozzie, and Gonzo check into the Happiness Hotel and meet up with Pops, the Electric Mayhem, and others. In this movie, the Muppets' success in apprehending the diamond thieves relies on their working together and combining their heterogeneous and unusual talents, but the plot of the film does not revolve around the congregation of the Muppet ensemble to the extent that the other two films do, nor does the film delve into the reasons why the group coheres.

4. This quote comes from the "Muppet Morsels" on-screen textual commentary feature of *The Muppet Show: Season One* DVD set. Goelz's statement appears seven minutes into the Sandy Duncan episode.

5. Fozzie also gets the chance to heckle Statler and Waldorf on other occasions such as the Steve Martin episode (*Season Two*), which contains numerous instances of the issues I explore here. For instance, Martin performs his closing number from the theater seats, and he is filmed from the stage, reversing the usual perspective by which the viewer accesses the Muppet theater.

Works Cited

Allen, Robert C. "Audience-Oriented Criticism and Television." *Channels of Discourse, Reassembled: Television and Contemporary Criticism*. 2nd ed. Ed. Robert C. Allen. Chapel Hill: University of North Carolina Press, 1992. 101–34.
Best of The Muppet Show, Featuring Peter Sellers / John Cleese / Dudley Moore. "Dudley Moore." Season Four, 1979-80. DVD. Time-Life Video / Jim Henson Home Entertainment, 2001.
Best of The Muppet Show, Featuring Tony Randall / Beverly Sills / Pearl Bailey. "Beverly Sills." Season Four, 1979-80. DVD. Time-Life Video / Jim Henson Home Entertainment, 2001.
Best of The Muppet Show, Featuring Steve Martin / Carol Burnett / Gilda Radner. "Steve Martin." Season Two, 1977-78. DVD. Time-Life Video / Jim Henson Home Entertainment, 2001.
Davis, Hugh H. "A Weirdo, a Rat, and a Humbug: The Literary Qualities of *The Muppet Christmas Carol*." *Studies in Popular Culture* 21.3 (1999): 95–105.
Dobrin, Sidney I. "'It's Not Easy Being Green': Jim Henson, the Muppets, and Ecological Literacy." *Wild Things: Children's Culture and Ecocriticism*. Ed. Sidney I. Dobrin and Kenneth B. Kidd. Detroit: Wayne State University Press, 2004. 232–53.
Durrett, Deanne. *The Importance of Jim Henson*. San Diego: Lucent, 1994.
Finch, Christopher. *Jim Henson, The Works: The Art, the Magic, the Imagination*. New York: Random House, 1993.
_____. *Of Muppets & Men: The Making of the Muppet Show*. New York: Alfred A. Knopf, 1981.

The Great Muppet Caper. 1981. Dir. Jim Henson. DVD. Walt Disney Pictures, 2005.
Groznic, Larry. "I Appreciate the Muppets on a Much Deeper Level Than You." *The Onion* 39.2 (2003). 2 July 2007. <http://www.theonion.com/content/node/25742>.
Harris, Judy. "Muppet Master: An Interview with Jim Henson." *Muppet Central.* 21 Sept. 1998. 4 Aug. 2007. <http://www.muppetcentral.com/articles/interviews/jim1.shtml>.
Kinder, Martha. *Playing with Power in Movies, Television, and Video Games: From Muppet Babies to Teenage Mutant Ninja Turtles.* Berkeley: University of California Press, 1991.
Michaels, Walter Benn. *The Trouble with Diversity: How We Learned to Love Identity and Ignore Inequality.* New York: Metropolitan, 2006.
Morrow, Robert W. *Sesame Street and the Reform of Children's Television.* Baltimore: Johns Hopkins University Press, 2006.
The Muppet Movie, 1979. Dir. James Frawley. DVD. Walt Disney Pictures, 2005.
The Muppet Show: Season One, 1976-77. DVD. Buena Vista Home Entertainment / Disney, 2005.
The Muppet Show: Season Two, 1977-78. DVD. Buena Vista Home Entertainment / Disney, 2007.
The Muppets Take Manhattan, 1984. Dir. Frank Oz. DVD. Jim Henson Home Entertainment / Tristar, 2001.
Parish, James Robert. *Jim Henson: Puppeteer and Filmmaker.* New York: Ferguson, 2006.
Saturday Night Live: The Complete First Season. 1975. DVD. Universal, 2006.
The Staff of Henson Associates. *The Art of the Muppets.* New York: Muppet Press / Bantam, 1980.

The Muppets as a Metaphor for the *Self*

Gideon Haberkorn

This article deals with *folk psychology*, which is "a set of more or less connected, more or less normative descriptions about how human beings 'tick,' what our own and other minds are like" (Bruner 35). Psychologists may study folk psychology, compare it to the way human beings *really* 'tick,' and, based on observation, possibly under experimental condition, develop a theory to explain its existence and persistence. Philosophers may study the conceptual issues that arise when we think about the mind, either in the context of folk or scientific psychology. Scholars of culture and art, finally, may investigate the way culture reflects, influences, and uses such concepts.

Art can reflect and affect our mental software. It can facilitate lateral thinking, i.e. help our mind shift sideways, changing the concepts of our *personal* folk psychology. The Muppets are especially useful when it comes to thinking about self and identity, both on the level of content and the level of discourse. Thus, on the first level, the Muppets offer a variety of patterns that may be adapted, adopted, and used as models in the everyday work of constructing the self. On the second level, they provide a useful meta-model for discussing the self. The Muppets, in short, can be a prism through which we reflect on and gain a deeper understanding of our selves.

The Self-Made Self

We live in a time when it is not only possible but necessary for us to become the architects and builders of our own selves. Societies, which were once closed, authoritative, binding systems, have developed into more open, flexible, democratic ones. As a result, the self has turned from a whole, independent, uniform substance, situated in the present, into a web of relations stretching back into the past and forward into the future. The network of the self is in constant tension, always pulled between singularity and society, continuity and variety, staying true to one's self and creating a better version of it (Keupp et al. 55–56, 69).

Rather than being constructed according to a unified and integrated plan, the self is based on a collection of patterns. Together, they form the *self-concept*—which is much like a library "without enough staff or shelves, so that some books are stored in a systematic, organized fashion while others are stacked haphazardly on the floor or shelved in the wrong place" (Baumeister 214). The self-concept is a collection of information, much of it usually not coherent. If contradictions become obvious, the result is *cognitive dissonance*.

People deal with such dissonances by ignoring them, or by working to create a new, less dissonant pattern, either by attempting to change any of the incongruent elements, or by adopting an overall pattern in which the dissonance can be resolved (Weber 118). Since only a small amount of the information making up the self-concept is in use at any given moment, most potential dissonances can safely be ignored. As a result, the information used most often tends to be the most consistent and coherent (Baumeister 214).

Cultural artifacts—such as novels, paintings, or sculptures—can help us gain a better understanding of our concepts simply by activating them. Human beings draw upon their conceptual libraries to make sense of any kind of experience, and in the appreciation of cultural artifacts we mobilize many of the same beliefs and emotions we use for making sense of everyday life. In the process, we may notice dissonances that we have successfully ignored so far, and we may also discover new ways of connecting beliefs which seemed unrelated before. Thus, cultural artifacts offer a chance to bring more order and coherence to our library of cultural concepts, and to become more confident in their application (Carroll 282–284). Such true consistency can acknowledge and encompass a certain degree of dissonance—as Whitman sings to himself: "Do I contradict myself? / Very well then I contradict myself, / (I am large, I contain multitudes.)" (88). The self-concept must necessarily contain a notion as to how much contradiction is acceptable.

If the Muppets can be a prism through which we reflect on and gain a deeper understanding of our selves, it is not only because they can in many ways be taken as metaphors for the processes of self-creation. As cultural artifacts, they also force us to negotiate and re-negotiate coherence between various concepts stored in our mental library and employed in the making of the self. As such, we should expect them to speak to problems of *individuality* and *identity*, of *normality* and *abnormality*, of *self* and *other*.

The Individual Identity of the Self

Self-concepts are used to construct the *individual*, i.e. the smallest social unit. It can be separated from everybody else, but can itself not be divided any further. It is literally *not dividable*. It may wear different *masks* in different circumstances, and it has to account for a wide range of domain-specific *personae*. Some of these *personae* may be officially part of the self, while others are disowned, depending on which domains of our life we regard as most significant. We may contain multitudes, but we do not own up to all of them.

Identity is a similar notion, describing the fact that we are who we are — that we are like ourselves, or at least similar enough to allow for *identification*. This may sound rather obvious, but it is not. Over the course of a few years, every molecule in the body is replaced; personalities change, memories fade. Things are not what they were; we are not what we have been. We are not even necessarily who we are. This rather disconcerting aspect of our physical and mental selves — their changeability, the fact that they will one day dissolve completely — is complemented by the realization that we can reinvent our *self*, at least to a certain degree.

By defining our identity and individuality, the *self* makes us particular and helps us draw the line between inside and outside, keeping out the *other*, i.e. everything that is different from our *self*. Indeed, one of the easiest ways of defining our *self* is to construct a dichotomy between self and other. The *self* can then be used to define *normality*, while the various *others* stand for varying degrees of *abnormality*. However, every culture incorporates some representations of the *other* into its tradition: Clowns and monsters patrol the edges of society, dancing on the margins in some form of carnival celebration. Such figures are both threatening and fascinating as they question and undermine our cultural concepts and categories, and thus the basis of our *self* (cf. Kearney 3–4, et al.; Cohen 6–16).

Carnival Virtues

Medieval carnival was dominated by a subversion and confirmation of social and political hierarchies (not, as Bakhtin has it, only or even mainly by the former). At such times, those of lower status dressed as kings and gods and clergy, those of higher status as peasants and beggars. There was "indiscriminate public mixing, dancing, singing, and parading of high and low classes and even of women, married or unmarried," and so conventional divisions of class and status and sex were questioned (Kinser 60). Simultaneously, "[o]fficials paraded or greeted the community at their residences or offices," and "[t]he military displayed their power in parades and the elites their prowess, above all in jousting," thus reaffirming the conventional hierarchies (60). In the most literal image of transgression, "all distinctions between the public and private were abolished; people ran in and out of houses and in and out of city gates" (60), as if to emphasize the *liminal* atmosphere — from the Latin *limen*, threshold. Carnival is at heart about the subversion and confirmation of society's conceptual mindscapes. It provides an institutional context for clowns and monsters to scamper around the margins of society and explore its conceptual structures.

Jim Henson's Muppets are hybrids of fools and monsters — *carnival incarnate*. They are a large and unruly family, but the core group can justifiably be limited to the denizens of *The Muppet Show*. The term *Muppet* is reportedly a portmanteau of *marionette* and *puppet* and properly covers all puppets made by Jim Henson or his Creature Shop (cf. Finch, *Jim Henson* 18). Characterizing them, as Mukerji does somewhat naively, via a supposed resemblance to "stuffed animals or colorful, stuffed monsters" (160) fails to account for creatures like those of *The Dark Crystal*, *Labyrinth*, or *The Storyteller*— and indeed a number of those featured on *The Muppet Show*. The prevailing characteristic of the Muppets is not so much their cuddly nature as their singular suitability for their appearance on television and film and the blending of the magic of film and television with the art of puppetry. Muppets are, in this sense, media puppets, and their ideal stage is the screen (cf. Finch, *Of Muppets and Men* 48).

The focus of this article is limited to *The Muppet Show* for two reasons, the first simply being its world-wide popularity: "By the fourth season [it] was the greatest international television hit of all time, being aired in more than 100 countries" (Finch, *Jim Henson* 119). The second reason is that *The Muppet Show*, because it is explicitly about the creation of a performance, foregrounds the artificial nature of a show, and focuses on the moment when it breaks down. It invites us to search for the little man behind the curtain, who in this case is likely to have his hand up a pig. The world of *The Muppet Show* is, as the opening number states, *muppetational*: It is the ideal context for the Muppets to perform their carnival. The show exists in a "universe of generally benign absurdity" — a world in which "characters may explode once in a while, or turn into chocolate layer cake, but they recover in time for the next performance" (Finch, *Of Muppets and Men* 27). It is perfectly normal in this world for tigers to show up at the North Pole, or for penguins to appear in tropical rainforests, usually wearing sunglasses. It is a carnival world, suspending all hierarchies, norms, and prohibitions — at least for the length of a half hour episode — and celebrating the temporary liberation from established order. Its inhabitants mostly take the mayhem for granted and accept it as the norm.

The fifth season (1980-1981) episode featuring Paul Simon (Episode 11) may serve as an example to illustrate the rules of the *Muppet* universe. The episode takes place mostly onstage and backstage, with a few scenes set in Paul Simon's dressing room and one — the first — just inside the theatre's entrance. There are a few shots of the audience, and, in the form of Waldorf and Statler, there is repeated audience commentary and heckling. *The Muppet Show* is either "a backstage drama punctuated by outlandish production numbers," or "a parody of a variety show frequently interrupted by backstage shenanigans" (Finch, *Of Muppets and Men* 28). There is constant movement from stage to backstage — even into the audience — with characters wandering about behind the scenes in costume, rehearsing their parts. At the same time, the more or less rehearsed production numbers are regularly infiltrated by the backstage mayhem. In this one single episode, there are roughly fifteen moves between stage, backstage, and audience. The *Muppet* madness spills from one setting into another, crossing the rather important thresholds between backstage, stage, and audience. The boundaries between these settings are not just spatial but conceptual. All of this makes the Muppet theatre a thoroughly liminal space. (The most ingenious instance of this in the Paul Simon episode may be when Veterinarian's Hospital begins with Piggy operating a puppet of herself.)[1]

The fact that the Muppet universe is inhabited by human-like puppets, animal puppets with human attributes, animal puppets with purely animal attributes, talking statues, talking food, and creatures of indeterminate provenance, as well as the occasional human, only underscores its strangeness (cf. Finch, *Of Muppets and Men* 31–32). Nevertheless, Tillis observes that it seems "as if Kermit and Miss Piggy were people who just happened to be animals" (*Aesthetics* 129), and indeed, all Muppets, right down to the singing vegetables and the juggling penguins, are basically people like you and me — apart from the fact that they display behavior which often cannot be integrated into conventional self-concepts. This leads Mukerji to mistakenly view them as embodiments of various cultural models of children (160). In fact, while children have not yet been completely socialized, and hence frequently do not adhere to a society's cultural patterns, the Muppets simply *refuse to be socialized*, and adhere to alternative patterns of their own.

Finch jokingly suggests a reading of *The Muppet Show* as "a docu-drama about a mental institution in which the inmates are encouraged to act out their neuroses while disguised as animals, vegetables or whatever happens to take their fancy" (*Of Muppets and Men* 28). This is interesting for two reasons: Firstly, societies tend to regard those who do not share their mindscapes as different or strange. The beliefs of such individuals or groups are often given a "negative ontological status," i.e. defined as less than real, and the individuals are often segregated in some way, either in order to subject them to some form of "therapy" in order to 'heal' them, or in order to "liquidate physically what one has liquidated conceptually" (Berger and Luckmann 133). At least metaphorically, those who see the world differently often wind up locked up in asylums or burned at the stake. Hence, the connection to the mental institution is interesting. Second, the notion of the Muppets as reified neuroses is noteworthy because, unlike actors, puppeteers cannot embody their roles—puppetry explicitly prevents a fusion of role and performer. Thus, the role remains a physical material handled by the performer, or, more explicitly, puppets are roles that have a physical existence separated from and independent of their performers (cf. Knoedgen 46–47). *The Muppet Show* is a pool of abnormal roles, a collection of *personae* that often do not fit the conventional cultural patterns.[2]

Puppet Peeves

Puppets have an image problem. They are always seen as hapless objects controlled by another, as in *puppet state*, or *puppet government*. It is certainly true that a puppet without a puppeteer is nothing but dead matter. This, in fact, is surely part of the appeal — that is to say, the audience clearly perceives puppets as manufactured objects, but as "objects that are given design, movement, and frequently, speech, in such a way that the audience imagines them to have life" (Tillis, *Aesthetics* 28). The inherent tension of the puppet is just that: The tension between "what it means to be an 'object' and what it means to have 'life'" (64). It is the nature of puppets to exist in the liminal space between object and life (cf. 65). The puppet proper, in fact, exists only when this liminal space opens up — it exists, therefore, only during the process of performance. A puppet is not just crude material; it is *performed material*.

Tillis emphasizes the performance and the performer, arguing that the puppet's inherent tension "is a reflection of the tension that exists between the operator who produces the signs and the material object upon which he sites them," and that the puppet "invariably exposes the presence of the operator behind it, even as it occludes that presence by taking focus as the site of the operator's performance" ("Actor" 115). Yet the puppet is not the material site of performance: By being performed material, by embodying all the performer's gestures, it becomes the manifestation of the role (cf. Knoedgen 46–47). This line of thought is highly reminiscent of a notion from gender studies, namely the idea of the body as "a peculiar nexus of culture and choice" (Butler 28), a situation for interpreting cultural concepts of gender. Gender thus becomes "an active style of living one's body in the world" (26), "and 'existing' one's body becomes a personal way of taking up and reinterpreting received gender norms" (29). Just so, the material is the situation in which the puppeteer can manifest the puppet as a reified role through performance.

Adding the Muppets to the usual set of stage metaphors used to conceptualize the *self* helps address a number of problems. On the level of discourse, the puppeteer and the puppet are more clearly separated than the actor and his role, and hence the separation between our *self* and the roles we inhabit is made more explicit. On the level of content, the Muppets continuously, and often fairly quickly, step into and out of various roles, all of which could be argued to be distilled versions of specific facets of their *self*. If Muppets perform roles from pre-existing sources, as in *The Muppet Christmas Carol*, they interpret them a lot more freely than is usual. The way Muppets deal with specific social roles and conventions is also noteworthy, and the cases of Miss Piggy and The Great Gonzo will serve as examples.

Gender Goes Hog Wild

The Muppets being the Muppets, and hence carnival incarnate, tend to become the site for fairly subversive interpretations of social models. One very good example is Miss Piggy, who may be the most obviously gendered Muppet, while at the same time refusing to fit any accepted gender pattern.[3] Mukerji emphasizes the way Piggy "continually undermines her gender identity with her voice, her actions, and her clear play-acting of feminine virtues" (173), and argues that the reason for the glamorous pig's problematic gender identity is the fact that "she is the invention of a male puppeteer," who projects his male self through a female puppet (174). As a result, claims Mukerji, Miss Piggy is "less like a girl and more like a drag queen or transvestite pretending to be what she is not (by nature)" (174). However, I cannot quite share Mukerji's reading.

Miss Piggy, I would argue, is not about pretension winning over nature. She is not unnatural. Rather, she provides a situation for negotiating gender against the background of cultural conventions. It is perfectly in keeping with the nature of the Muppets that Piggy should subvert the traditional female gender model. Often, she will pretend to be more or less traditionally female, but it is obvious that she is much more honest when she displays aggression, ego, and her hunger for fame and glamour. While many of these characteristics are traditionally associated with men rather than women, this association is cultural — there is nothing natural about it. Miss Piggy is not unnatural; she is pig-headed. She is not so much about a man pretending to be a woman, against nature, but rather about an individual dropping all pretense and displaying traits which do not fit the traditional model.

The sow *fatale* lives her body in the world, and instead of simply reifying a role through performance, her puppeteer, Frank Oz, opens up a situation in which roles can be questioned and reinterpreted. Her character began to crystallize at a point when Oz, who had already been playing her for a number of shows, intuitively improvised: the script called for her to slap Kermit, and Oz had her "puff out her ample chest, assume that attitude of offended rage that would become so familiar, and deliver a vicious karate chop, accompanied by an appropriate, blood-curdling yell" (cf. Finch, *Jim Henson* 110). While neither action is inherently male or female, the slap is encoded as a form of violence acceptable in women in the Western world's social mindscape, whereas the karate hit most certainly is not. There is another telling scene in the Paul Simon episode, where she begins singing "Scarborough Fair" in a strained, high-pitched voice, but soon reverts to a more natural lower register. The essence of Piggy is obviously not the pretension to be what she is not (by nature), but rather the letting go of such pretension. Miss Piggy is not so much about denying nature as resisting culture. Because she is at the same time still labeled as obviously female, Miss Piggy encourages viewers to revise their cultural concepts of a female self. This may make it possible to resolve dissonances caused by any behavior or characteristic that does not fit the more traditional gender model.

Normality Goes Hay-Wire

Another very good example of an abnormal performance is the Great Gonzo, who may well be the most grotesque Muppet. Gonzo invents and performs impossible stunts that can only result in disaster and pain for him, leading Finch to suggest that he may well be a masochist (*Jim Henson* 104). In any case, he is a perfectionist and a visionary, who can work up an enthusiasm for anything from training Mexican jumping beans to shooting himself from a cannon or performing an underwater heart transplant on himself.

The Great Gonzo is an extreme personality, and he revels in being different, other, unique. His character truly came together for his puppeteer Dave Goelz when, after a failed audition for dancing chickens, he had Gonzo turn to the camera and ad-lib, 'Nice legs, though' (cf. Finch, *Jim Henson* 104). It says a lot about the character that his sexual preference for poultry is merely an odd, rather charming, detail.

Gonzo resists categorization. He resembles no identifiable animal or plant, although he does have a beak. In the Paul Simon episode, during Veterinarian's Hospital, he is asked what he would like to reincarnate as, and he admits that he does not even know what he is this time around. In the second Muppet movie, *The Great Muppet Caper* (Henson, 1981), the characters are thrown from the freight hold of an airliner, in boxes labeled *Bear*, *Frog*, and so on. Gonzo's box is labeled *Whatever* (cf. Finch, *Jim Henson* 131).

The Great Gonzo provides a situation for negotiating, questioning, and reinterpreting normality as such. His essence is the defiance of norms and boundaries, fervent commitment, and a strong belief in himself. He is never half-hearted or reluctant. When he presents his own compositions to Paul Simon, it does not matter to him that they are very different, to put it mildly — he is convinced of their value, just as he is convinced that Simon's guitar is a clarinet. Gonzo is queer in the old-fashioned sense of strange, odd, bizarre, unconventional, abnormal, and just plain freaky. He embodies queer pride, content to be seriously weird even by Muppet standards, and his example encourages viewers to revise their cultural concepts of what exactly is normal, acceptable, or natural. He also provides a model for accepting and treasuring what makes us different and unique, instead of striving to fit in and become more conventional. To anyone striving to integrate unconventional elements into a self-concept, Gonzo provides a more flexible model that may help resolve cognitive dissonances.

This, incidentally, is why *Muppets from Space* was a disaster for Gonzo's character: Giving him a longing to belong and providing him with a family turned the Great Gonzo from one of a kind into one of a group. Suddenly, Gonzo was no longer a Muppet defying categorization. The film ended with him happily joining a group of Muppets that looked just like him, and it began with him explicitly longing for this. Instead of celebrating his weirdness, he was openly unhappy with it. The Great Gonzo, champion for the unconventional, wanted nothing more than to become conventional. The change is disturbingly reminiscent of the one that turns Jack Nicholson's McMurphy in *One Flew Over the Cuckoo's Nest*, but thankfully, it does not seem to have blunted the character's power as a cultural model.

Body Building

The Muppets provide alternative role models that the audience can use in constructing their own *selves*. Their refusal to accept cultural conventions and categories is echoed by the fact that they are very obviously puppets, lifeless matter which insists on coming to life. They are performed material — and, in using them as a metaphor for thinking about the *self*, we are forced to acknowledge that, when all is said and done, we, too, are lifeless matter which insists on coming to life. Just as the material is the situation in which the puppeteer can exist the puppet through performance, our bodies are the site of our performed selves.

Because puppet theater works with a manufactured body, it is easy to assume that the largest — or most important — part of the work consists in the creation of that body: The physical puppet seems to be the most significant element (cf. Knoedgen 11, 44). One tends to forget that the puppet is not merely the physical material: Both Miss Piggy and the Great Gonzo developed as characters not only based on their physical bodies, but also based on improvised performances. Similarly, it is tempting to reduce human beings to their bodies, to judge them based on their biological material and not necessarily on their performance. As a consequence, people have always altered their bodies to better fit their self-concept or to affect or at least reflect a change in that concept—using cosmetics to hide perceived defects or signs of age, painting and tattooing to mark rites of passage, piercing various parts of the anatomy to attach items of jewelry, and even surgically augmenting, enhancing, and rearranging parts of their bodies (cf. Weber 60, 63, 69, 72, et al.). While it seems unlikely that physical change alone can do more than mask the self, certainly not change it radically, there is undoubtedly some degree of interaction. When it comes to Muppet bodies, Dave Houseman of Jim Henson's Creature Shop insists that it is his job to build a *natural user interface* for the puppeteers—an object through which they can channel their performance without having to think about it (cf. Bacon 99, 101). This suggests the body as a medium through which we perform our *selves*, an interface for gesturing the *self* to the world.

Yet, bodies are not just situations in which we perform our identity through a collection of gestures; they also gesture themselves. Some performances are made more difficult, if not impossible, because of the bodies they are to be situated in. Once again, The Great Gonzo proves a useful example. All through the first season of *The Muppet Show*, the character did not quite work. His failed stunts were not funny but painful. Dave Goelz realized that the problem was Gonzo's face, which could only express gloom. Between seasons he built a new version of the Muppet, including an eye mechanism that enabled him to look excited, thus making it possible to develop the enthusiastic side of Gonzo's character, which led the writers in turn to adapt the way they wrote for Gonzo (cf. Finch, *Of Muppets and Men* 37). The Muppet model of the *self* apparently includes the ability to influence the self-concept by changing the body. It also offers an interesting perspective on the more extreme cases of plastic surgery: Besides the regular characters, there is also a group of Muppets called *Whatnots*. These are simple torsos and heads that— with the help of a library of eyes, noses, wigs, and costumes—can be transformed into just about any character the script calls for (cf. Finch, *Jim Henson* 64). The point is that *Whatnots* pay for maximum flexibility with a near-total loss of identity and individuality.

Mind Matters

If we use the Muppets as a basis for constructing our mental model of the *self* in general and our own *self* in particular, then we can see our bodies as interfaces for gesturing our *self* to the world — interfaces which may also produce their own gestures, influencing or limiting our performance, but by no means dictating it. Of course, it may turn out at some point in the future that our genetic makeup determines our mindscape and our *self*. Until then, however, it seems more useful to focus on what we do rather than who we are and what we are made of, if for no other reason than simply because it seems to go against a common default assumption.

There is apparently a tendency to believe that we do as we are. The way Lakoff describes it, this is a basic human tendency: "We commonly understand people metaphorically as if they were objects made of substances that determine how they will behave," conceiving "of a person as if he had an essence or a collection of essences that determined his behavior" (*Moral Politics* 87). This understanding is, Lakoff argues, based on the experience that "[p]hysical objects are made of substances, and how they behave depends on what they are made of" (87). Because this is a basic human experience, available to all human beings at all times, it should be a basic human assumption that people do as they are. This entails, among others, the notions that people cannot fundamentally change, and that we can predict and judge people once we know what they are made of. Foucault, on the other hand, maintains that, at least in the case of sexuality, mindscapes fundamentally changed in the 19th century, when the concept of sodomy gave way to that of homosexuality: While "sodomy was a category of forbidden acts," the homosexual was a person — "[t]he sodomite had been a temporary aberration," while "the homosexual was [...] a species" (*History of Sexuality* 43). Generalizing from this change, the belief that we do as we are would seem to be not particular to humanity but to this society, at this specific time. Whichever way it is, both views allow our mindscape the ability to change, in Foucault's case by changing the discourse, and in Lakoff's case by having new experiences on which to base our mental model of *selves* and *self*. Experiencing the Muppets should suggest a model based on the belief that we are as we do.

However, the metaphor of the Muppet as *self* also emphasizes the importance of our bodies — much more clearly so, in fact, than the metaphor of the role. A role, after all, is a role, and it is easy to forget that it needs an actor to even exist. The Muppets clearly illustrate that there would be no performance without material.

Now, it is important not to carry the metaphor too far. It is fairly flexible, but at some point, it will break. For example, unlike the Muppet body, the human body holds not just the potential of all future performances, but also the record of all past performances: Our wrinkles record, etched into our faces, all our smiles and all our frowns. Our fatty deposits are as much fossil evidence of laziness and fast food as our well-developed muscles are of discipline and exercise. Muppet bodies never change, unless the performer wants them to. Similarly, the gender reading becomes complicated once Piggy and Kermit are shown, in *The Muppet Christmas Carol* (Brian Henson, 1992), to have children: Leaving aside the questionable mechanics of procreation involved, we note that the boys are all frogs, like their father, while the girls are all pigs, like their mother. Yet species cannot be read as equivalent of biological sex, since there are several male pigs on the *Muppet Show*, including Link, the caricature manly man hero type. There are, notably, no female frogs.[4] While the Muppet body can in many cases be compared to the human body, it is also an embodied role, a physical manifestation of character. In that sense, Muppets have no unambiguous physical sexual markers. The puppeteer and the performance are the ultimate source of both sex *and* gender.

Script Supervision

So far, using the Muppets as a basis for constructing our mental model of *selves* in general and in particular suggests the *self* as an intersection of body and performance. However, like our own *self*, the *Muppet Show* is not improvised but largely scripted, and this fact is still missing from the model. Finch hints at the need for puppeteers and writers to agree on a Muppet's personality (cf. Finch, *Of Muppets and Men* 34). Jim Henson felt that the right puppet and the right performer would come together and bring the script to life (cf. Finch, *Of Muppets and Men* 41). A Muppet is, then, neither simply a performance, or a scripted part, or a puppet. A Muppet is a scripted character interpreted by a performer through a physical object. It exists only in the event of all three working together in performance.

This brings us back to the beginning. Our minds are not alone; they live in social mindscapes. The collection of patterns we use to construct our mental models exists against the background of these social mindscapes, the collection of patterns our society uses to make sense of the world. All our performances take place in the context of these social scripts. The network of our *self* is in constant tension, always pulled between singularity and society, continuity and variety, staying true to one's self and becoming a better version of it.

We live in a time when it is not only possible but necessary to be the builders and architects of our own *selves*. If we adopt the Muppet model as a framework for thinking about our *selves*, it implies that we are not our bodies, nor our social roles and scripts, nor simply our own free will. We are not what we are: We are what we do, how we perform our roles through bodies in our own idiosyncratic ways. Our *self* exists at the intersection of culture, nature, and performance. The Muppets, as cultural artifacts, are a prism through which we can both rethink our self-concept and gain a better understanding of what a *self* is.

Notes

1. Nevertheless, the madness is in fact bound within a fairly rigid frame: It all takes place in an enclosed set, containing a clearly regulated collection of possible events. The only case in which this framework is broken in this episode is the "Muppet Newsflash."

2. Geertz notes that "[t]he drama analogy for social life has [...] been around in a casual sort of way — all the world's a stage and we but poor players who strut and so on — for a very long time," and the respective metaphors, "most notably 'role,'" have been staples of sociological discourse since at least the 1930s" (26; cf. also Edgar, "Roles" 341, and Hartley, "Performance" 173). A classic in this vein is *The Presentation of Self in Everyday Life* by Goffman, which is still much referred to. Undoubtedly, it can be useful to analyze emancipation as women refusing to perform roles scripted by men, and colonialism and the politics of racial suppression can be discussed as the forceful casting of those suppressed in roles scripted by the colonizers, often complete with pre-defined styles of performance. All of these would be attempts to catch the self in a net of metaphors.

The problem with the metaphor is that it is misleading. McAdams argues that Goffman's focus on social roles fails to take into account the identity behind the roles people play: "For Goffman," he maintains, "nothing transcends the particular behavioral performance we enact" (126). Jauss draws attention to the differences between life and theatre: Actors are allowed only one role per play, real life casts us in numerous roles, frequently several at the same time; actors engage in play and make-believe, real people are serious about their roles; actors are very restricted in the way they can interpret their role, real people have a lot of leeway (601, 603–604). Finally, Geertz notes that, while "Goffman also employs the language of the stage quite extensively," he seems to see theatre as "an oddly mannered kind of interaction game — ping-pong in masks," and therefore "his work is not, at base, really dramaturgical" (24). Metaphors are dangerous because they tend to distort and exclude. Yet they are still useful in exploring and mapping an area, as they entail possible questions and directions. The set of stage metaphors commonly used to understand the self has its uses and should not be discarded too hastily.

3. See also "The Uniquely Strong but Feminine Miss Piggy" by Maryanne Fisher and Anthony Cox in this collection.

4. There are some who take Jill, Bill and Gil from *The Muppets Take Manhattan* for frogs, making them the only adult frogs beside Kermit, and Jill the only female Frog in the Muppet universe. However, they are not green, like Kermit, or his nephew Robin and the unidentified adolescent frog playing Peter Cratchit in *The Muppet Christmas Carol*. Nor do they have the same distinctly shaped pupils as Kermit. Judging from Kermit and his nephew, *Muppet* frogs are green and, when grown up, develop uniquely shaped pupils. Jill, Bill and Gil share neither of these characteristics, and there is no evidence to support a characterization of them as frogs.

Works Cited and Consulted

Bacon, Matt. *No Strings Attached: The Inside Story of Jim Henson's Creature Shop*. New York: Macmillan, 1997.
Baumeister, Roy F. *The Cultural Animal: Human Nature, Meaning, and Social Life*. New York: Oxford University Press, 2005.

Bell, John. "Puppets, Masks, and Performing Objects at the End of the Century." *The Drama Review* 43.3 (1999) 15–27.
Berger, Peter L., and Thomas Luckmann. *The Social Construction of Reality: A Treatise in the Sociology of Knowledge.* London: Penguin, 1967.
Bruner, Jerome. *Acts of Meaning.* Cambridge: Harvard University Press, 1990.
Butler, Judith. "Variations on Sex and Gender: Beauvoir, Wittig, Foucault." *The Judith Butler Reader.* Eds. Sara Salih and Judith Butler. Malden: Blackwell, 2004. 23–37.
Carroll, Noël "Art, Narrative, and Moral Understanding." *Beyond Aesthetics: Philosophical Essays.* Cambridge: Cambridge University Press, 2001. 270–293.
Cohen, Jeffrey Jerome. "Monster Culture (Seven Theses)." *Monster Theory.* Ed. Jeffrey Jerome Cohen. Minneapolis: University of Minnesota Press, 1996. 3–25.
Culler, Jonathan. *Structuralist Poetics: Structuralism, Linguistics and the Study of Literature.* 1975. New York: Routledge, 2002.
D'Andrale, Roy. "A Folk Model of the Mind." *Cultural Models in Language and Thought.* Eds. Dorothy Holland and Naomi Quinn. Cambridge: Cambridge University Press, 1987. 112–148.
Edgar, Andrew. "Roles." *Key Concepts in Cultural Theory.* Eds. Andrew Edgar and Peter Sedgwick. London: Routledge, 1999. 341–342.
Finch, Christopher. *Jim Henson: The Works. The Art, the Magic, the Imagination.* New York: Random House, 1993.
_____. *Of Muppets and Men: The Making of the Muppet Show.* New York: Alfred A. Knopf, 1981.
Foucault, Michel. *The History of Sexuality. Vol. I: The Will to Knowledge.* 1976. London: Penguin, 1998.
Goffman, Ervin. *The Presentation of Self in Everyday Life.* New York: Anchor, 1959.
Hartley, John. "Performance." *Communication, Cultural and Media Studies: The Key Concepts.* London: Routledge, 2002. 173.
Jauss, Hans Robert. "Soziologischer und ästhetischer Rollenbegriff." *Identität.* Eds. Odo Marquard and Karlheinz Stierle. München: Wilhelm Fink, 1979. 599–607.
Kearney, Richard. *Strangers, Gods and Monsters: Interpreting Otherness.* London: Routledge, 2003.
Keupp, Heiner et al. *Identitätskonstruktionen: Das Patchwork der Identitäten in der Spätmoderne.* 1999. Reinbek: Rowolt, 2006.
Kinser, Samuel. "Carnival." *Medieval Folklore: A Guide to Myths, Legends, Tales, Beliefs, and Customs.* Eds. Carl Lindahl, John McNamara and John Lindow. Oxford: Oxford University Press, 2002. 59–61.
Knoedgen, Werner. *Das Unmögliche Theater: Zur Phänomenologie des Figurentheaters.* Stuttgart: Urachhaus, 1990.
Lakoff, George. *Moral Politics: How Liberals and Conservatives Think.* 1996. Chicago: University of Chicago Press, 2002.
_____. *Women, Fire, and Dangerous Things: What Categories Reveal About the Mind.* Chicago: University of Chicago Press, 1987.
Lakoff, George, and Mark Johnson. *Metaphors We Live By.* Chicago: University of Chicago Press, 1981.
McAdams, Dan P. *The Stories We Live By: Personal Myths and the Making of the Self.* 1993. New York: Guildford Press, 1997.
Meschke, Michael. *Grenzüberschreitungen: Zur Ästhetik des Puppentheaters.* Frankfurt am Main: Nold, 1996.
Mukerji, Chandra. "Animals, Monsters, and Muppets" in Elizabeth Long, *Cultural Studies and the Sociology of Culture.* Malden: Blackwell, 1997. 155–184.
Reeve, Johnmarshall. *Understanding Motivation and Emotion.* Hoboken: Wiley, 2005.
Shepherd, Simon, and Mick Wallis. *Drama / Theatre / Performance.* London: Routledge, 2004.
Tillis, Steve. "The Actor Occluded: Puppet Theatre and Acting Theory." *Theatre Topics* 6.2 (1996) 109–119.

_____. *Toward an Aesthetics of the Puppet: Puppetry as a Theatrical Art.* Westport: Greenwood Press, 1992.
Weber, Robert J. *The Created Self: Reinventing Body, Persona, and Spirit.* New York: Norton, 2000.
Whitman, Walt. "Song of Myself." *Leaves of Grass.* Ed. Sculley Bradley. New York: Norton, 1973. 28–89.
Zerubavel, Eviatar. *Social Mindscapes: An Invitation to Cognitive Sociology.* Cambridge: Harvard University Press, 1997.

Stuffed Suits and Hog-Wild Desire

Lynne D. Schneider

> STATLER: *You think this show was educational?*
> WALDORF: *Yes, it will drive people to read books!*

Two grouchy, but dapper, old puppets perch in the upper balcony box, stage left. Glimpsed askance from the wings, a favorite camera vantage, they appear to occupy the proscenium arch. Who are these octogenarians, and why do they heckle at the threshold of the stage? The theater's most faithful customers, Waldorf and Statler (as seen on TV), attend *The Muppet Show* week after week, not as patrons but as if it were their job. While whimsical critters and balls of fluff work onstage to enact the Muppet World of make-believe, together these two sleepy old men actually do existential double duty. Statler and Waldorf represent not only the Muppet realm and the "real world" of the television audience, these two elderly gents in their exclusive plush balcony also embody the threshold between the two. If the proscenium arch is the mouth of the stage, Statler and Waldorf are its voice. Their theatrical and paradoxical "job" is to speak for something *almost* as old as they are: the revolutionary role of compassion in art.

Unlikely avatars of compassion, together they amount to a rather grumbly Janus-figure stationed at the permeable boundary between the routine workaday world and the unpredictable nighttime realm of the *carnivale*. They look both to the world of quantities, girded with three-piece suits and four-in-hand ties, and to the landscape of qualities that we can only enter in dance, jest and dream.

As threshold characters, stationed within the invisible proscenium "wall," the two old men frame the show's *dramatis personae* of critical binaries. Acting as a deliberate contrast to the stage cast, their tidy business suits contrast with Fozzie Bear's beat-up hat, the hip threads and shades of Dr. Teeth and his band, or the satin gown and feather-boa style of evening wear from *At the Ball* which Miss Piggy sports as everyday wear. These tired, old men highlight the exuberance and youth of the cast, especially Kermit's tiny nephew, Robin. High and low culture, differentials in class, age and gender, and the human/not-exactly-human divide account for a few of "the usual suspects" rounded up for interrogation in theoretical discourse. Such binaries threaten to draw attention to the differences between the actors and the audience, but our dyad of stodgy curmudgeons bridges those gulfs and draws the TV-viewing eye instead to the permeable borders between Us and Them.

Visually, the proscenium arch suggests the idea of "boundary," but the geezers' plush velvet theater box melds messages from both sides of the stage divide. Linear quantities commingle with nonlinear qualities: commodities, earnings, and predictable Newtonian "causation" mix with color, light, harmony and movement. Representing a cozy, comfortable crucible, the box stands for that gaze on the edge between worlds that draws together disparate impulses through catalytic associative energies such as allegory, symbol and satire, and magic. The alchemical fire that melts and realigns both sides of the divide is unbridled-unleashed-unpenned *Eros*. Who better to highlight the active, central and ever-young forces of life than two old men stationed on the brink of the great beyond?

These elders in their box perform the cultural problem they highlight with respect to powerful life energies. This problem is tenaciously old, most often overlooked, but perpetually current and urgent. This overlooked emergency is most clearly demonstrated when either Statler or Waldorf, unbeknownst to the other, has fallen out of the box and dangles by one skinny arm, clinging to the balcony rail by one geezer claw.

> WALDORF: Did you fall?
> STATLER: No, my upper plate fell, and I jumped after it! [*TMS*, 1.21].

The problem is that we want to play, too. Whatever part of us falls for the corniness of the jokes, the rest of us jumps after it. Laughing at or even with those old men, these special bridge characters, bring us *into* play.

This desire, poignant when the show debuted, has lost none of its luster. The year *The Muppet Show* appeared on television, the American president, Gerald Ford, had not been elected to any national office. American troops had mostly come home from Viet Nam, but not in clear-cut victory. The nation struggled with recession and inflation. 1976 also saw just a brief rebound on Wall Street from the 1972–74 bear market (Cox et al). Morale and the economy hung on by the nails. Adults needed to know that childish and destructive (irrational) mayhem was well-buttoned up. *The Muppet Show* also answered a more pressing and very adult need to feel childlike again, if only for one half-hour per week.

Mediating such opposing needs only proved more imperative after the war. In 1976, sexual counterculture busily burst (albeit "off-screen" for many Americans) out of its bi-coastal "closet" in much the same way dressing room chaos erupts before the footlights, despite all the deft stage management Kermit brings to normalizing that energy with his Host act. That presidential election year, the nation scrutinized all over again the curtain between the nation's staged and backstage dramas. People had seen how Nixon's 1974 resignation, followed by Gerald R. Ford's act of pardon, "vanished" any performative consequences for potential "high crimes and misdemeanors."

America's backstage haunted the nation the way Uncle Deadly haunts the theater. The critique of macro-scale representation, already staged in the highest halls of American power, voiced itself within the micro-scale of the Muppet world. Despite the steady increase in small black bombs popping off within the TV-confines of *The Muppet Show*, Statler and Waldorf stage-manage the explosive problem of drama as both representation and real action as carefully as Kermit manages the palette of acts. We hear their message-management in grouching and occasional enthusiasm from these two representatives of American capitalist power, ex-businessmen most notable for their sighing over conspicuous and inevitable losses,

> STATLER: Every week this show looks better to me.
> WALDORF: Every week your eyesight gets worse [*TMS*, 1.21].

This voice of loss flips into the loss of voice:

> STATLER: Hey, Waldorf, I was wondering if you... [mouth moves, but no sound is heard]
> WALDORF: I guess I better get the batteries replaced in my hearing aid.
> STATLER: Ha ha ha! I fool him every time! [*TMS*, 1.1].

When a fellow cannot trust his closest associates, whose word can he trust? This dueling duo subtly raises anxiety over truth and trustworthiness within the proscenium, which they represent.

If art opens up a new way of relating to life, are two old geezers the best advocates of that strategy? Certainly, cooking up a new way to be in the world is not simply the bailiwick of the (culinarily-defunct) Swedish Chef. The composite of skits tests and deconstructs several approaches, leaving viewers with the enigma of the early modern chorus that is more than simply a commentary.

Of course, *The Muppet Show* is an experiment, but apparently not a successful physics or chemistry one, represented by Muppet Labs, Bunson Honeydew, and his allegorical partner Beaker, nor a bio-medical operation, represented by Veterinary Hospital, where the patients routinely explode, vanish, or find themselves subject to astonishing abuse and neglect. Life science students would not be surprised, at any rate, that the experiment is performed first on a frog:

> JULIET PROWSE: I never talked to a frog before.... I never knew frogs had a sense of humor.
> KERMIT: Let's face it, Julie, a frog without a sense of humor is a green lump [*TMS*, 1.1].

This exchange hints at a central theorem of *The Muppet Show* (if there is one!): *Eros* may not be conflated with wildlife. In the Muppet World, actual animals amount to a reminder of nonverbal Nature. In that realm, all that is humanly conscious speaks. For example, Muppy, the show's "eponymic" dog, is sometimes a real pooch who pads around the backstage and sometimes a puppet-puppy. As a flesh dog, he is seen and not heard. Only as a Muppet does Muppy "speak." Consciously, expressively and intelligently, he *bites, barks, licks* and *wags* (and sucks up all of Kermit's milk through the frog's straw). In Muppet Space, wild life is not *animalistic*. It is animistic. Put simply, as Kris Kristofferson opines to his co-star and wife Rita Coolidge, "Everything on this show walks and talks — animal, vegetable, and — A talking boulder — Mineral?" (*TMS*, 3.1)

Within the world of commodities, all of that life force feels dangerously centrifugal. Any brand of anarchy on Wall Street provokes panic. The business-as-usual *ethos* demands that buttons stay buttoned and ties tightly tied! Statler and Waldorf represent that world, both in terms of their appearance and the histories of their real namesakes, but they are also Muppets. As such, representation for them is problematic. Unlike much of the working cast, they are not feathery or furry critters. Rather, they are conspicuous wearers of suits. Members of the Muppet World, they also represent real human history.

Their names and attire speak of a conjoined American and British history, of business and power and success and luxury. Bearing rather time-honored high-brow names in American culture and business, Statler and Waldorf at first fain to look down on the low-brow mayhem onstage. Their names bear the hefty history of people as rich and powerful as these Muppets are old. Statler and Waldorf, as names, mean "luxury" and "American hospitality" and carry a legacy of robber baron privilege and the aftershocks of the Gilded Age, but beneath that surface similarity lies an opposition that touches the heart of their role as *vox populi*.

Waldorf is reminiscent of William Waldorf Astor, son of John Jacob Astor, the wealthiest man in America in his day. The younger Astor served as ambassador to Italy under Chester Arthur and built the Waldorf Hotel. When his father died in 1890, his inheritance made him the richest man in America. Yet, he repudiated the land that made his family rich; he was quoted as saying "America is not a fit place for a gentleman to live" (Sykes). Later to be knighted the 1st Viscount Astor of Great Britain, in 1899, William Waldorf became a British subject. In 1903 he bought Hever Castle, the childhood home of Anne Boleyn, where he spent his latter years (it was said) sleeping with two revolvers at his side and looking for her ghost. By the time *The Muppet Show* debuted in 1976, the name "Waldorf" served up a whole menu of incongruent connotations *prix fixe*: anthroposophic/naturalistic education with a side of creamy salad made from firm bits of walnut and crisp slivers of apple and celery.

In contrast to Waldorf's old money legacy, Statler is the namesake of Ellsworth Milton (E.M.) Statler, who launched his fortune with enormous temporary hotels in the blue collar towns of Buffalo and St. Louis to serve the great turn-of-the-century hoi-polloi expositions mounted in those cities. Despite setbacks—lousy weather, President McKinley's assassination—Statler turned a modest profit on the first venture and, if it were not too tasteless a pun, one might say he made a killing on the second. With his pockets lined, he shuffled off to Buffalo, his home, to erect his first permanent hotel. The workingman's city loved his catchy slogan: "A Room and a Bath for a Dollar and a Half" (Jarman). His goal was to provide a decent place to stay for average people, who typically shared a bath with many other travelers when they stayed in a hotel. He made comfort possible for the average traveler. This motive stands in marked contrast to Waldorf, erstwhile-American, who finally installed a moat and a drawbridge at his English home and forbade even his high-class friends to stay as overnight guests (Miller).

While Statler and Waldorf stand for money and social cachet, they also sit for all of that phallic power paled by time:

>WALDORF: I'd sure like to get close to Connie Stevens, but I'm already too close to something else.
>STATLER: What's that?
>WALDORF: 90 [*TMS*, 1.2].

The high tide of commerce seems to have washed them up and withdrawn. Once cosmopolitan titans, they now have nothing better to do than to witness a show as colorful, energetic, and ultimately as futile and silly as life must appear to them. Why watch with them what they watch? We watch both them and the stage show because they foreshadow our ineluctable condition and we need to see what they see that makes it worth their while to show up show after show. We might just be a little curious to know what makes it worthwhile to go on living.

The Muppet Show behaves a lot like an allegorical pageant of life through their eyes. They peer out of their velvet-lined box, itself an evocation of what is to come for us all (provided we have the wherewithal to line our boxes in velvet). If we are lucky, we will grow as old and rich as they, but lucky or not, we share their implied condition: one foot in the grave since the day they were made.

Like us, the television audience, they sit alongside the show. By Season Three, the show opens with a look at their box along with the theater audience, the whole singing together. Until they develop their connection to the *hoi polloi*, they are fence-sitters, in effect, between stage and audience. Until they forge a relationship with us, through Fozzie Bear as I describe anon, Statler and Waldorf are as alienated and yet enticed a group of viewers as we are. By turns, they grouse, cheer and doze on the threshold between the variety show of life and what comes after the last "commercial break." Together we wait and watch at the proscenium, the mouth of the great invisible divide between show and what comes after. And for a moment, but only for a moment, these two old men shelter us from the paradox of *Eros* within death.

They juxtapose their outrageous age between the audience and all the youthful energy that erupts in song and dance and bomb blasts. They bridge the gulf between the actions of men and Punch and Judy *commedia del arte* violence and caresses, all without real consequences. They impose brown-suited judgment on antics performed by puppets, children's playthings, arrayed in crayon bright colors. Presiding over that explosion of vivaciousness, Statler sighs over the depredations of age. Onstage, 38-year-old Connie Stevens sings a rock-n-roll oldie in her 1950s-era poodle skirt, tight white angora sweater and push-up bra (*TMS*, 1.2). She pretends to be a girl reminiscent of *Grease*, then a five-year-old Broadway musical that critiqued the sexual repression in the 1950s and contextualized the free-love movement of the 1960s. Statler sighs with unfulfilled desire. The energy of regret, lost opportunity, and lost time, threatens to overwhelm us with *Weltschmerz*, in post-war 1970s as well as now. Waldorf reacts as quickly to contain Statler's erotic grief. Cruelty as kindness accords with the paradoxical nature of their relationship; Waldorf implies that Statler need not grieve his loss because he has lost nothing:

> STATLER: I remember being a teenager in love.
> WALDORF: Yeah, but Queen Victoria wouldn't have you! [*TMS*, 1.2].

He was an impotent geezer romantically sidelined long before the sexual revolution ever took its first shot. For us, they proffer assurance of a "safe distance" from the mayhem that marks the edge between goals of business and the anarchic threat of erotic chaos. Stuffed suits struggle to contain Hog-Wild Desire. After all, loosing *Eros* is like unleashing Animal, who devours even a "live" TV (*TMS*, 3.1).

Before we label the notion of anarchic terror as histrionic, we might glance at the history of the proscenium arch, and how it has stood as proof of, and proof against, the Stuffed-Suit/Hog-Wild-Desire dichotomy that characterizes *The Muppet Show* as a whole, with Statler and Waldorf as its chief representative dyad.

One of the mightiest passive tools for artistic control, the proscenium is the frame around the opening of the stage, rendering theater into the form of a great big Punch-and-Judy puppet show. The arch and the curtain that close off view of the action confine play within a sort of recessed box, placing actors behind the barrier of the footlights. The audience views the action from only one direction. In the early 17th century, when this was a structural innovation, what the audience saw within that lit-up box swiftly mattered more than words. The proscenium arch enforced viewer passivity. It created an impassible distance, captivating spectacle, pretty and moveable scenery, pageantry and action — the arch bridged the highway to television, itself a kind of proscenium.

The Muppet Show takes this tool for passivity and effectively explodes it. Statler and Waldorf confront their complicity in the explosion:

> WALDORF: The thing I always thought was so weird about the Muppets is that they think explosions are funny. Explosions are not funny!
> [Statler's cigar explodes]
> WALDORF: Although some of them are really quite droll! [*TMS*, 1.1].

Before there was the television, there was the proscenium arch and before Inigo Jones, a favorite of King James I, built the arch into English theater design early in the king's reign, Standing Room Only "groundlings" crowded around a 40-foot wide stage that reached 25 feet into the audience. They could loaf alongside the tragedian boards, and a player could walk downstage and chat (Styan). Sixteenth-Century theater drama used few properties and even less scenery. Language nuance trumped visual spectacle. Cheap ticket prices, crowded free-form audience space, free verbal exchange between actors and audience (inaudible to higher-priced bench and box-seat holders) were common; judging by the number of book-burnings, arrests for conspiracy and treason and theater closures (even without the help of plague outbreaks), we can presume that the Tudor court, at least, felt that a lot more than clowning was going on in Elizabethan theaters. James I took care of that with Inigo Jones's proscenium arch.

In a deft subversion of that almost-400-year-old control-mechanism, *The Muppet Show* turns that artifice of separation between audience and play-action into a magnifying lens. The television screen is the proscenium arch. The cathode ray tube sits, transparent, between television-viewing audience (mostly human) and the players (mostly critters of felt, feather, yarn, etc). While the proscenium arch "lens" looks sometimes outward, at the puppet theater audience as symbolic of the viewing public, and ofttimes inward, at the backstage mayhem, the active proscenium "eye" of *The Muppet Show*, its special gaze, maintains a continuous focus on the interplay between art and audience, cultural artifact and consumer.

The Muppet Show visual lens cranks up the display to the point of absurdity while it tunes in on the unspeakable aspects of culture. The proscenium, a potent tool of repression and crowd control, can become a magnifying lens and a conduit when it opens channels between fantasy desires and real gratification. *The Muppet Show* proscenium, with Statler and Waldorf to voice that divide, focuses on those channels as the keys both to freedom and security. When Statler and Waldorf open their soft, felted mouths to kibitz, they reinforce their combined role as voice of that controversial threshold. Foremost, they focus attention on impotence and its opposite.

In the working world, the audience members are active and consequential. In the playhouse, they relinquish their active roles when they buy a ticket and confer their own part onto a false representative of the world, the players. This exchange inversion, in effect, takes place across the proscenium divide. When the passive-audience/play-action inversion breaks down, history has shown that political anarchy can ensue, even in post-industrial/modern America. I cite here, in particular, the Shakespeare Riots of May 10, 1849, examined in Nigel Cliff's 2007 work *The Shakespeare Riots*.

The riots took place, significantly for us, in Astor Place, namesake of W. Waldorf Astor. The problem arose over who was the better Shakespearean, high-art British actor William Macready or populist/popular American actor Edwin Forrest. Cliff claims this was the last moment Shakespeare was truly popular in America. The crowd rioted, determined not to give the stage to a British actor. Monied, powerful men of business took the matter into their hands, men the Muppets Statler and Waldorf ironically represent (for even monied, powerful men get old, deaf, sleepy and ultimately impotent). Such titans of business called in the National Guard, who fired live ammunition into the rioting crowd. Thirty died. Many more were wounded. Nothing could be more terrifying than the rise of a populist Shakespeare within American society, I suspect, because perhaps no playwright comprehends the centrifugal subterfuge of the staged-real dichotomy as does the work of W.S., the initials of the elderly male-personified dialectic-in-the-box.

Foremost for Shakespeare and for *The Muppet Show*, sexual energy blurs boundaries. The first to go is the human-Muppet divide. Female guests caress the host liberally. Juliet Prowse kisses Kermit. Connie Stevens, Florence Henderson, Ruth Buzzi, and Valerie Harper pet and stroke the frog just as if he were a good luck charm or a repressed prince. Miss Piggy validates these women's attentions to the frog by the violence of her jealousy, expressed in the obvious visual pun of her "pork chops." Human guests dance, joke and sing their way across the human-Muppet divide with human-sized Muppets.

Fittingly, the first season ends with *Mummenschantz* as guest stars, a dance troupe in which the human and the puppet are wholly melded into three black-clothed performers who lack human faces.

Always loitering close to the edge, Statler and Waldorf both define and defy the human-Muppet divide. The deep verity of living/non-living comprises one border over which Statler and Waldorf seem to stand guard. A vigilant eye is necessary. In *The Muppet Show,* life erupts from *anywhere.* The trouble is that old men do not always manage to stay awake. After a long, loud, day-glow, trippy disco piece with dancing boas and a singing former feather duster with only a very toothy mouth:

> STATLER: Was that a great number?
> WALDORF: I don't know. I slept through it.
> STATLER: So did I. That's why I asked [*TMS*, 1.21].

Perhaps when they doze, the stage fills with their dreams just as it filled with the allegory of life's vanity when they were awake. Then, when they are off-camera and we do not see them, we view instead the wildly alive things they dream.

The divide between waking and dream, between Us and Them, fades when feathery-ended day-glo tubes look out at us through their big eyes and dance a little scenario of social justice (*TMS*, 1.21). Two tubes are the same shape, same colors, but one is bigger. Because his large size renders him unable to see how he is just like the little guy, he wins several battles but loses the war. As long as the little tube cannot dance to the music, the big tube stomps him down. When the little tube dances to the beat, he beats the big tube (he shoots the big tube). Utterly incapacitated, stagehands and actors carry the vanquished tube off stage on a stretcher. When the just inversion is complete, the old men wake. Within *The Muppet Show*'s play with sleep and waking, two once-powerful men doze in their impotent age and dream of justice. When Harvey Korman complains that he is the only human, the Muppets turn him into a chicken (*TMS* 1.10).

Across the proscenium divide, the differential between Life and Non-Life is the most fundamental of deconstructed dichotomies. From the first episode, when tall green noodles shaped like giraffes dance with the guest star poking wry fun at how 5'11" Juliet Prowse was once thought too tall to be a serious dancer — any identity presumption, starting with the expectation of an absolute divide between human-guest and puppet-host, dissolves like Prowse herself at the end of the scene.

The expectation that Statler and Waldorf will hold that line, however, proves flawed — as both "human" and "puppet," they represent the first assault on ontological fundamentalism. They prove to be as "in on" the eroticized Muppet World as Kermit himself. If we enter the adult world of Muppets with any presumption of a stable puppet-human dichotomy, an amicable separation of "life-forms" and "lifelike-forms," we fool ourselves. Likewise, our reliance upon a preference for the creative over the created reveals a Flesh-Felt chauvinism. When life imbues all things, consciousness resides in all skins; whether cellulose or cellular, the Flesh-Felt Binary must give way to the Felt Flesh Continuum.

Even the proscenium participates in that Continuum. When the theater picture synchronizes with the TV cathode-ray tube frame, the map of the Muppet World connects seamlessly with the map of the living, TV-watching world: "[I]t is no longer a question of either maps or territories. Something has disappeared: the sovereign difference, between one and the other..." (Baudrillard 2). This occurs most obviously when Fozzie Bear is doing a stand-up act. This identification — Muppet World = TV Viewer World — opens the channels for Statler and Waldorf to mediate, as they do faithfully when Fozzie takes the stage. As dialectic expression of the proscenium and the worlds that lie on either side of that invisible divide, we turn to our beloved geezers for some reference point. This is their job on the show: they mediate between worlds. They always interrupt Fozzie Bear because he stands for vaudeville, for populist theater, or even for street theater just barely buttoned up, tie knotted and hauled indoors.

As the voice-box of both stage (*vox proscenii*) and audience (*box populi*?), they draw attention to the phenomenon of the dissolving divide between the "real" and the "representational." Apropos to that *box populi-vox proscenii* function, Statler and Waldorf not only draw attention to actions like Juliet Prowse's dissolution in word; they also enact the dissolution.

> WALDORF: She vanished! How did she do that?
> STATLER: Probably like this. [Statler takes a deep breath and fades himself out]
> WALDORF: [to the television audience] That's probably how she did it [*TMS* 1.1].

If even two impotent old men can do this vanishing act, it stands to reason that anyone can. In the real world, the television audience has already seen that anyone and anything can vanish, including guilt and responsible redress, if men are powerful enough to make it so. Our avatars of business demonstrate that the audience can also vanish — but in the world of Muppets, it is only by our own choice.

If we willingly suspend disbelief, animistic power *might* arc across the social membrane of the proscenium into the "real" precincts of these suited gents and, by proxy, to us. Discomfort with that power might prompt us to hang onto our skepticism, so that we can feel comfortably *unlike* the Muppets. As long as *We* are not *They*, we might feel safe from the chaos that choice and power imply. Then Statler and Waldorf undermine our misgivings. They sigh over lost love or the need to "stretch their legs," and we are united in our humanity. The pair enacts a paradox. Just when we touch close to the facts of our existence, we drift dreamily on the ontological frontier of satire, no closer than ever to a definitive division between "real" and "make-believe."

Eros blurs that line. Old men sighing for love contains that desire up to a point. We expect old men to sit and to sigh. Muppet *Eros* is so potent that it overflows the banks of normative sexuality. Wayne and Wanda, representatives of normality, regularly fail to finish so much as one line of a song. Unfettered sound and movement flood their space and drown them out. That same subversive energy courses through the routine *At the Ball* scenes in the form of slapstick violence: Animal routinely "dips" his dance partner so hard she hits the floor, but she remarks, "Say, that was FUN!" Rowlf the dog dances with the human girl, her long hair momentarily obscuring a collar that is much thicker, blacker, and more formal than the flea collar Rowlf suggests it is. Even "old folk" Muppets like George the Handyman cannot resist the current of energy, bumping in missionary rhythm. All the while, dancers toss off tension-moderating jokes. Referring to high-culture icons in a campy (not to say cannibalistic) manner refocuses the carnality of the situation:

> MISS PIGGY: Do you prefer Shakespeare to Bacon?
> MISTER PIG: I prefer *anything* to BACON! [*TMS* 1.1].

The frankly corny, absurd or silly verbal context deflects attention from orgiastic visuals.

The bacchanalia feels under control as long as the old men sit tight in the balcony, yet true to the free-association ethos of *The Muppet Show*, one or both soon leave their analytical safe-distance box. First, Statler and Waldorf enter *At the Ball* together. Dancing is still an obvious visual metaphor for sex when, apparently not for the first time, Statler and Waldorf waltz in one another's arms and argue over their gender roles.

> STATLER: You said I could lead this time!
> WALDORF: *You* said you were going to wear the pink taffeta! [*TMS* 1.21].

Once they have opened the verbal door to cross-dressing, it is only a matter of time before word becomes deed and the show performs the realignment of norms.

Most basic of all norms is the presumption of old men's sexual passivity. Statler and Waldorf shake that surety when they "shake it" "At the Ball," but they topple it when they argue over meeting the beautiful, young Valerie Harper. Both want to do more than *think* out of the box. Both agree that only one should venture to meet her. They agree to "flip" for it — the implied coin flip becomes two different sorts of flipping. One is the slapstick standard visual literalization of a verbal expression: Statler suddenly flies up out of his chair, turns in the air and flops back to the box. The other sort of "flip" took place when both Statler and Waldorf evinced an *active* interest in a woman. Although Statler wins the "flip," he represents both of them, and (by proxy) us. So far he has been presumed impotent. Now he proves otherwise.

He asserts himself backstage, a potted flower in his lap. This contained bit of flora must not be watered, or it will grow out of control. *Eros*, barely leashed in this theater of desire, imbues even old Statler's bud. A little accidental moisture activates the plant. The vine grows into an imperializing monster. Statler's phallic potential expresses itself in a leafy stalk so fecund that it fills the theater with its flora. The quickly-lengthening rope of leaves both highlights and obliterates boundaries. The vine borders doorways and staircases, but it violates persons. Statler's "vegetable love" proves awfully kinky. The flower chases Muppets and humans, ties them up, gags them, collars them, hauls them on and off stage and, finally, spawns a suitably phallic "son"-flower (*TMS*, 1.20).

Statler's disappearance and his "flip" engender tension over whether he, as the audience that represents us, in fact, *is* us. If we easily accepted that we could not take a deep breath and vanish, can we feel so complacent about Statler's "flip"? If he can "flip" his passivity, can we? If we embody any aspect of the power of the life force expressed most poignantly in two enfeebled old men, the subversive potential for personal change looks pretty nearly unlimited. That personal empowerment, if it is united with deep urgings for social change, feels ... like a new kind of scary. No wonder *The Muppet Show* teems with monsters. The theater itself spawned its very own blue-faced, tuxedoed phantom, presumably out of the composite fear of sex and success, ironically named Uncle Deadly.

In 1905, when the historical Statler and Waldorf were young and powerful men, Sigmund Freud explored libidinal energy in terms of social constructs in *Jokes and their Relation to the Unconscious* and *Three Essays on the Theory of Sexuality*, building on his 1900 work, *The Interpretation of Dreams*. In his work on humor, he connects the narcissism of the psyche, the inner person, with the individual's social relations and external networks of meaning, such that humor amounts to a sudden self-recognition in terms of the external world: "The comic arises in the first instance as an unintended discovery derived from human social relations" (Freud 234). Repressed libidinal tension produces humor when it is released into view. Release is terrifying in its potential for disorder, shame, violence, obliteration, but far worse, it might be *fun*. In other words, anxiety-production rises precisely in proportion with the possibility for delight, communion, thrill, pleasure and humor. Statler and Waldorf, doing double-duty, mediate both the potential for violence and for hilarity to release a particular hidden potential that lurked in all that roiling energy.

Of course, they perform their greatest alchemy with their dramatic foil, Fozzie Bear. The old men have devoted whole episodes to abusing Fozzie: "You're doing impressions? We'd like to see you do an impression of a bare stage!"—to which Fozzie dutifully responds by doing a BEAR stage. A people-pleaser by trade, when his people abandon him, Fozzie abandons that role. We have already seen that when Statler leaves his box, his leafy stalk grows. Stalking Valerie Harper, his stem of love turns from passive to aggressive. Viewers as regular as Statler wonder if Fozzie abandons his usual pleaser role, will his vengeance and scorn similarly engulf the theater? Yet, who best deserves Fozzie's vengeful scorn, and who is left when everyone leaves him? If anyone should handle this crisis of confidence, it must be Statler and Waldorf, his constant tormentors and companions.

They are constant in several ways. As the voice of the relational "wall" between audience and players, they cannot leave until the curtain falls. When "Ig-glue" attaches them, they cannot leave even then — they become an inseparable part of the theater upholstery (*TMS* 3.4). However, they have regularly used Fozzie rather harshly. Besides begging for a bare (not bear) stage, Statler and Waldorf ask for his promise that his last joke was really his *last* joke. They get their wish. Plaintively, Fozzie drops the jesting: "Hey, how come you two guys are still there? Did you lose your beds at the Old Fools' Home?" (*TMS* 1.22). Surprisingly, when the forced jokes stop, the two old men laugh sincerely. They enjoy his quip at their expense. They avert the threat of escalating acrimony by laughing at themselves. Fozzie waves his hand dismissively and despondently at them, and at the emptied theater, where no jokes, much less riots, will now take place. Sadly, the libidinal energy of riot and chaos is the same life force that fuels the spontaneous laughter of crowds, and the whole spectrum of that animism is denied him. Fozzie claims, "Ah, it's TOO LATE!" Suddenly, at that moment, it is no longer too late. Waldorf and Statler applaud Fozzie. They laugh *with* him.

Wonderfully, Statler and Waldorf transfigure abandonment into sympathy for the rejected individual. Chaos and criticism transmute into acceptance and appreciation. Statler and Waldorf redeem the crowd's repudiation of the audience-player relationship. They stay and laugh warmly, not derisively. The relationship is no longer about blowing off tension in laughter, symbolized by small black hand bombs with sparking fuses, or ramping up erotic chaos to find the centrifugal fly-off point. Statler and Waldorf *did not* abandon Fozzie and, through them, neither did we.

Through our mutual friends, we recognize the importance of tenderness. Through Statler and Waldorf, we have [safely!] experienced life's raw energy, the violence and passion of joining, of song and dance, and now we enter a complementary emotional space. We join with Fozzie in sorrow for the abandoned individual who tried so hard to please. Through Statler and Waldorf, a shared sympathy closes the curtain over sadness. They are the ever-present guardians of that threshold. It is not too late. If we wonder, *What would happen if the suit and vest were unbuttoned, the Windsor knot untied? Would hog-wild desire loose the dogs of revolution upon us?* Statler and Waldorf, Muppet-Men, our curmudgeon heroes show us that out of the unfettered heart flows compassion.

>WALDORF: Eh, what do you think?
>STATLER: Beats sitting home watching TV! [*TMS* 1.1].

Works Cited

Baudrillard, Jean. *Simulacra and Simulation*. Trans. Sheila Faria Glaser. Ann Arbor: University of Michigan Press, 1994.
Cliff, Nigel. *The Shakespeare Riots: Revenge, Drama and Death in Nineteenth Century America*. New York: Random House, 2007.
Cowles, Virginia. *The Astors*. New York: Alfred A. Knopf, 1979.
Cox, Amanda, Xaquin G.V. Leonhardt, and David Leonhardt. "Bear Markets." *The New York Times*. 10.11.2008: <http://www.nytimes.com/interactive/2008/10/11/business/20081011_BEAR_MARKETS.html>.
Darlington, William Aubrey. *Through the Fourth Wall*. Freeport, NY: Books for Libraries Press, 1968.
Freud, Sigmund. *The Interpretation of Dreams*. Trans. Joyce Crick. Oxford: Oxford University Press, 1999.
_____. *Jokes and Their Relation to the Unconscious*. Trans. James Strachey. New York: Norton, 1963.
_____. *Three Essays on the Theory of Sexuality*. Trans. James Strachey. New York: Basic Books, 2000.
Jarman, Rufus. *A Bed for the Night — Story of E.M. Statler and His Remarkable Hotels*. New York: Harper, 1952.
Miller, Floyd. *Statler, America's Extraordinary Hotelman*. New York: The Statler Foundation, 1968.
The Muppet Show Season One (Special Edition) 1976-77. DVD. Buena Vista Home Entertainment. 2005.
Styan, J.L. *Shakespeare's Stagecraft*. Cambridge: Cambridge University Press, 1967.
Sykes, Bonnie Marie. "William Waldorf Astor." *American National Biography Online*. Oxford, England: Oxford University Press. Feb. 2000 <http://www.anb.org/articles/10/10-00059.html>.

The Muppet Show Re-forms the Fringe
Anissa M. Graham

> *"There's just one thing I gotta remember. I ... am ... normal."*
> Jean Stapleton, *The Muppet Show*

The Fringe on Top

The story of the Muppets and their impact on popular culture is intertwined with the story of television itself. By the late 1950s the television had quickly replaced the radio as the central icon of the family home. Its position as living room centerpiece encouraged everyone to focus attention on it. Parents, who began to see their children absorbed by television shows (both those created especially for them and those that were not), worried and fretted over the sort of television little Billy and Suzy watched. While typical worries centered on the sexual and violent content of prime-time TV programming, parents felt they needn't worry about programming created specifically for children, like *The Howdy Doody Show, Kukla, Fran, and Ollie,* and *Sky King*, because they focused on imaginative play or on fantastic adventures. During the 1960s and 1970s, animated programming slowly began to replace formats that relied on human actors; shows such as *The Jetsons* and *The Flintstones* became the new standard for children's programming (Alexander). The 1970s also saw the emergence of parenting guides influenced by the work of Dr. Benjamin Spock; these guides, with their focus on the cognitive and psychological development of the child, refocused critical lenses on television shows. That focus continues in the era of No Child Left Behind; strictly educational shows, like *Sesame Street* and *Blue's Clues*, are held to a certain standard regarding intellectual content, but shows meant primarily to entertain, like *Spongebob Squarepants, Fairly Oddparents, Hannah Mon-*

tana, or *Camp Lazlo*, need not require any critical thinking at all. Such stratification of programming is not limited to children's television, but early emphasis on the gap between intellect and entertainment creates an audience of adult viewers who often consciously avoid anything labeled "intellectual" or "cultural." As Jennifer C. Garlen observes in her essay in this anthology, *The Muppet Show* from its inception has seamlessly and hilariously blended high and low culture into entertainment for both adults and children. Intellect and frivolity work together in a wonderfully weird harmony on the show. In addition to blending high and low culture, *The Muppet Show* brings fringe culture into the home. It normalizes the often frightening elements of those on the outside and in some cases "weirdifies" the normal.

Early Forays into the Fringe

Perhaps it is not particularly surprising that the Muppets embraced those on the outside and, in particular, elements of counter-culture. A quick review of the early performances of Jim Henson and the Muppets makes clear that they did not need to bring the fringe in with them; the Muppets were already there. For instance, a skit involving an early version of Kermit examined the problems of visual thinking; the skit, which appeared several times in the Muppets' early performances in the 1960s, puts a spotlight on the surreal world in which the Muppets live. What the Muppets visualize is quite literally visual as it is drawn on-screen for the television audience to see. In each version of the sketch, an accomplished visual thinker (Kermit on *The Ed Sullivan Show*) must show a straight man just learning the craft (Grump on *The Ed Sullivan Show*) how this visual thinking thing is done. The lesson quickly gets out of control as the visualized thoughts take over the screen, obscuring the characters. The sketch emphasizes the "in" nature of the hipster with his use of scat rhythms making the staid normality of the square appear abnormal (*Muppets Magic*).

Another early example of re-forming the fringe into the normal can be seen in the early puppet Yorick. Yorick is nothing more than a head with an appetite, reminiscent of any of the all-consuming movie monsters-of-the-week from screens big and small. In a sketch involving the ur–Kermit, Yorick slowly devours the in-drag Kermit as he/she sings "I've Grown Accustomed to Your Face," a variation on the closing number of Allan Jay Lerner and Frederick Lowe's 1956 musical *My Fair Lady*. In its original form, the stiff Professor Higgins suddenly realizes that he has fallen in love with the once cultural outsider, Eliza Doolittle. Higgins, himself simultaneously an insider and an outsider, through the course of the song comes to terms with his desire to continue his relationship with the once socially inappropriate Eliza (Lerner and Loewe). While the original song highlights acceptance of the unusual by the normal, the Muppet skit rejects acceptance in favor of consumption. Yorick, as the outsider, doesn't want Kermit to accept him. While Eliza becomes normal through internalizing patterns of speech, Yorick literally internalizes the normal by consuming Kermit. However, the fringe act of consumption negates any normalizing effect Kermit might have had (*Muppets Magic*).

Muppets as the Fringe

In its debut season in 1976-77, *The Muppet Show* continued the Muppets' forays into the fringe. While their earlier journeys involved Muppets-centered interactions, *The Muppet Show* with its variety show format allowed the characters to bring human actors into or out from the fringes. Guest stars on the show became participants in any number of unusual moments that reconfigured their status as stars and as people. For instance, Ethel Merman's appearance in Season One follows an already established pattern for female guest stars—competition with Miss Piggy for star status. The gauntlet is thrown in Kermit's opening monologue, when Piggy interrupts to let him know that she will be performing a medley of Ethel Merman's greatest hits. Kermit asks, "Why would anyone want to hear you sing Miss Merman's songs when Miss Merman is here to sing them herself?" (1.22). Piggy, not to be put off, replies that since she had rehearsed them, she'd perform them anyway and call it a tribute to Irving Berlin. Piggy's sense of her own stardom in thinking that a performance of someone else's work by her would be an honor is typical of the sort of star tinkering the Muppets do throughout the show's run. Instead of Piggy's performance, Ethel Merman performs a series of duets featuring some of her signature songs. She and Piggy sing a portion of "Anything You Can Do" from *Annie Get Your Gun*. Piggy's performance begins as the others do with Merman looking at her through a dressing room tabletop mirror frame. Here Piggy and the other performers are ostensible reflections of Merman herself. However, Piggy, unlike the other performers who worked in the mirror for this sketch, comes out of the fixed frame to become adversary rather than reflection. Piggy ultimately wins the contest by singing higher than Merman can, albeit off-key.

While this interaction between Merman and the Muppets pulls an established star into the fringe, the star seems relatively comfortable there as is evidenced by her closing number "There's No Business Like Show Business." In this number, Merman brings the Muppets (the fringe) into the norm by including them in the "showpeople" category. The Muppets are part of the community of performers to which Merman herself belongs; this community, like the Muppets, functions as insiders and outsiders. Merman's final statement highlights the inside status of the outsider as showperson: "You know, you don't have to be crazy to do this show. [Pause] But it helps." (1.22) The "You don't have to be crazy to..." gag certainly wasn't a new joke when the show appeared; however, its use in the closing moments emphasizes Merman's acceptance of her new community. She has done the show, and based on the logic of the assertion, her performances work because she, like her castmates the Muppets, is crazy.

Blended Fringe — Outsiders on the In

In addition to bringing insiders out, the first season of *The Muppet Show* embraced a moment of the fringe with an appearance by Vincent Price, the "crown prince of terror." Price's appearance on the show allowed the Muppets to explore some of their fringe tendencies more overtly. The guest list preceding Price included performers like Jim Nabors, Florence Henderson, Peter Ustinov, and Ben Vereen. While these performers were subjected to all manner of oddities in their performances on the show, like Peter Ustinov's conversations with a hat rack, for instance, the fringe elements in the episodes are merely odd, not terrifying. Vincent Price's appearance, on the other hand, offered an opportunity for the Muppets to explore the macabre in new ways.

Price's early career was littered with a wide variety of roles designed to terrify and intimidate. His appearances in films like *House of Wax* (1953), *House on Haunted Hill* (1959), *The Tingler* (1959), and a successful series of films loosely connected to the works of Edgar A. Poe and Nathaniel Hawthorne for scream king Roger Corman established his creepy credentials. Like Boris Karloff and some of his other contemporaries in the Gothic-horror set, Price was also willing to find the comedic in the horrific. Appearances in films like *Dr. Goldfoot and the Bikini Machine* (1965) and on TV series like *F Troop* play on the audience's expectations for a Price character and set those expectations on their ears. In 1967 Price appeared on the situation comedy *F Troop* in an episode entitled "V is for Vampire." In the episode Price plays Transylvanian immigrant Count Sfoza. This character and Price's performance illustrate the shift in his career as well as a shift in response to the Count Dracula pattern of monster; the Count arrives at the beginning of the episode driving a black hearse with black horses wearing a black opera cape complete with blood red silk lining. His first line is clearly an allusion to Bela Lugosi's first line in Tod Browning's 1931 *Dracula;* instead of being creepy, the line is rendered comic as is evidenced by the ubiquitous laugh track and Price's heavy pancake makeup. Horror and creepiness are reduced to sight gags.

Price's work wasn't all horror though; other elements of his career served to temper his scary résumé. In 1962 Price began working with Sears and Roebuck to bring fine art to the masses. "The Vincent Price Collection of Fine Art" was a successful program for Sears that ran for nine years putting "more than 50,000 pieces of fine art [...] into American homes and offices" ("Sears and Fine Art"). The success of this program brought to the public eye Price's knowledge of art, a knowledge cultivated through study at Yale and the University of London ("Sears and Fine Art"). In the late 1960s, he co-authored a series of cookbooks with then-wife Mary that highlighted the best of American cuisine.

In contrast to the slightly silly *F Troop* vampire and Price as art critic and chef were the villains in the popular horror films that emerged around Price's 1977 appearance on *The Muppet Show*. Films, like *The Exorcist, The Texas Chainsaw Massacre, Carrie,* and *Halloween,* featured villains who happily and tragically splattered blood; the age of the slasher picture had taken hold leaving behind the atmospheric 18th-century Gothic inspired films *(The Abominable Dr. Phibes)* or the science horror films *(The Fly, The Tingler)* of Price's early career. Price's body of work throughout the 1960s and 1970s represents an interesting phenomenon with regards to fringe culture. Having been so outrageously abnormal for so long, Price had become normal and funny by the late 1970s. Many of the adult viewers of his *Muppet Show* appearance might not recognize him from his horror work but rather from his stint as Egghead on the *Batman* series. Younger audience members might recognize his voice from *Here Comes Peter Cottontail* in which he voiced the "villain" January Q. Irontail. These performances as well as his hobbies were so far removed from the labs and castles of his films that perhaps the only scary thing left about him was his voice.

In the year before his appearance on *The Muppet Show,* Price was called upon to lend that scary voice and presence to a TV special starring none other than Alice Cooper; Price played the spirit of the nightmare to Cooper's Steven, a persona inspired by Cooper's song, "Welcome to My Nightmare." (*"Alice Cooper: The Nightmare"*). Like his appearance with Cooper, Price's *Muppet Show* appearance allowed him to rekindle some of that ability to scare an audience and to satirize, not the fringe he was once a part of, but the normal he had been embraced by.

Price's *Muppet Show* appearance plays with all of these roles moving the actor in and out of the fringe. He appears in three major sketches through the course of the episode. The first sketch is entitled "The House of Horror" co-starring the bastion of the weird, Gonzo, and the desperate comedian, Fozzie Bear. Fozzie and Gonzo rent a "summer cottage" in the mountains of Transylvania, which Gonzo had seen advertised in the *Wampire Veekly.* While they bemoan their frightening new home complete with haunts, a knock at the door brings in Price in full Dracula attire — fluffy white shirt, medallion on a red satin sash, black dress pants, and an opera cape (a virtual duplicate of his Count Sforza costume). After a series of one-liners, some of which mock notions of beauty, the real punchline of the sketch appears. We, along with Fozzie and Gonzo, learn that Price will turn into a "screaming, maniacal, demonic, raging, blood-lusting animal" at the stroke of midnight (1. 19). In the distance we hear the chiming of an old clock, and Price's "beautiful" assistant, played by the Phantom of the Muppet Show also known as Uncle Deadly, attempts to assist his master during his transformation and is horrified to discover that it is New Year's Eve. Price's transformation on New Year's is a special one; instead of a monster, he turns into Guy Lombardo, with strains of "Auld Lang Syne" playing in the background. This transformation, which involves Price putting on a party hat, grabbing a baton, and blowing on a noisemaker, so terrifies Fozzie, Gonzo, and the assistant that they run screaming into the night. From 1929 until 1976, Guy Lombardo hosted an annual New Year's Eve show broadcast live from New York; his last performance came mere months after this episode was filmed. Lombardo was famous for his rendition of "Auld Lang Syne." The nostalgic nature of "Auld Lang Syne" with its sentimental attachment to the past as well as Lombardo's annual appearance worked to make him a perfect icon of mainstream culture for the Muppets to take a swing at. In this sketch, Price and the Muppets mock an American institution. In modern terms, it would be the equivalent of mocking Dick Clark and his Rockin' New Year's Eve. Based on the response of Fozzie, Gonzo, and the assistant, we should reject figures like Lombardo. By fleeing the Lombardo/Price monster, the Muppets tell their child audience that it's potentially okay to turn away from what parents consider "normal" and "good" entertainment. In the British version and in the versions available on DVD, Price turns into Jack Parnell. The joke in this case is that Parnell is the composer of *The Muppet Show's* theme. Instead of mocking the American mainstream, the Muppets now mock themselves as elements of the normal through the rejection of their own composer.

The second sketch is a roundtable discussion with Price, French chef Pierre LaCousse, and Muppet Monster Gorgon Heap. Interestingly, both the chef **and** the monster are close friends of Price. Price again embraces both acceptable (LaCousse) and fringe (Gorgon Heap) culture here. Kermit emphasizes the cultural nature of this segment in his conversation with Price by saying it will "raise the intellectual level" of the program (1.19). Instead of an intellectual discussion, however, Muppet cannibalism ensues as Heap eats both LaCousse and Kermit. Price too attempts to eat his host. The horror of the consumption of our green surrogate is diffused somewhat by Price's admission that he knows "I'm a bit of a devil, but I do love frog's legs" as he hams up licking his lips (1.19). As with other cannibalistic moments in the series, consumption serves to alienate and assimilate. The roundtable discussion focuses on the art of French cuisine, and the use of frogs' legs in French recipes is a subtle subtext here. French cuisine, once the realm of the elite, had been brought into the homes of everyday people by Julia Childs starting in the early 1960s and by Price himself. Not attempting to eat Kermit becomes abnormal based on the context of French fine dining. However, Kermit is also the host of the program, a being capable of reasoning and speech, and eating the rational host puts the scene back into the fringe.

The final sketch has Price being interviewed by Kermit, who has emerged unharmed by his consumption by Gorgon Heap in the previous sketch. Kermit asks Price how he can so convincingly transform himself into a vampire. Price gives a rather lengthy explanation of the actor's craft, and when he finishes, Price asks Kermit if he understands. Kermit nods, baring a set of impressive fangs in his froggy mouth, and then lunges for Price's throat. Kermit's transformation into a monster in the final sketch is yet another example of the Muppet tendency to normalize the fringe. Of all the characters on the show, Kermit is most like his audience. As host, it is his job to serve as mediator between the audience and the acts. He intervenes on the behalf of both when things get weird or otherwise out of hand. In those rare moments when Kermit becomes performer, the audience is led on a journey of self-discovery. By becoming a frog-vampire, Kermit emphasizes that there's a little fringe in all of us; thereby proving what Dr. Jeff Q. Bostic and his colleagues posit in an essay about the influence of anti-heroes on adolescent behavior which includes a discussion on one of the Muppets' later guest stars, Alice Cooper. Bostic and his colleagues assert that the fringes remain outside of the mainstream for only a finite time before the mainstream "invariably reequilibrates to them" (57). The Muppets are simply doing the work of the mainstream by normalizing the outlandish on their show.

Scary Fringes

Season Three of *The Muppet Show* sees a return to the scary fringe with guest star, Alice Cooper. Throughout the episode, Cooper will be rendered both horrific and comic through his interactions with the cast. In particular, Statler and Waldorf, everyone's favorite hecklers, do much to normalize the very fringe Cooper. Cooper's threat to the normal was well established by the time of his *Muppet Show* appearance in 1978. Vincent Furnier had been creating a spectacle of himself since his days with his high school rock band, The Earwigs. Much of the spectacle was created through the use of mascara and weird costumes punctuated by the liberal use of explosions and stage blood during live performances. From the onset Cooper's work can be seen as a carefully constructed performance; however, an appearance at the 1969 Toronto Rock N Roll Revival would forever blur the lines between performance and reality. Jeffrey Morgan recounts the event in his biographical essay of Cooper once posted on the artist's official website. During the Alice Cooper Group's performance, someone threw a live chicken onstage; Cooper reflexively threw it back. In attempts to explain later why he threw the chicken to the audience, Cooper claimed he thought chickens could fly. Unfortunately for the '69 Toronto chicken, it didn't; the chicken was pulled apart by rabid fans. The ASPCA, among other organizations, would dog and continues to dog Cooper for the violent and rather horrific death of the chicken, labeling him as a sick, demented monster (Morgan). While no chickens were harmed in his appearance on *The Muppet Show*, Cooper does threaten the souls of three of the cast — Kermit, Gonzo, and Piggy.

Kermit sets the tone of the program with his introduction of Cooper: he asks the audience to welcome "one of the world's most talented but frightening performers" (3.7). Kermit's introduction immediately establishes Cooper's actions as performance. In his segue to the first sketch, Kermit offers the following bit of advice: "So beware of ghoulies and ghosties and long-legged beasties and things that go bump in the night" (3.7). By evoking a traditional Scottish prayer in his introduction, Kermit establishes Cooper as otherwordly; the prayer asks God to "preserve us" from the terrors of the night. Kermit's lines cause the audience to wonder if Cooper is as dangerous as the rumors surrounding him claim; these lines create additional tension between the normal and the fringe. Just where is Cooper in the continuum we wonder. Following Kermit's introduction, Cooper and his band of monstrous Muppets perform "Welcome to My Nightmare."

The sketch is set in a dungeon with Cooper rising from a coffin, and like Price in both his *Muppet Show* appearance and his appearance on *F Troop*, Cooper is decked out in Dracula garb. Cooper's costume is more like Frank Langella's from his appearance in 1977 in the Broadway revival of *Dracula* than the Lugosi-inspired costume of Price; it looks more like a stylized tuxedo than a throwback to sensationalized Victoriana. Cooper glides across the stage, summoning a ghost to dance with him as he sings this 1975 hit. The lyrics are enough to reinforce the notion that the gap between mainstream and fringe is quite small indeed. Cooper tells us that we will "like it" in his nightmare, that we "are gonna feel right at home" and that we "belong" (Alice Cooper). The fringe, unlike the mainstream, is inclusive rather than exclusive. Cooper and his band disappear at song's end: such dissolves are a staple of this episode and emphasize one of the scary components of Cooper's stage persona for adults, his association with the demonic.

Cooper's connection with the devil is stressed through allusions to a mysterious boss and a Faustian contract. The reference to the tale of Doctor

Faustus adds an air of intellectualism to the show; adult audiences might remember Faust from school readings of either eponymous works by Christopher Marlowe or Johann Wolfgang von Goethe. However, one need not know either of these works to know the story of a bargain in which the cost is greater than the gain. The Faust story is introduced when Cooper offers to make Kermit a rock star or an astronaut if he signs a contract; this fame and fortune are to be provided by a "friend" of Cooper. Kermit rejects Cooper's offer, but Gonzo and Miss Piggy are tempted to sign.

Gonzo's desperate desire to be recognized and loved leads to comedy as he begs for a pen to sign Cooper's contract: "I'll sell ya my soul for a pen. No wait, I have plans for that" (3.7). Gonzo's needs weirdly echo those of Faustus in Marlowe's play. Faust, too, longs for love; one of his last requests of Mephostophilis is to have Helen of Troy as his lover (Marlowe, *Doctor Faustus*, V.1.115). Also like Faustus, Gonzo is willing to barter away something priceless in a haphazard manner. Gonzo, however, never gets a pen, and his soul is safe.

Later, Cooper and a rainbow-feathered metallic Muppet perform a duet together, the 1977 "You and Me," which begins with the line "For I have touched you and made you beautiful" (*The Muppet Show*, 2.7). At the end of the sketch, we discover that the feathers hide Miss Piggy who does not like her makeover at all. She calls Cooper a creep and demands to be changed back. Piggy, in this instance standing in for more mainstream elements, refuses to embrace the fringe notion of beauty or of love as defined in the song; her rejection of Cooper, like Gonzo's desperate pleas for a pen, creates comedy as Cooper asks his mysterious boss via a two-way radio if he gets a commission for hourly rentals of souls. The answer, we learn, is a no, punctuated by a tongue of flame (3.7).

Each of these moments serves to remove the terror of the rather frightening idea that the Devil or some sort of evil agent is out to destroy us. This Devil could easily be a member of the fringe (i.e. Cooper) who moves among us. Yet, the comedy that results from Cooper's attempts to win over the Muppets undercuts that terror of losing the soul. The very nature of the Muppets themselves lessens the threat of Cooper's soul stealing. What sort of a soul do felt and fur puppets have, and why would the Devil want one? The perceived silliness in the notion of Muppet souls allows Cooper to simultaneously act as the threatening fringe and as a member of the normal world. Because the Muppets (probably) don't have souls, Cooper is only an actor pretending to be an agent of evil, and while it doesn't strictly make one normal, being an actor does make Cooper a part of the community of "normal" people.

Perhaps the most telling Muppet interaction in this episode is Cooper's confrontation with Sam the Eagle. Sam, whose patriotism and rigid social values are often the source of much mockery, establishes himself as the voice of decency very early in *The Muppet Show*'s run. In fact, in the Vincent Price episode Sam introduces the singing act of Wayne and Wanda as a countermeasure to the weirdness of Price; he refers to Wayne and Wanda as "very natural" and "very normal" (1.19). Natural and normal are certainly not elements of Cooper's appearance on the show. Sam confronts Cooper in his dressing room, coming up behind Cooper who is refreshing his mascara. Sam tells Cooper: "You sir are a demented, sick, degenerate, barbaric, naughty freako!" Cooper replies with a smile and a cheery "Thank you." Sam departs head in feathers muttering "Freakos—1, Civilization—0" (3.7). By having this confrontation take place in a dressing room, the Muppets highlight that Cooper's threat is largely a performance. He's not really leading all the kiddies to hell; he's just stretching their notions of normalcy.

The show's conclusion undoes Cooper's demonic threat entirely by having Gonzo appear onstage in a puff of brimstone-like smoke. Kermit worries that Gonzo has signed the Faustian pact, but, the piece of paper Gonzo holds is actually the special effects bill. In the ensuing laughter, we are reassured that the "ghoulies and ghosties and long-legged beasties" are just clever camera tricks and not threats to our immortal souls. The ultimate indignity is visited upon Cooper in Statler and Waldorf's parting joke: Statler—"So that was Alice Cooper." Waldorf—"You should see his sister, James Fennimore" (3.7). Cooper is now linked with an author who helped to establish the myth of the American frontier, an author very much a part of mainstream culture. Nobody who gets heckled so magnificently could possibly be dangerous.

Altering the Audience

In their appearances on the show, both Price and Cooper take the Muppets seriously as performers; they interact with them as though they were other human actors. In his article on *The Muppet Show* for *The Radio Times Guide to Television Comedy,* Mark Lewisohn notes this tendency as "one of the great strengths" of the show, commenting that the guests "[converse and interact] with the furry creatures as if it was perfectly normal." This sense of normalcy transfers itself to the ways in which the Muppets treat their guests. Because the Muppets treat even the most outlandish guest as normal, the audience is encouraged to do so as well. We embrace the weird because it does not seem all that different from the normal.

The short term effects of the appearances of performers, like Vincent Price and Alice Cooper, are simple enough to identify. Within the context of a thirty-minute episode, the adult and child audience take the fringe in and accept it as normal. However, the long-term effects might be a little more difficult to see. A look at the younger audience members and their responses to fringe culture as they aged can offer a way to assess the Muppets' ability to alter perceptions of the fringe. Denise Matthews in her article "Media Memories: The First Cable/VCR Generation Recalls Their Childhood and Adolescent Media Viewing" looked at the essays of college students majoring or otherwise involved in the study of Mass Communication who were young children between 1980–85; these children would have been exposed to the final season of *The Muppet Show*. Additionally they may have seen reruns of the series, which were common in the U.S. on cable from 1988 to roughly 2001 (De Bolt). Matthews' study highlights the impact television and shows like *The Muppet Show* can have on the formation of an individual's identity. The study using a symbolic interactionist approach examines how the participants "now [construct] and [interpret] recollections of their childhood and adolescent media-viewing experiences, particularly how they recall engaging with mediated content and characters within the context of parental communication" (Matthews 220). Since *The Muppet Show* would have been a series with cross-over appeal, the findings here seem relevant to an interpretation of the series' later impact on the audience.

Key to the theory used in Matthews' study is the notion that an individual can examine herself in the same way she can examine any distinct object, like a car or a book (221). Through such an examination one can discover just how the self of the "now" came to be. Matthews divides the development of self into three stages: play, game and reference group (222); this middle stage, the game stage — typical in children six to ten years old — is the most likely stage for the bulk of *The Muppet Show*'s child audience. In the game stage, children roleplay in an effort to internalize social norms, sometimes using real-life as their models for play, and sometimes drawing from television (222). The concept of the Muppets themselves as role models might seem outlandish; however, a discussion with Muppet fans often reveals close identification with at least one of the characters. Jordan Schildcrout in his essay "The Performance of Nonconformity in *The Muppet Show*" discusses how *The Muppet Show* worked in his own life: "As a child, I knew that every Sunday night, I could witness the triumph of the weirdoes in the Muppet Theatre, and in my imagination become one of them and join in their triumph" (833–834). Additionally, behavior, like Piggy's karate chops or Kermit's frustrated arm waving, can be seen in mature adults. Such behaviors reinforce Matthews' conclusions regarding the participants in the study and those like them: "They [the participants] vividly described childhood and adolescent situations that as memories remain salient and are therefore available to the ongoing construction of their biographical selves. These autobiographical data provide impressive evidence that *childhood media viewing impacts the individual's socialization and thereby exerts long-term influence*" (236 my emphasis). *The Muppet Show's* original child audience is now part of the adult audience. The choices made by that audience in terms of viewing are no doubt influenced by early childhood habits.

Muppets in the Fringe

In these early years of the 21st century, the influence of the Muppets has not lessened as is evidenced by their appearances in commercials and TV specials. The original cast of the show still has enough perceived star power to encourage consumerism. Additionally, elements of *The Muppet Show*, including signature musical numbers, have been invoked to connect audiences with social movements like environmentalism. Kermit's "Bein' Green" has been used to sell Ford Hybrid cars (Musial), and one of the song's lines (and Kermit's catchphrase) "It's not easy being green" was used by the BBC for a television documentary chronicling a family's attempts to have a more eco-friendly house. Before it was used for environmentalism, the song was used to emphasize racial equality especially in performances by Ray Charles (1975 on *The Cher Show*) and Lena Horne (1976 on *Sesame Street*). In its use on *The Muppet Show* in Seasons One and Two, Kermit sings "Bein' Green" to work through difficulties presented by his job as manager of the Muppets; here the song is about empowering the individual.

Given its varied appropriations, it's not all that surprising that the song appears in an episode of *Angel*, a Joss Whedon-David Greenwalt series about a vampire with a soul working as a detective/paranormal eliminations expert in Los Angeles; however, its use in the episode pulls the Muppets into the world of the fringe through appropriation by a demon. In "The House Always Wins," Lorne, a demon from an alternate dimension called Pylea, belts out this tune as part of a Las Vegas nightclub act at the Tropicana. Lorne is the ultimate fringe element even in a show that routinely features otherworldly characters. Lorne with his green skin and red horns stands out from his audience, and there is little he can do to disguise his appearance in order to blend in. The stage show at the Tropicana attempts to lessen the weirdness of Lorne's appearance by having his back up singers appear with horns and green pancake makeup: the illusion doesn't quite work, for both the television audience and select members of the Tropicana audience know the truth. Still the majority of the audience buys into the notion that Lorne, like Alice Cooper, is simply a performer pretending to be something otherworldly and threatening. A conversation between Lorne's friends who happen, by chance, to be in the audience highlights the performative aspect of Lorne's appearance:

> GUNN: No one seems to be bothered by the fact that he's a demon.
> FRED: They must think it's all makeup. Like the Blue Man Group. [Pauses and turns to Angel] You don't think the Blue Man Group...
> ANGEL: Only two of them ["The House Always Wins"].

The reference to Blue Man Group, a well-known avant-garde theatrical group, brings the outlandish situation of a demon in Las Vegas into the real world. Again, as in the Cooper episode of *The Muppet Show*, normal and fringe keep slipping in and out of each other's worlds. Blue Man Group is a real group of performers; Lorne is a character in a television series. Because their performances stretch the boundaries of standard theatrical song and dance performance, The Blue Man Group also belongs in the fantasy world of the fringe; Lorne, on the other hand, performs his numbers in traditional Vegas-style making him part of the "normal" world of performers referenced in the Ethel Merman episode. Yet Lorne remains fringe because of his demonic appearance.

Lorne's performance of "Bein' Green" taps into the literal meaning of the song: it's difficult to be a green-skinned demon in LA or in this case Las Vegas, just as it is difficult to be a frog in show business. Ironically in his home realm of Pylea, Lorne is fringe as well. Because he embraces melody and song, he is shunned by his family and others of his race. Through this performance, Lorne embraces Kermit's use of this song as an anthem of self-acceptance. Even the staging of his performance calls to mind Kermit's performance in Season One; while Kermit performs on a stage alone on a box with a painted forest background, Lorne's stage is barren with the exception of his chair and a background filled with twinkling lights. The isolation of both singers onstage echoes their isolation or perceived isolation offstage. Neither is truly alone as the audience well knows: Lorne's friends await him in the audience, and Kermit's friends await him backstage. Each group cares for their "outsider" friend unconditionally. Through song, Lorne and we are reminded that individuality or "bein' green" is okay as well.

Even in a show like *Angel* where a vampire with a soul attempts to redeem himself, the Muppet influence is at work. Writer David Fury may have chosen "Bein' Green" for its comic potential — a green demon sings a song about being green originally performed by a frog on a 1970s "kid's" program. Its impact on the audience is potentially greater than mere comedy though. As Matthews' study shows, the memories of childhood viewing affect the ways in which individuals view the world of the "now." By including Kermit's signature number, Fury creates a subtext for his audience. "Bein' Green" ultimately conveys its positive message about self, about notions of race, about the environment because of its associations with its original performer, Kermit. We empathize with Lorne and the fringe because we once empathized with Kermit.

The exchange between fringe and mainstream culture continues. The former guest stars of *The Muppet Show* are a part of this ebb and flow process. In 2008, Bluewater Productions released a comic entitled *Vincent Price Presents,* which taps into Price's rich early career. Like Price's performance on *The Muppet Show,* Darren G. Davis, publisher of Bluewater Productions, sees Price's role in the new comic series as representative of Price's popular culture impact: " 'Vincent Price will serve as a host who introduces the stories, the inspirational muse for the series, and as an iconic player who lingers in the backgrounds in some stories, and steps forward as the leading man in other stories'" (qtd. in Biggers 1). Readers of the comic are exposed to the scary Price; viewers of *The Muppet Show* Season One collection see the "normal" Price. Both men exist simultaneously in the mind, neither taking precedence. In recent months, Alice Cooper has returned to the fringe with the promotional material for his latest album, *Along Came a Spider.* Cooper is back in mascara and stage blood looking menacing and quite frightening (*Alice Cooper: The Official Website*). Cooper's new album, tour and web presence reemphasize his fringe status, but like Price, Cooper's *Muppet Show* appearance exists in not only the memories of his audience, but also in their DVD collections, making him less scary.

These simultaneous experiences with fringe culture and mainstream culture are at the heart of the normalizing influence that *The Muppet Show* can and does have. Performers like Cooper and Price retain their outsider status because of their connections to horror and yet are rendered normal by their inclusion in the Muppet family. Their treatment at the hands/paws/claws of the Muppets allows the human audience to interact with the scary in a safe way. The outside is brought in, is given a family, and is ultimately rescued — all because we see the divisions between normal and fringe fall apart when confronted by the "most sensational, inspirational, Muppetational" show of all.

Works Cited

Alexander, Allison. "Children and Television" *The Museum of Broadcast Communications.* <http://www.museum.tv/archives/etv/C/htmlC/childrenand/childrenand.htm>. 23 May 2008.
Alice Cooper. "Welcome to My Nightmare." *Welcome to My Nightmare.* Atlantic, 1975.
Alice Cooper: The Official Website. 2008. Alice Cooper.com. 23 December 2008 <http://www.alicecooper.com/index.php>
"Alice Cooper: The Nightmare." *The Internet Movie Database.* 17 December 2008. <http://www.imdb.com/title/tt0072624/>
Biggers, Cliff. "The Price Is Right." *Comic Shop News* 1095. (2007): 1.
Bostic, Jeff Q., et al. "From Alice Cooper to Marilyn Manson: The Significance of Adolescent Antiheroes." *Academic Psychiatry.* 27.1 (2003): 54–62. http://ap.psychiatryonline.org/cgi/reprint/27/1/54. 24 July 2008.

DeBolt, Doug. "DVD Review: *The Muppet Show: The Complete Third Season*" *The Trades.* 23 June 2008. http://www.the-trades.com/article.php?id=10390. 25 July 2008.
"The House Always Wins." *Angel: Season Four.* Writ. Joss Whedon, David Greenwalt and David Fury. Dir. Marita Grabiak. WB. 20 October 2002. DVD. 20th Century–Fox, 2004.
"*It's Not Easy Being Green.*" *BBC Lifestyle TV and Radio.* http://www.bbc.co.uk/lifestyle/tv_and_radio/green/. 25 July 2008.
Lerner, Alan Jay, and Frederick Loewe. "I've Grown Accustomed to Her Face." *My Fair Lady: 1956 Original Broadway Cast.* Sony, 2002.
Lewisohn, Mark. "*The Muppet Show.*" *The bbc.co.uk Guide to Comedy.* <www.bbc.co.uk/comedy/guide/articles/m/muppetshowthe_7774625.shtml>. 26 August 2006.
Marlowe, Christopher. *Doctor Faustus.* Ed. Sylvan Barnet. New York: Signet Classics, 1969.
Morgan, Jeffrey. "Alcohol and Razor Blades, Poison and Needles: The Glorious Wretched Excess of Alice Cooper, All-American." *Alice Cooper: The Official Site.* <http://www.alicecooper.com/bio.html>. 20 August 2007.
Muppets Magic from The Ed Sullivan Show! Perf. Ed Sullivan, Jim Henson, Frank Oz. DVD. Sofa, 2003.
The Muppet Show Season One (Special Edition). 1976-77. DVD. Buena Vista Home Entertainment. 9 August 2005.
The Muppet Show: The Complete Third Season. 1978-79. DVD. Walt Disney Video. 20 May 2008.
Musial, Robert. "Ford Escape Hybrid Ads Feature Kermit the Frog." *Ford Motor Company.* 20 April 2007. <http://media.ford.com/newsroom/feature_display.cfm?release=25176>. 25 July 2008.
Schildcrout, Jordan. "The Performance of Nonconformity on The Muppet Show — or, How Kermit Made Me Queer." *The Journal of Popular Culture* 41.5 (2008): 823–835.
"Sears and Fine Art." *Sears Archives.* <http://www.searsarchives.com/history/art/>. 20 July 2008.
"V Is for Vampire." *F Troop.* Writ. Austin Kalish and Irma Kalish. Dir. Hollingsworth Morse. ABC. 2 February 1967. Warner Bros. *AOL Video.* 24 July 2008. <http://video.aol.com/video/v-is-for-vampire/1722309>

Part Two

Adaptation and Performance

From Muppetry to Puppetry
Jennifer Stoessner

For many people, *The Muppet Show* and *Sesame Street* are the first things that pop into mind when one says "puppetry." However, puppetry is a diverse area of performance, with variations existing in all aspects of design and technique. The great assortment of puppet types, from marionette to shadow to rod to water puppet, is matched by the incredible array of ways in which the object may be manipulated. Puppetry crosses international boundaries, with indigenous puppet styles and themes for almost every nation on earth. It is one of the oldest performing arts in the world, but at the same time, it is one of the most adaptable to new technology. The fusion of old and new ideas makes puppetry a fertile soil for the creation of artistic work and the exploration of form and function. Jim Henson became an advocate for puppetry several years after he first began working with puppets, but once he had established himself in that advocacy, he was a continual contributor to the community of puppeteers.

When Jim Henson began working on his first successful television program, *Sam and Friends* in 1955, puppetry was already a well-established source for inexpensive daily programming content (Finch *The Works* 15). Experiments with puppetry on television began as early as 1930, with the idea that a puppet's size would match the small frame of the television screen (McPharlin 378–9) Programs such as *The Howdy Doody Show* and *Kukla, Fran, and Ollie* had been successful since 1947, and adults as well as children enjoyed viewing the puppet on the small screen. *Sam and Friends*, airing in Washington, D.C., from 1955 until 1961, featured puppets that Henson designed specifically for the television (Durrett 8). Daughter Cheryl Henson says, "It had never been done before. It had never been done before because no one had actually ever thought to build puppets in a special way for this new medium of television. They had taken puppets that were built for the theatre and put them on television" ("Biography Close-Up"). Henson began to work with puppets as a way to get into television, a medium that fascinated him.

As son Brian Henson expresses it, "He created the Muppets to get into television. He didn't create the Muppets and somebody said, 'Wow, those Muppets are great. We gotta put them on television.' It was all calculated the other way" ("People Profiles"). The quirky appeal of the puppets that Henson created resulted in a five year run in Washington, D.C., and their being engaged in advertising campaigns locally and nationally.

Like many Americans, Henson was largely unaware that puppetry had such a rich history and international tradition. On a trip to Europe in 1958, he discovered that puppets could be a means of entertaining a cross-section of society rather than just a family or child audience (Parish 42). Henson said, "I saw that puppetry was truly an art form in Europe. It was something that could be done artistically, with creativity. Back home, there weren't all that many puppeteers, but in Europe they are everywhere and everybody goes to puppet shows. It's an integral part of their lives..." (Durrett 26). Henson returned from Europe and began to pursue puppetry with more intensity and focus. He said, "It was at that point I realized that puppetry was an art form, a valid way to do interesting things. I came back from that trip all fired up to do wonderful puppetry" (Inches 32). To learn more about the craft of puppetry and to meet other puppet enthusiasts, he made a connection with the Puppeteers of America. The Puppeteers of America is a national organization devoted to linking puppeteers with each other and promoting the art form. He later served as president of the group from 1962 until 1963. At age twenty-six, he was the youngest person to ever hold the office (Eide 57).

During the 1960s as his involvement with puppetry organizations continued, Henson also continued to develop puppets that capitalized on the tricks of the televised show. He had by this time eliminated the proscenium arch of the theatrical puppet show in favor of using the frame of the television screen. He used monitors to allow a puppeteer to see the puppet as he or she manipulated it, showing the performer exactly what the home audience saw on the screen. The puppets' mouths moved with lip-sync, rather than being stationary like some puppets or "jabbering" like others. Jane Henson says, "Puppets on the television screen was a whole different way of approaching puppets.... [Jim] was particularly intrigued with little, tiny movements. He felt that the puppet face on the screen filled the screen in as important a way as any human face and then, because it was an abstracted face, the puppet was really able to do super human things or beyond human or get away with anything" ("Henson's Place"). Henson's quirky sense of humor and his attention to detail got his Muppets a great deal of attention and work on national television. Rowlf the Dog was a regular feature on *The Jimmy Dean Show* from 1963 to 1966, Ed Sullivan and Jack Paar invited the Muppets to perform variety material on their shows, and a new program called *Sesame Street* was developed in collaboration with Jim Henson and his company in

1969. Increasingly, the face of American puppetry was that of a goggle-eyed, fleece-covered Muppet.

By the time the Muppets had achieved worldwide fame with *The Muppet Show* in 1976, Henson was aware that other talented puppeteers were not able to receive such widespread and immediate exposure. In his effort to feature other talented puppeteers and other puppetry performance styles, Henson invited puppeteers Bruce Schwartz and Richard Bradshaw to appear as guest artists on *The Muppet Show*. Richard Bradshaw is an Australian puppeteer whose specializes in opaque shadow puppets. Bradshaw appeared on the Ethel Merman episode of the show in Season One on April 9, 1977. Kermit's introduction of the performer begins, "We on *The Muppet Show* are very interested in puppets, for some strange reason." He continues by saying that Bradshaw produces the "world's funniest shadows" ("Ethel Merman"). Following Kermit's introduction, Bradshaw presents a piece that is a standard feature of his own live shadow show, which he has been performing in Australia and internationally since the 1960s (Blumenthal 95). Bradshaw's shadows differ from the traditional shadow figures of Indonesia, Turkey, and China in that they appear on the shadow screen as simple black silhouettes rather than elaborately detailed or translucent figures. His performances incorporate songs such as "Old MacDonald" and "I Bought Me a Cat," short stories, and visual trickery using custom designed transformation figures (Bradshaw). Bradshaw offers workshops on shadow puppetry at festivals and in schools. He additionally is credited with the revival and preservation of a classic shadow puppet routine from the eighteenth and nineteenth centuries called "The Broken Bridge" (Periale and Smythe).

In Season Two, the Muppets would feature guest puppeteer Bruce D. Schwartz on the episode starring singer Cleo Laine. It originally aired in the United States on January 15, 1978. Schwartz had established himself as a captivating puppet artist in New York City during the 1970s. *Puppetry: A World History* describes his work as "graceful scenarios of love, longing and loss, using delicate-featured puppets—and also knock-down, crude, lewd handpuppet farces" (Blumenthal 107). His sources of material ranged from Irish ballads to the traditional puppet characters of Pierrot and Punch, as well as material derived from international puppetry styles. Schwartz's work earned him multiple UNIMA "Citations of Excellence," an award that recognizes brilliance in the art of puppetry, to "shows that touch their audiences deeply; that totally engage, enchant and enthrall" (Powell and Shore 9). This award had been proposed by Jim Henson and adopted by UNIMA-USA, the American branch of the Union Internationale de la Marionette in 1975 (Eide 57). Schwartz also received a MacArthur Genius Grant in 1988 before he made the decision to cease his puppetry activities in favor of a more anonymous life on the West Coast as a yoga instructor ("Bruce Schwartz").

Kermit's introduction of Schwartz recalls the self-aware humor of the Bradshaw intro from the previous season. "Ladies and gentlemen," he begins, "it's very seldom that we have a guest puppeteer on the show. In fact, between you and me, it's rare that we have *any* puppeteer on the show" ("Cleo Laine"). He continues to introduce Schwartz's first performance, an elegant puppet that dances a mini ballet. Unlike Bradshaw and the Muppet performers, Schwartz is visible to the home audience during his performance. He directly manipulates the puppet's head and neck while using black rods to move her arms and, in a deft example of efficient puppet movement, her legs as well. The camera rarely cuts to a close shot of the puppet, enabling the viewer to see not only the mechanics of the manipulation but also Schwartz's intense focus and concentration. Schwartz also appears in the closing number of the episode where his puppet figures illustrate Laine's performance of the song, "If."

Henson continued to work with the Puppeteers of America and UNIMA-USA, but it would be several years before a guest puppeteer would make another appearance on *The Muppet Show*. During the fifth season, on November 23, 1980, the guest star for the episode was Señor Wences. Wences had been a popular variety performer in vaudeville and on television, with 23 appearances on *The Ed Sullivan Show* alone (Leonard 255). A ventriloquist and juggler, Wences had a unique sense of humor, and his figures were a great representation of his unusual approach to material. Most famous, of course, was Johnny, a little boy character formed by Wences, "folding his hand into a fist, adding the wig and eyes, then drawing the lips and nose" (Blumenthal 78). The illusion was completed with the addition of a stationary doll body beneath Johnny's head/Wences's hand. The employment of Wences's own body as his figure was different from other ventriloquists' rigid doll-like figures. Another of his characters, Pedro, utilized the traditional mechanical head of a vent figure but it was housed in a box, having no body at all. Brian Henson said in his introduction to the episode with the 2000 Time Life video release that a bizarre character like Pedro "proved that Señor Wences was sufficiently insane to work with the Muppets" ("Best of *The Muppet Show*"). Insane or not, it is from this character that Wences's signature "'S all right? 'S all right" routine derived. Wences's appearance on *The Muppet Show* was the second appearance by a ventriloquist. Edgar Bergen appeared in the second season of the series on November 11, 1977.

Kermit introduces the show, saying that in honor of Wences's presence it will be a complete change of pace from other episodes. "Tonight," he says, "we're going to do a puppet show! Yes, yes, it's a real first" ("Señor Wences"). The episode highlights puppetry with Wences performing excerpts of his variety act as well as another guest appearance by Bruce Schwartz performing a Japanese ghost story. Henson and the Muppet writers also use the episode as a showcase for world puppetry traditions. It begins with Pinocchio performing "Puppetman" with the choral support of a workshop full of puppet toys. Pinocchio is, after Kermit the Frog and Mr. Punch, perhaps the most well known puppet in the world. Created by Carlo Collodi in 1881 and published in book form in 1883, *Pinocchio* has become an enduring story of morality and valor, interpreted into a film version by Walt Disney in 1940 and is a constant favorite with puppet theatres. Collodi's Pinocchio was a marionette, operated by strings, but the Muppet version is operated in the Henson style as a hand and mouth puppet. Although Pinocchio is not a marionette in the piece, there is a shot where the character is seen full body, an image infrequent in the waist-up Muppet world. Several puppeteers, assisting Steve Whitmire as the lead performer, manipulate Pinocchio's arms and legs. The effect is an example of Henson mixing traditional manipulation techniques, in this case the teamwork approach of Japanese bunraku, with the technology afforded by the television medium. The dancing figure of Pinocchio is matted into the shot, using Chromakey technology and rendering the puppeteers invisible (Finch *Of Muppets and Men* 174). As his career developed, Henson became known for techniques blending puppetry tricks with technical wizardry.

Another nod to the rich global puppetry tradition comes through a performance of Punch and Judy by Beauregard, the sweet but dim-witted janitor, played by Dave Goelz. Punch is one of the most familiar puppets in the world. Mr. Punch was first recorded as being seen in England in 1662 by Samuel Pepys but had originated earlier in the *commedia dell'arte* tradition of Italy, as Pulcinella around 1600 (McPharlin 116). His original puppet incarnation was as a marionette, but today he is most recognizable as a hand puppet. Punch is a "nasty fellow, low cunning trickster given to coarse speech and almost revolting cruelty" (Beaumont 15). Despite his flaws, he is the hero of the common man and outdoes his adversaries, often figures of authority, through wit or more often through blows with his stick. In fact, the plot of any Punch performance is driven by the use of the stick to dispatch the opposing figure, enabling one performer to move through a quick succession of characters. The crocodile traditionally opposes Punch and manages to carry him off to Hell to meet with the most threatening of adversaries, the Devil himself. The inclusion of Punch in *The Muppet Show* is a bow to the popular puppet theatre form as well as a nod to the show's host culture in England where Punch and Judy remains a popular seaside entertainment.

The Punch and Judy segment also acknowledges what I will call "metapuppetry," puppetry performed by a puppet. When Beau begins his performance, he tells Kermit that he will go behind his stage, the backstage balcony area, to perform. He accidentally lowers Punch and remarks, "Oops, wrong one," and he himself disappears behind the stage. Beau's comment acknowledges that he is also a puppet, albeit not the one featured in this backstage performance. Once the situation is sorted and Beau has prepared for his show, Kermit shouts, "Bravo!" prompting Beau to rise to receive the plaudit. Kermit tells him that he was not saying bravo for Beau but rather for Punch, yet another nod to the puppeteer's art, which often renders him or her a nonentity in comparison to the puppets. Henson himself appeared in an advertisement for American Express, capitalizing on his own invisibility as a puppeteer and the supposed inability to be recognized without the identification of the credit card ("American Express Commercial").

During Beau's performance, Miss Piggy enters and sees the violent, knockabout actions of the puppets. She expresses her displeasure that she is not appearing in the show, in favor of "dolls." Kermit informs her that puppets are not just dolls and that puppetry is an art form. Piggy replies, "You call that violence art?" Kermit explains, "Violence belongs with puppets. That's Punch and Judy. They've always been violent. It's good. It's a good aggressive behavior." As he and Piggy squabble, Beau stops his own show and begins to watch their fight. Piggy finally tells Kermit that she will show him aggressive behavior and administers a karate chop to the frog, who crumples to the ground. As Piggy storms off the screen, saying with disgust, "Punch and Judy," Beau cries out, "Bravo! Bravo!" During this exchange, Henson is once again playing with the Muppets as puppets. Beau's meta-puppet show ceases, and he watches the puppet show before him, literally foregrounding Kermit and Piggy as actual puppets, rather than as their established characters.

Piggy's final line brings an additional layer of meaning to the scene. While she is verbally dismissing Beau's performance (and puppetry as a whole), she is also claiming a part of the same heritage as Punch and Judy. Punch, though English, is not the exclusive possession of the Brits. Every European nation has its own version of this mischievous clown. The appeal of the everyman hero, coarse and witty, resulted in the creation of Guignol in Lyon, Polichinelle elsewhere in France, Hanswurst in Germany, Kasparek in the Czech Republic, Petrouchka in Russia, and Pulcinella in Italy (Baird 96–111). This moment between the pig and her frog effectively identifies the pair as the American Punch and Judy. Though connections to the form have been made to Burr Tilstrom's beloved creations, Kukla and Ollie — both hand puppets, one a not un-crocodilian dragon — the actions, alternately affectionate and aggressive, of Kermit and Piggy certainly represent another version of the same model, albeit fuzzier and less deadly in the long run ("The American Puppet").

Other Muppets who get into the act on the Señor Wences episode are the Swedish Chef and Fozzie Bear. The Swedish Chef performs traditional "Swedish bread lump" puppetry, to his own sung accompaniment of the song,

"These Boots are Made for Walking." Frank Oz, the hands of the Henson performed Chef, places bread dough on his fingertips to make shoes and more dough on the back of his hand for a body while performing this finger puppet routine. It is silly, certainly, but exposes the home viewer to an additional type of puppetry, again different from the Muppet style, the standard finger puppet. Fozzie is much more ambitious, deciding to perform with marionettes. Fozzie had previously built a ventriloquist figure named Chucky on the Edgar Bergen episode, failing to understand that the secret to ventriloquism was the performer's ability to throw his or her voice ("Edgar Bergen"). Kermit greets his enthusiasm for puppetry with apprehension, as the frog remembers the disasters of Fozzie's previous performances. Fozzie's performance in the latter half of the show highlights the complications of marionettes-tangled strings and a fight with gravity as the bear is pulled to the stage by his rebellious dancing clown puppet. Though the performance is not a success, Fozzie's interest in puppetry is not quelled. By the end of the episode, his puppet has attached strings to the bear and the meta-puppeteer role has been reversed.

While many of the Muppets embrace puppets, Miss Piggy is not alone in her skepticism of the appeal of puppetry. Gonzo the Great, invited by Fozzie to join his marionette act, asks Kermit what a puppet is. Kermit tells him, "It's a doll that's made to look alive by wiggling strings or putting your hand inside it." Gonzo considers this for a moment and rejects the act, saying, "What a stupid idea. Who wants to watch dolls wiggle? I mean, even I wouldn't do an act like that. Doll wiggling, talk about boring." As Gonzo leaves, Kermit turns to the camera to say, "I didn't have the heart to tell him." When Fozzie is ready to perform, Kermit leaves to introduce Fozzie. Gonzo re-enters to reflect, "Wiggling dolls is weird. In fact, it might even be sick." However, Fozzie's failed performance convinces Gonzo that puppetry might be worth some additional consideration. Indeed, by the end of the show, everyone has gotten into the act. The final sting of the closing titles finds Statler and Waldorf humming "*The Muppet Show* Theme" while playing with finger puppets. Of course, the self-reflective puppet fun must come to an end and the grumpy pair tosses the puppets from their hands into the void beneath their balcony.

The Muppet Show lasted five seasons, but Henson had other puppetry projects to create, including *The Dark Crystal*, one of the first live action films to be produced where no human beings appear. The technical magic and the incredible puppetry of the film reflect the crystallization of Henson's experiments with puppetry and film technique when it was released in 1982 (Harris). This year also marked the beginning of the Jim Henson Foundation, "the only grant-making institution with a mission to promote puppetry in the United States." The Henson Foundation's website says that it "introduces thousands of adults and families to the magic of puppet theater through grantmaking, artist advocacy and public awareness efforts, and other outreach activities" ("The Jim Henson Foundation"). Henson wanted to preserve the live theatrical puppetry legacy that had inspired him during his interim with the POA and on his international travels. He had long been developing a Broadway show and had performed a live stage show in Las Vegas in 1971 (Harris, Inches 82). Though the Broadway performance never made it to fruition, the Foundation provided funding to Julie Taymor, the director of the acclaimed *Lion King*, in its first set of grant awards as well as in subsequent years ("Grant Archives"). "Jim was a big supporter of Julie Taymor toward the end and the stuff she wound up doing. He would have been so pleased to see it because he always wanted to get puppets on Broadway," said Muppet head writer Jerry Juhl (Eide and Abrams 4). In 2004, *Avenue Q*, a musical featuring furry-faced and foul-mouthed Muppet-style puppets, won the Tony Award for Best New Musical. The triumph of the show further validates Henson's belief that puppets could be viable on the Broadway stage.

To celebrate the live stage traditions that inspired his televised innovations, Henson also made a six-part television special called *Jim Henson Presents: The World of Puppetry*. Each episode featured a puppet artist from a different country, each with a vastly different vision of the art form. Bruce Schwartz and Richard Bradshaw were each the subject of an episode when it was produced in 1985 ("Jim Henson's World of Television" 42–4). These recorded performances by Bradshaw, Schwartz, and the other featured puppeteers from the series have been archived and are available to puppeteers, researchers, and the interested public. The Paley Center for Media, formerly the Museum of Television and Radio, has a large video archive of Henson's work called "Jim Henson's World of Television," and *Jim Henson Presents...* is a part of the collection. Additionally, the six episodes are available for review at the New York Puppet Library for the Performing Arts at Lincoln Center. In its Theater on Film and Tape Archive is the Jim Henson Collection of Puppet Theater. Along with *Jim Henson Presents...*, the collection includes nearly seventy tapes of performances featured in the Jim Henson Foundation's International Festival of Puppet Theater. The Festival ran during even numbered years from 1992 though 2000 and did much to increase the visibility of world puppetry in New York City and across the country. Cheryl Henson emphasized the importance of the documentation of live puppetry performance, saying, "You have a very live form of theatre—how you see work, how you continue to be inspired by individual's work as opposed to how you actually imitate somebody's work" ("What Makes...?"). The entire collection serves the academic and artistic community by "enhancing awareness and understanding of the field among theater students and professionals, the primary users of the archives" ("About the Foundation"). That the performances are documented is a testament to Jim Henson and the Foundation's diligence and appreciation for the ephemeral nature of performance even when artifacts, the puppets themselves, remain.

A further acknowledgment of Jim Henson's devotion to puppetry was made by the Puppeteers of America in 1997 when the "Vice-President's Award for Innovation" was renamed the "Jim Henson Award" (Thompson 73). The award "recognizes innovation in puppetry that is technological, dramaturgical, or collaborative in nature" (Thompson 72). The most recent recipient of the award was Brian Windsor, an artist who combines motion-capture technology with real-time puppetry, all driven by modified video game controllers. By building puppetry into the computer, Windsor has been able to expand people's understanding of what puppetry is and of what it can be. Henson's legacy is present. Although technology may be viewed as either a blessing or a curse in art, Jim Henson "brought an ancient art form into the twentieth century and set the standards by which anyone working with puppets on television will have to be judged" (Finch *Of Muppets and Men* 69). Yet despite all of the advances that Henson made technologically, he still maintained the primacy of the puppeteer. "...The performance is where the humanity is, where the relationship is and I think that has to stay at the heart of it all," said Henson (qtd. in Harris). The relationship of puppet, puppeteer, and audience is a magical one, one that Henson revered. *The Muppet Show* was just another way to share that magic.

Works Cited

"About the Foundation." Jim Henson Foundation. New York. 2006. 13 Feb 2007 <http://www.hensonfoundation.org>.
"American Express commercial." YouTube. 2 Jun 2007. YouTube.com. 8 Dec 2007. <http://www.youtube.com/watch?v=skor2mwvAAw>.
"The American Puppet." VHS. Mazzarella Bros. Productions, 2001.
"Avenue Q Awards." *Internet Broadway Database* 2001–2008. The Broadway League. 13 Feb 2008 <http://www.ibdb.com/awardproduction.asp?id=13502>.
Baird, Bil. *The Art of the Puppet*. New York: Macmillan, 1965.
Beaumont, Cyril. *Puppets and Puppetry*. London: The Studio Limited, 1958.
Bell, John. *Strings, Hands, Shadows: A Modern Puppet History*. Detroit: Detroit Institute of the Arts, 2000.
Best of The Muppet Show. Video Recording. Perf. Frank Oz, Jim Henson, Jerry Nelson. Jim Henson Home Entertainment & Time Life Video, 2000.
Biography Close-up: Sesame Street. Host and interviewer Harry Smith. Interviewees Cheryl Henson, Steve Whitmire, Joan Ganz. Biography Channel, New York. 18 Mar 2001.
Blumenthal, Eileen. *Puppetry: A World History*. New York: Abrams, 2005.
Borgenicht, David. *Sesame Street Unpaved*. New York: Children's Television Workshop, 1998.
Bradshaw, Richard. "Richard Bradshaw and His Shadow Puppets." 2001: A Puppet Odyssey, Puppeteers of America Festival. University of Tampa, Florida, 8 July 2001.
"Bruce Schwartz." Wikipedia, the Free Encyclopedia. 10 August 2007, Wikipedia Foundation, 26 September 2007 <http://en.wikipedia.org/wiki/Bruce_Schwartz>.

"Bruce Schwartz." *World Puppetry Festival 1980* (Washington, DC: Puppeteers of America, 1980).

"Cleo Laine." *The Muppet Show*. Perf. Jim Henson, Frank Oz, Dave Goelz, Jerry Nelson, and Richard Hunt. 15 January 1978.

Durrett, Deanne. *The Importance of Jim Henson*. San Diego: Lucent Books, 1994.

"Edgar Bergen." *The Muppet Show*. Perf. Jim Henson, Frank Oz, Dave Goelz, Jerry Nelson, and Richard Hunt. 11 November 1977.

Eide, Paul, with Alan Cook and Steve Abrams, editor. *A Timeline of Puppetry in America*. Special Edition of *Puppetry Journal*. Minneapolis: Puppeteers of America, 2003.

Eide, Paul, with Steve Abrams. "In the Company of Genius—50 Years of Jim Henson's Muppets." *Puppetry Journal* 57.1 (Fall 2005): 2–9.

"Ethel Merman." *The Muppet Show*. Perf. Jim Henson, Frank Oz, Dave Goelz, Jerry Nelson, and Richard Hunt. 9 April 1977.

Finch, Christopher. *Jim Henson: The Works*. New York: Random House, 1993.

_____. *Of Muppets and Men*. New York: Knopf, 1981.

"Grant Archives." 2006. *The Jim Henson Foundation*. New York. 13 Feb 2007. <http://www.hensonfoundation.org>.

Harris, Judy. "Muppet Master: An Interview with Jim Henson." *Muppet Central*. Articles. Transcript of Telephone Interview. 21 Sep 1998. Muppet Central.Com. 24 Apr 2007 <http://www.muppetcentral.com/articles>.

Henson, Jim. *It's Not Easy Being Green and Other Things to Consider*. New York: Hyperion, 2005.

Henson's Place: The Man Behind the Muppets. Director. David A. Goldsmith. interviewees Jane Henson, Jim Henson, Frank Oz. Platypus Production, England, 1984.

Inches, Alison. *Jim Henson's Designs and Doodles*. New York: Abrams, 2001.

The Jim Henson Foundation. 2006. The Jim Henson Foundation. 13 Feb 2007 <www.hensonfoundation.org>.

Jim Henson's World of Television. Museum Guide. New York: Museum of Television & Radio, 1992.

Leonard, John. *A Really Big Show: A Visual History of* The Ed Sullivan Show. Eds. Claudia Falkenburg and Andrew Solt. USA: Sarah Lazin Books, 1992.

Mazzarella, Mark. *The American Puppet*. Mazzarella Bros. Productions, 2001.

McPharlin, Paul. *The Puppet Theatre in America, A History: 1524 to Now*. USA: Harper & Brothers, 1949.

Parish, James Robert. *Jim Henson, Puppeteer and Filmmaker*. New York: Infobase, 2006.

"*People* Profiles: Jim Henson." Host. Willow Bay. interviewees Jane Henson Candice Bergen, Brian Henson. CNN, 1999.

Periale, Andrew, and Robert Smythe. "Fantoccini and the Future of Puppetry." Puppet Rampage 2007. Puppeteers of America National Festival, Concordia University, Minnesota, 21 July 2007.

Puppeteers of America Membership Handbook and Directory. Ed. Fred Thompson. Connecticut: Puppeteers of America, 2006–7.

"Señor Wences." *The Muppet Show*. Perf. Jim Henson, Frank Oz, Dave Goelz, Jerry Nelson, and Richard Hunt. 23 November 1980.

Thompson, Fred. Puppeteers of America Membership Handbook and Directory. Connecticut: Puppeteers of America, 2006–7.

UNIMA-USA Membership Directory. Eds. Lia and Philip Shore Powell. Atlanta: UNIMA-USA, 2006.

"What Makes a Puppet Play?" Transcriber Bonny Hall. 1996 International Festival of Puppet Theater, Bruno Walter Auditorium, New York. 16 Sept 1996.

Windsor, Brian. Personal Interview. 24 September 2007.

The Muppets and Shakespeare
Hugh H. Davis

On the "Red Carpet" before the 2004 Emmy Awards broadcast, actor William H. Macy joked with Kermit the Frog that "we should do *Hamlet*." While Macy (or at least the writers for this patter) likely thought the idea of a Muppet performing Shakespeare would be humorous, the Muppets actually have a long history with the Bard. The majority of their literary forays are from the Victorian era — feature-length films of Charles Dickens' *A Christmas Carol* and Robert Louis Stevenson's *Treasure Island*, a full episode of *The Muppet Show* based on Lewis Carroll's *Alice in Wonderland*,[1] and a television-movie adaptation of L. Frank Baum's *Wizard of Oz*— but the author with whom the Muppets have shown the most affinity is William Shakespeare. Throughout their fifty-plus years, Jim Henson's Muppet characters have referenced, alluded to, parodied, and paid homage to a vast array of cultural and pop cultural concepts. Muppet programming, in turn, exists on a multitude of levels, allowing enjoyment by different age groups. The Muppets have often aimed for literary targets, starting with Grimm's Fairy Tales but often going beyond these children's stories into the literary canon, and one recurring subject from that canon has been Shakespeare. Muppet-inspired Shakespeare is hardly a surprise, given the popularity of the subject in both intellectual and pop cultural venues, but the regularity of such segments and the varying uses of Shakespeare are both noteworthy.

The parallel paradises of the blessed isle and the sunny Sesame Street ("where everything's a-ok!") provide a pair of ideal locations, but the connections between these two blessed plots — Shakespeare and John of Gaunt's England and Henson's Sesame Street — serve as mere starting points for the many overlaps the two form, and, indeed, the theater of *The Muppet Show* reveals a stage in which the worlds of William Shakespeare and Jim Henson, as well as their myriad creations and subsequent adaptations and transformations, interact. Allusions are made; plays are rewritten; Shakespearean characters appear. An Elizabethan-dressed Patrick Stewart recites a "Soliloquy on B," contemplating if the letter he holds in his hand is "a B or not a B." Three Anything Muppets[2] witches learn cooperation while evoking *Macbeth* (Borgenicht 55). "The Alligator King" number—a musical sequence presented both in animated and live-action/puppet form—presents a simplified *King Lear* (Borgenicht 62–63) for children's consumption. Big Bird tells Prairie Dawn that his "Grannybird once said, 'The Whole World's a Stage,'" recalling *As You Like It*; Big Bird and Prairie Dawn then decide to use that stage to "put on a show" in the special *Sesame Street Jam: A Musical Celebration*. The *Masterpiece Theater* spoof "Monsterpiece Theater" includes such segments as "Much Ado About Nothing" and "Monsters of Venice," recalling Shakespearean titles and productions. Children viewers are not provided explanatory footnotes or narrators clarifying the origin of these allusions. Instead, the viewers are asked to view and accept the segments as they are, and, as such, these early introductions to Shakespearean elements merit consideration.

In *Unspeakable ShaXXXspeares,* his assessment of "American kiddie culture" (his term), Richard Burt discusses that part of the appeal for *Sesame Street* is its ability to appeal to both adults and children. Adults are able to understand the allusions and references, while children enjoy the typical silliness and mayhem offered by the Muppets (232). Children watch *Sesame Street* with their parents (presumably also regular PBS viewers), and the result is multi-layered entertainment. The hallmark of long-standing children's entertainment, including programs like *The Bullwinkle Show* and *Looney Tunes,* is a sophisticated approach to its humor, and the Muppets exemplify this sophistication through their use of Shakespearean allusion within segments on their educational show.

The aforementioned "Monsterpiece Theater" has provided the most fully realized Shakespearean moments on *Sesame Street.* Alastair Cookie (an avatar of Cookie Monster and an exemplar of culture) introduces each segment, and his introductions suggest the traditional view of Shakespeare as cultural icon. On one occasion he announced, "Tonight, Monsterpiece Theater proud to present classic play, *The Taming of the Shoe,* by William Shoespeare, famous podiatrist. Trust me" (qtd. in Borgenicht 69). These recognitions—that the segment spoofs a classic play, as well as the reassurance of the audience to trust this storyteller about the variations presented—reveal a self-referential understanding of the literary task at stake. To transform Shakespeare's comedy into the tale of Grover's unruly clog borders on the absurd (a Muppet specialty), but the postmodern recognition of this inherent absurdity unveils the Muppet sensibility about such textual appropriations. Cookie ends the segment by advising his listeners, "To thine ownself be shoe," evoking Polonius' advice in *Hamlet* while also recalling the tendency to rely upon quotations to define and denote knowledge of Shakespeare. The Monsterpiece

Theater segment reminds viewers of the original, thus reinforcing the existence of that source material.

Further textual reinforcement is provided in the longest of the *Sesame Street* Shakespeare sketches. In a 1991 episode, Alastair Cookie pronounces:

> Tonight, me proud to present one of best-loved classics in whole world. A play that explores feelings that bubble deep inside all of us. Yes, me proud to present *Hamlet, Prince of Denmark.* It not get classier than this [qtd in Borgenicht 68].

The introduction itself recalls the image of Shakespeare as the cultural apex for production; Shakespeare's reputation — along with this play's — extends easily through the neighborhood of Sesame Street, creating a cultured air for the segment before it even begins. When the skit does begin, viewers first see popular character Elmo on a castle set, who then sees Hamlet (Mel Gibson, reprising his role from Zeffirelli's film). The sequence then unfolds in mock-Shakespearean dialogue:

> ELMO: Forsooth! Elmo spotteth Hamlet, Prince of Denmark. Reading a book. *(Mel laughs.)* A funny book! It maketh him happy! Oh Hamlet, what doth thou read that maketh thou so happy?
> HAMLET: *(Happily)* Words, words, words.

This dialogue continues, with Gibson's Hamlet revealing a series of emotions through facial expressions, answering Elmo's questions with the same line from the play, only adjusting the tone according to his emotions. "Feddeth up," Elmo leaves the scene, returning shortly with his own book, which makes him laugh. When asked what doth he read, the popular monster Muppet simply explains that, as a child, he cannot read, and, instead, "Elmo's looking at pictures, pictures, pictures!"

Hamlet's desire that Elmo "Get thee to a Library!" provides the basis for this entire sequence: Shakespeare is an outlet for words, and reading produces a gamut of emotions. As Richard Burt says, the importance of reading is illustrated with *Hamlet* "made safe as a classic" (234), although this classic remains one far beyond the scope of its viewers. *Sesame Street* is an educational show for preschoolers, many of whom, like Elmo, cannot read words by themselves, much less entire tragedies. Thus, although these segments do provide "literal version[s] of Shakespeare's entry into American ... youth culture" (3), these allusions can serve only as introductions of titles and ideas. Children, therefore, view these sketches and meet Hamlet for the first time, as Jim Henson's creations provide the means to open dialogue about the plays.

Gibson's appearance as Hamlet reminds viewers of the pop cultural echoes of Shakespeare. Gibson is one of now hundreds of celebrities to guest star on *Sesame Street,* but his presence as this particular character — recreating one of his more (arguably) "artistic" roles, rather than stepping from the frames of *Mad Max* or *Lethal Weapon* — is noteworthy; preschool viewers might recognize Gibson's face or voice from his other work, including Disney's 1995 film, *Pocahontas*, but Hamlet is not presumably a character they know. While popular fictional characters might appear on *Sesame Street* (such as Henry Winkler as the Fonz or Lily Tomlin as Ernestine), classic literary characters are less likely.[3] Casting Gibson is deliberate, for it reminds all viewers of the existence of other versions of the text, thus recalling the nature of adaptation, and then recalling the original text itself. Hamlet is moved by words; when he shares his experience with Elmo, the viewer is reminded then of Shakespeare's original words.

Sesame Street is but a part of the Muppets' connection to Shakespeare. Hamlet and Shakespeare both appear elsewhere. The comedy of the Muppets is wide-ranging but literate, and Henson programs provide intertextual allusions to literature, often using allusions for gags, rather than just didactic lessons. In the 1950s, the first regular Muppet program, *Sam and Friends,* aired locally in Washington, D.C.; this puppet show, which aired during the same hour as the news, featured sophisticated humor. One character in this show's menagerie was a skull puppet named Yorick, a forerunner of later characters like Cookie Monster and Animal, representing a form of "living hunger," consuming any and everything in its path (Henson Associates 22). In its six-year run (from 1955 to 1961), Yorick's main humor was based on his appetite, but the *Hamlet* allusion was noted. In a script from October 13, 1959, Kermit the Frog introduced this skull by saying, "Of course, there's Yorick, as in Shakespeare's 'alas, poor Yorick — don't eat my laughmeter'" (qtd. in DellaVedova 30 July). Even in a possibly literary moment, Yorick's hunger overtakes him, but, regardless of the punchline, the allusion exists and clearly suggests the literary connections for the Muppets even in this early stage.

A sketch on *The Jimmy Dean Show* from 1963 has Rowlf the Dog, the first nationally-recognized Muppet, reciting "To be or not to be" and attributing the line to Shakespeare's dog, thus offering a canine twist on the authorship debate and keeping alive the idea of shaking up Shakespeare and other literature as a source for humor. The literary endeavors for Henson and his colleagues have continued through the years, with the Muppet Shakespearean segments continuing as well. The importance of reading remains a common theme for the Muppets. The primary theme of the *Muppet Babies* cartoon, along with, in its own way, the *Storyteller* specials based on European folktales and myths, is the importance of individual reading and learning. Following in this tradition, Ann Brown's Muppet Kids book, *TV or Not TV,* emphasizes imagination for children while also alluding to Hamlet's most-famed soliloquy. These productions suggest that an assumption of knowledge, basing jokes on allusion, and the concept of Shakespeare as cultural icon (even among pop cultural icons such as the Muppets) persists.

The first two seasons of *The Muppet Show,* in particular, provide a plethora of Shakespearean references. Two are perhaps coincidental: Ethel Merman and Kermit's duet of "You're the Tops!" includes the line, "You're a sonnet by Shakespeare," with Kermit offended by the next line, calling him Mickey Mouse (*TMS*, "Ethel Merman"); a chorus of pigs performs "That's Entertainment!" and sings of "some great Shakespearean scene where a ghost and a prince meet and everyone ends up mincemeat" (*TMS*, "Cloris Leachman"). In both cases, the songs are simply appropriated by the Muppets, but both also recall Shakespeare as an element of mass culture.

The concept of Shakespeare's difficulty recurs in one of the first episodes, guest starring Twiggy. The Phantom of the Muppet Show (later renamed Uncle Deadly) is upset the Muppets have taken over his theater. He explains to Kermit, "My Hamlet was acclaimed as the greatest ever. Then I played my most difficult role ... Othello. On opening night, I was killed." When asked who killed him, the bitter thespian replies, "The critics." Uncle Deadly's treatment at the hands of the critics has left him angry, proclaiming none should perform at this theater. Shakespearean expectations brought this character his doom, as his Othello failed to live up to critics' desires. In ensuing episodes, Uncle Deadly joined the ensemble and returned to acting, but he did not try Shakespeare again.

On another occasion, the hope for an intellectual discussion unravels. With Florence Henderson as the guest, Kermit hosts a panel on "Was William Shakespeare in fact Bacon?" Instead of managing a debate on the ever-vexing authorship issue, Miss Piggy ends all intellectual activity when she takes offense at perceived pig slurs. Kermit's attempt to clarify he meant Francis Bacon falls on deaf ears, as Piggy attempts to unite the pigs of the world.

Sam the Eagle claims "culture is culture" (having thought Rudolf Nureyev was an opera singer), and the Muppets tend to be irreverent with all culture, poking fun at all pretension. Fozzie Bear introduces diva Beverly Sills as "Bev Sills, 'Queen of Nashville,'" who then proceeds to perform "When It's Roundup Time in Texas"; Nureyev dances with a giant pig in "Swine Lake"; unable to obtain a film by Ingmar Bergman, the Muppets present one by his brother Gummo. Such irreverence defines the Muppets and their similar takes on Shakespeare. Even while making fun of the cultural weight carried by Shakespearean literature, the Muppets expect an audience capable of understanding their allusions and references. As Jennifer C. Garlen deftly addresses elsewhere in this collection, one trait of the Muppets is their tendency to conflate high and low culture, and Shakespeare is but one element in a tapestry of allusions.

A "Veterinarian's Hospital" skit (from the Nureyev episode), featuring Dr. Bob (Rowlf the Dog), Nurse Piggy, Nurse Janice, and a pig patient, is a tongue-in-cheek tribute to the Bard, often using mock–Shakespearean dialogue. Dr. Bob asks, "Prithee Nurse, who be-eth our next patient?" When shown he is to help "this little piglet," Bob corrects, "Not piglet, Hamlet. We're doing Shakespeare here," at which point the doctor is reminded, "It sounds more like Bacon." A transfusion is needed, and Janice thinks the blood type is 2B. Ever quick, Dr. Bob asks, "Well, is it 2B or not 2B?," prompting Piggy's response, "Methinks they have no shame." Dr. Bob makes puns on the Elizabethan words "zounds" ("Zounds terrible!"), "shrew" ("timing of the shrew" and "if the shrew fits...") and on "Yorick" ("Alas! Poor Po-rk!" he tells the pig patient). Reminded he is a doctor first, Bob clarifies, "Doctor first, Richard II, Henry the Fourth." Apparently offended at the irreverent play on Shakespearean concepts, Statler bemoans, "I'm a student of Shakespeare," to which Waldorf retorts, "You were a student with Shakespeare." The humor of this entire skit is based in literate knowledge of Shakespeare, and cultural lines blur, as a tribute to Shakespeare becomes a series of quick-hitting puns, while critics defending the Bard and his appropriation are mocked for their advanced age.

Other Shakespearean sequences from Season Two suggest Shakespeare's presence as a provider of artistic quality or *avant garde* possibilities for performance. In an episode guest-starring Teresa Brewer, the Great Gonzo attempts to recite Shakespeare "while suspended by his nose from a feather boa 9 feet in the air." He begins, "*The Merchant of Venice.* Act one, scene one. Antonio speaks: In sooth, I know not why I am so sad. It wearies me. You sa—sa—[sneezes] ah ah ahaaachooooo!" He then falls to the floor (qtd in DellaVedova 31 July).[4] Gonzo's experimental theater is then recalled in the episode guest-starring Peter Sellers, when Sellers announces to Kermit (while dressed as a Viking, prepping to impersonate Queen Victoria) a newly perfected act (he promises, "it's original"), where he will recite the soliloquy from *Richard III* "whilst—and at the same time—playing tuned chickens." Announcing, "Once more into the breach," he begins:

> Now is the winter of our discontent *[flaps chickens under his arms]*
> Made glorious summer by this son of York;
> And all the clouds that low'r'd upon our House
> In the deep bosom of the ocean buried *[plays "Shave and a Haircut" with chickens].*
> (*TMS*, "Peter Sellers")

Explaining to Kermit, "I enjoy a good chicken," Sellers is surprised when Kermit tells him "You can't do that on our show.... Gonzo just did it last month." Entering, Gonzo tells him, "It died here. It was terrible. I mean, they've got no taste around here." Sellers agrees they have "no taste at all." The inherent suggestion is that experimental theater is too much for the audience, but Shakespeare is the means which artists, such as Gonzo and Sellers, use to begin experimentation. Shakespeare provides cultural capital.

In the third season, Shakespeare was invoked as cultural (and possibly financial) capital. In a "storybook" episode starring Lynn Redgrave, the Muppets present a tale of Robin Hood and his Merry Men. At the show's midpoint, the Bard is introduced in an interval by Sam the Eagle. This Shakespeare, wearing a business suit and smoking a cigar, speaks in a New York accent while quizzed by Sam, the self-appointed arbiter of culture for the show. Telling Sam he is "*a* William Shakespeare," the interviewee has to disappoint his fan,[5] telling him that the Bard's name is only his "nom de plum" and that the real playwright is dead. Asked by the stunned Sam if the lately departed author left a wife and children, this incarnation of Shakespeare explains, "As far as I'm awares, he left just about everything, including an unfinished play, *Henry VIII*." With Sam saying all of this news is "a tragedy," the New Yorker Shakespeare tells him, "Well, it ain't a comedy."

After this Shakespeare pronounces his desire to gain royalties, Sam implores him to recite from his work, but he instead recruits the Swedish Chef to present the "To be or not to be" speech. Sam tells the viewers, "I didn't understand all of it, but I'm certain the English people enjoyed it." Shakespeare never wrote a play about Robin Hood,[6] and, while the authorship question of *Henry VIII* is still not certain, it was certainly completed, having appeared in the first folio. However, Shakespeare has again become cultural high mark. Validity for the production is supposedly offered by the introduction of Shakespeare, albeit a cigar-chomping hack; Sam's lack of true knowledge about Shakespeare recalls the debunking of academics/critics and firmly places Shakespeare in mass cultural circles.

In its fourth season, *The Muppet Show* offered its final twist on the Bard, playing again with the cultural baggage associated with such productions. Gonzo, ever the artist, appears in Elizabethan dress but with his nose bandaged and announces he cannot perform the first act *of Hamlet* while hanging from his nose, having sprained it. A panicked Kermit recruits the episode's guest star, the silver-screen Superman Christopher Reeve, to fill in; after a quick costume change in a phone booth,[7] Reeve tells Kermit in a slightly affected British accent, "You may introduce me, my good frog." On a castle set, Reeve then begins the "To be or not to be" soliloquy, with Fozzie cuing him. With the performance interrupted by Beauregard,[8] who hands the guest star a skull prop, Reeve switches to the Yorick soliloquy. When he calls Yorick a fellow "of most excellent fancy" (5.1.185), the skull comes to life and recalls, "Ma always said I was the plain one." The now-alert Yorick complains that he is "carrying the whole scene," prompting the Muppets to suggest, "We're not ready for Shakespeare" (prompting Yorick's response "He's not ready for you either"). Instead, the performers sing Cole Porter's "Brush Up Your Shakespeare." Their very scene disproves the suggestion that Shakespeare is beyond them, for their humor is based in knowledge of the text. The scene establishes Shakespeare as a factor in mass culture, not simply the high arts.

In the third season of *The Muppet Show*, Raquel Welch is seen studying a copy of *The Merchant of Venice* in her dressing room, for she hopes to change her image. Scooter the gopher tells her she has no need to worry, for she can do what she wants on the show and does not have to wear any of her more typically revealing costumes "unless you really want to." A chorus of Muppets then beg her, "Please want to!" The opening reference is the episode's lone allusion to Shakespeare, yet Welch's desire to use Shakespeare while appearing in the Muppet Theater as a way to revamp and control her image suggests a vaulted position for both the Bard and these felt-and-foam performers. Through her appearance on this variety show, Welch hopes to be seen in a new light, with the filter of Muppet-based Shakespeare allowing that new light to shine upon her.

From 1996 to 1997, the Muppets appeared on network television in *Muppets Tonight!*, an updated *Muppet Show*. This program aired as part of ABC's "TGIF" lineup of family programming. While the Muppets remained irreverent as ever, an interesting theme emerged on the new series, as guest stars, following in the tradition of Raquel Welch, hope the Muppets will allow them to perform differently than normal. The use of the Muppets for experimentation further recalls Peter Sellers' Shakespearean plans, as well as the use of Christopher Reeve not as Superman but as Hamlet. On *MT!*, Arsenio wants to play the clown in *Pagliacci;* Heather Locklear, long cast as a bimbo, hopes to appear in something "intelligent and sophisticated."[9] Garth Brooks, in turn, desires to do something other than country music, resulting in a Tom Jones impression, a scene from *Fiddler on the Roof,* and a mambo number, along with, not surprisingly a Shakespearean sequence.

Brooks plays Romeo to Miss Piggy's unsuspecting Juliet (she expects to sing "Surry with a Fringe on Top") in a version of the balcony scene. Piggy agrees to play along, but her poor eyesight (apparently the result of advanced age) results in misread cue cards ("Oh Romero, Romero"); her nephews Andy and Randy enter, proclaiming, "Wefore art thou the Two Gentleman of Bologna." When Piggy insults them, they ask, "If you prick us, do we not bleed? If you tickle us, do we not laugh?" As the scene continues with Piggy's malapropism "Parking is such sweet sparrow ... whoever wrote this should be shot," Randy and Andy remove a beam, and the balcony collapses, bringing the scene literally crashing down. Statler, once again offended, complains, "Shakespeare would have hated that," only to prompt Waldorf's line, "You should know; you dated his sister." This time, however, Statler does not leave the insult alone, and he replies, "Boy, was she ugly." The joke is a fairly obvious one, meant to mock Statler's age, but the idea of Shakespeare's sister, a postulation from Virginia Woolf's *A Room of One's Own*, further proves the multi-layered humor of the Muppets. While Judith Shakespeare is not further discussed, the allusion here reveals the writers' trust in their audience's intelligence.

Shakespeare and the Muppets provide Brooks an opportunity to expand his horizons (a trend he continued with appearances on *Saturday Night Live*), and Shakespeare here remains cultural baseline for humor. The writers assume viewers will understand the basics behind the jokes. The Shakespearean humor is self-referential and intertextual, and the Muppets provide the springboard for adaptation and variance.

In a 1997 episode, *Muppets Tonight!* offered one final (for the time being) statement on the relevance of Shakespeare. Ernst Stavros Grouper (a one-eyed mogul recalling, ironically, both Rupert Murdoch and Bond villain Ernst Stavro Blofeld) is buying out their show, and the Muppets are asked to show what hip programming they produce. Kermit and Clifford show a clip from "The Two Homies of Verona," starring guest star Coolio and Gonzo (the Muppets' most-experienced Shakespearean).

> COOLIO: Make haste, homey.
> GONZO: What ho!
> COOLIO : A rival gang of watchers draw nigh.
> GONZO : 'Tis a gallop-by. Cover thyself. *[Both duck; an arrow flies in]*
> COOLIO : Yo-eth! Chilleth out. I prithee thine actions do reveal thou art whack.
> GONZO : Yea, verily whack. *[High-five each other.]*
> COOLIO : Word up.

Grouper wants to bury this "trash." Of chief interest is the fact that the Muppets use a Shakespearean-inspired skit to justify their relevance and hipness. This episode aired as the program itself fought low ratings, and the writers revealed their own cultural insight. Shakespeare provides cultural credibility; that cultural capital is universally recognized. However, the Muppets also call upon a Shakespearean moment for immediate credibility, thus suggesting how intertwined these facets of our cultural tapestry are. Shakespeare, iconic symbol of high/artistic culture, enables the Muppets, icons of popular culture and at times symbols of capitalistic pursuits, to intermingle and serve each other.

One near production might have fully developed the connection between the Muppets and Shakespeare. In 1999, Jeff Marx and Bobby Lopez, who would go on to write the Tony-winning Broadway musical *Avenue Q*, wrote a screenplay treatment with eight songs for *Kermit, Prince of Denmark*, a film designed to adapt *Hamlet*, following in the tradition of *The Muppet Christmas Carol*[10] and *Muppet Treasure Island*. The unproduced film, which would have at least fulfilled William H. Macy's suggestion, would have involved a confusion of identity, a combination of human and Muppet thespians taking on the roles from the tragedy (including Miss Piggy, in a highly bizarre move of double-casting, as both Gertrude and Ophelia), and a variety of songs combining both Shakespearean-based humor and Muppet-based frivolity ("Kermit, Prince of Denmark").

Shakespeare's literary stature and history lend credibility, even in parody, to skits revealing an inherent knowledge of the canon (a knowledge required by both writer and viewer); artistic experimentation is allowed first through Shakespeare and then through Shakespearean-inspired humor. The Muppets, in turn, offer a mass audience to Shakespearean-based skits. Allusions and intertextual references inform the Muppet shows, and viewers in turn are reminded to return to the text as the original source.

The trend may also reverse. In director Lenka Udovicky's production of *The Tempest* for the Globe Theatre London in 2000 (a production most universally known for its casting of Vanessa Redgrave as Prospero), actor Jasper Britton evoked the Muppets. While playing the creature Caliban, Britton flung fish at the Groundlings (along with such other outrageous acts as biting the head off a fish). This act recalls the Muppet character Lew Zealand, whose vaudeville-inspired act involved throwing "boomerang fish" at the audience. Invariably, the fish do not return to the thrower's hands, and Zealand, like this Caliban, rains fish upon his onlookers. While this connection may be merely coincidental, with Caliban perhaps more an out-of-control performance artist than vaudevillian Muppet, the link suggests the further blurring of high and pop culture. In the new millennium, Shakespearean stage productions evoke and allude to pop cultural icons, just as elements of popular culture evoke and allude to Shakespeare.

William Shakespeare and his works are continually reinvented and reimagined for different times and places. Jim Henson and his Muppets have taken elements from Shakespeare and offered them to a wide audience. Just as the use of Shakespeare affords the Muppets credibility (as they invoke legitimate theater of the canon), so too does this introduction to a broad-based audience serve Shakespeare. Shakespeare is kept in the eyes of a mass audience who need knowledge of him to understand the basis for the humor. The Bard serves as a springboard for experimentation artistically, and the Muppets make full use of the inherent potential in using Shakespeare to entertain. Children watching the Muppets are thus introduced to Shakespeare at an early age. Just as *Sesame Street* viewers continue watching the Muppets as they mature, so too can they grow as viewers and appreciators of Shakespeare. With the Muppets now a part of Disney's empire, their catalog of productions is being made and kept available, so children young and old can discover and revisit the Muppet trips to the sceptered isle. As escapism, the Muppets take viewers to sunny days and a place protected against infection; Shakespeare's "earth of majesty" is a fertile field for Muppet adaptation.

Notes

1. Recent straight-to-DVD productions for *Sesame Street* have included the Victorian literary adaptations *A Sesame Street Christmas Carol* (2006) and *Abby in Wonderland* (2008).
2. "Anything Muppets" are "unadorned puppet torsos and heads that could be turned into anything a script required by adding the right eyes, the right nose, the right wig, the right costume" (Finch 64).
3. In a similar vein, Gordon Jackson and Jean Marsh recreated their *Upstairs, Downstairs* roles in some segments, tying *Masterpiece Theatre*—a decidedly artistic program for PBS viewers—into the tapestry of allusions.
4. In a posting to the Shakespeare listserv, Dana Shilling suggests further Muppet possibilities with *Merchant*, listing a potential casting of *Sesame Street* and *Muppet Show* regulars as characters in the play, with Cookie Monster nominated for the role of Shylock.
5. The ever-pompous but often culturally-confused Sam the Eagle excitedly tells Shakespeare that he has seen *The Sound of Music* "a dozen times."
6. Some suggest *As You Like It* was inspired by May-Day plays which traditionally included Robin Hood.
7. "[J]ust hanging around the phone booth in case trouble breaks out," the stage-trained Reeve admits this "won't be my first time in tights," acknowledging his big-screen stardom as a superhero.
8. Beau interrupts to get all props on stage before his impending coffee break, causing Reeve to realize that the grounds upon which his acting has been halted were "Coffee Grounds?!"
9. Locklear may have found disappointment in the resulting product: "'The Hardy Pig Boys in the Mystery of the Zombie Queen of the Amazon Outer Space Jungle Bee Woman Case,' based on a novel by Jane Austen, written by Andy and Randy Pig."
10. A bust of Shakespeare appears in the classroom scene in the Dickens adaptation.

Works Cited

Borgenicht, David. *Sesame Street Unpaved: Scripts, Stories, Secrets, and Songs.* New York: Hyperion, 1998.
Burt, Richard. *Unspeakable ShaXXXspeares: Queer Theory and American Kiddie Culture.* New York: St. Martin's Press, 1998.
DellaVedova, Carla. "Re: Muppets & Shakespeare." E-mail to Hugh Davis. 30 July 2001.
_____. "Re: Muppets & Shakespeare." E-mail to Hugh Davis. 31 July 2001.
Finch, Christopher. *Jim Henson: The Works—The Art, The Magic, The Imagination.* New York: Random House, 1993.
Henson Associates. *The Art of the Muppets: A Retrospective Look at Twenty-Five Years of Muppet Magic.* New York: Muppet Press/Bantam, 1980.
"Kermit, Prince of Denmark." *Muppet Wiki.* 24 Feb 2008. <http://muppet.wikia.com/wiki/Kermit%2C_Prince_of_Denmark>
Shakespeare, William. *Hamlet* in *The Complete Works of William Shakespeare.* 4th ed. Ed. David Bevington. New York: Harper Collins, 1992. 1065–1116.
_____. *The Merchant of Venice* in *The Complete Works of William Shakespeare.* 4th ed. Ed. David Bevington. New York: Harper Collins, 1992. 182–215.
_____. *Richard II* in *The Complete Works of William Shakespeare.* 4th ed. Ed. David Bevington. New York: Harper Collins, 1992. 725–762.
_____. *Richard III* in *The Complete Works of William Shakespeare.* 4th ed. Ed. David Bevington. New York: Harper Collins, 1992. 631–681.
Shilling, Dana. "The Price of Swine." Online posting #9793. 16 Jan 2000. The Shakespeare Electronic Conference. 16 Aug. 2001. <SHAKSPER@WS.BOWIESTATE.EDU>.

"Starring Kermit the Frog as Bob Cratchit": Muppets as Actors
Ginger Stelle

Most people have heard stories of crazed fans who are unable to separate characters from the actors who play them. A soap opera fan throws a drink or shouts an obscenity at the woman who plays the soap opera vixen; fans write impassioned love letters addressed, not to the medical drama actor, but to the dreamy doctor he plays. This has even become a popular plotline for films, television shows, or plays dealing with the entertainment industry. The cliché aside, however, most people have no real difficulties separating the actor from the role. Television-watching and film-going audiences are accustomed to watching human actors portraying characters. Consequently, when Brad Pitt appears onscreen, people accept that he is no longer the "Brad Pitt" they were just reading about on the pages of that tabloid while they were waiting in line at the supermarket. They see him as the character he plays, at least until the movie ends. The next time they see him at an awards show or on the pages of that supermarket tabloid, they understand that he is Brad Pitt, not the character in the movie they just watched. Infatuated teenagers can easily watch several movies in a row starring their favorite actor in wildly different roles without getting confused. When married performers appear together in a film, even though the audience may be aware of their off-screen relationship, that off-screen involvement does not necessarily translate to the film. Typically, characters exist apart from their real-life personae.

What happens, however, when the actors are themselves characters? Since their creation, Jim Henson's Muppets have existed as specific characters. Though people know the Muppets have human controllers, most casual fans would be unable to identify which Muppets were performed by Jim Henson and which by Frank Oz. However, they would be able to identify Kermit the

Frog or Miss Piggy without difficulty because they exist as part of the contemporary cultural lexicon and are clearly recognizable. Kermit the Frog is Kermit the Frog. Miss Piggy is Miss Piggy. The Great Gonzo is The Great Gonzo. And so on. Nor is it only the well-known and most popular Muppets; many of the "Muppet Morsels" (a fun-fact subtitle track on *The Muppet Show* Season One DVDs) are devoted to identifying the various Muppets by name. Each Muppet has an identifiable and permanent persona, with a particular and unique personality. Gonzo is the weirdo; Kermit is the sane one, the leader. Miss Piggy sees herself as a glamorous star, loved by everyone. Fozzie tells bad jokes but has a heart of gold. Additionally, over the years, the relationships between the Muppets have crystallized into recognizable patterns. The on-again-off-again love affair between Kermit and Miss Piggy has been going for three decades, for example.

Despite the fact that they are, ultimately, puppets, for decades audiences have been asked to accept these characters, these Muppet personae, as actors and performers in their own right. *The Muppet Show* was a variety show with many of the standard variety show roles: a host (Kermit), a resident stand-up comic (Fozzie), an eccentric performance artist (Gonzo), a diva (Miss Piggy), a band (Dr. Teeth and the Electric Mayhem), a crooner (Rowlf), and a host of other acts. They perform musical numbers, dance numbers, and comedy sketches. They interact with human guest stars, both on and off the stage. *The Muppet Show* establishes that they are not mere singers, dancers, and comedians, but "people" who perform. A frog puppet that sings and dances is one thing; a frog puppet who sings and dances and flirts backstage (or on stage) with female guest stars and gets karate chopped by his pig "girlfriend" is something else! *The Muppet Show's* mix of onstage and backstage further complicates the picture because the Muppets exist simultaneously as characters and performers. As actors, furthermore, the Muppets sometimes participate in typical "celebrity" functions: they appear on late-night talk shows, present at awards shows, and endorse products by appearing in commercials. They even make movies.

The Muppet movies represent the greatest display of this phenomenon as the films ask audiences to accept the Muppets on the same terms as human actors. As previously mentioned, when Brad Pitt appears in a movie, audiences see him as the character he plays. The Muppet movies ostensibly ask audiences to see the Muppets as their on-screen characters rather than as their off-screen personae. However, the Muppets bring their characters with them. In *The Muppet Movie* (1979), *The Great Muppet Caper* (1981), and *The Muppets Take Manhattan* (1984), the Muppets "play" themselves, though not necessarily with the same back-story. In the first movie, Kermit sets out for Hollywood, meeting the others along the way. In *Caper*, Kermit, Fozzie, and Gonzo play themselves as reporters, and they meet Miss Piggy while on assignment. In *Manhattan*, the crew, recent college graduates, try to get their show on Broadway. While the Muppets may not necessarily be playing their fully developed characters, they still play a version of themselves, and the existing relationships are still present, even if in slightly different form. In *Manhattan*, for example, Kermit is still the leader. Miss Piggy still looks on jealously when Kermit talks to Jenny, the waitress (Juliana Donald). Dr. Teeth and the Electric Mayhem stay together when the larger group breaks up, as do Gonzo and Camilla. Similar dynamics exist in the other films, as well. It was not until *The Muppet Christmas Carol* (1992) that Kermit and his fellows actually stepped outside their traditional roles and truly "acted." Though they have since appeared in *Muppet Treasure Island* (1996) and *The Muppets' Wizard of Oz* (2005), *Carol* presents the most illuminating insights into the ability of the Muppets to become actors.

In choosing to adapt Charles Dickens' Christmas classic, *A Christmas Carol* (1843), Jim Henson Productions and director Brian Henson had to deal with a truly iconic story. In his study *The Life and Times of Ebenezer Scrooge*, Paul Davis explains: "My acquaintance with Scrooge feels preliterate, different from my sense of Dick and Jane, Dr. Doolittle, or Robinson Crusoe. I remember when I first met the Hardy Boys, but I feel as if I've always known Scrooge and Tiny Tim" (3). The tale of the miser who encounters the Ghosts of Christmas Past, Present, and Yet to Come and who subsequently undergoes a fundamental character change is deeply ingrained upon the contemporary cultural psyche. Since its initial appearance *A Christmas Carol* "has been adapted, revised, condensed, retold, reoriginated and modernized more than any other work of English literature" (P. Davis 4). In the twentieth century alone, "more than twenty films and a hundred and forty televisions productions [were] based on Dickens's tale" (Norden 188). By joining this re-visioning tradition, the Muppets, though cultural icons themselves, nonetheless had to deal with a century-and-a-half's worth of cultural expectation.

Hugh Davis argues that *The Muppet Christmas Carol* is one of the most faithful adaptations of Dickens' novella in existence (96). Ironically, however, he suggests that the film's success as an adaptation comes at the expense of its Muppet-ness:

> [I]t uses one of the most amazing calls for suspension of disbelief in film history to tell its dramatic tale. The audience is asked to forget that Kermit and Piggy are on the screen and, instead, see Bob and Mrs. Cratchit, as played by two actors [...]. The fact that the Muppet character Kermit [...] participates in press interviews illustrates the nature of the suspension of disbelief which must occur for the film to succeed. The puppets create a surreal atmosphere initially, but once the movie starts, the audience is captured by the story and accepts Kermit the Frog as a character different from "just" Kermit [97–98].

He further contends that although "a successful mix of Muppet and literature occurs," the resulting film is somewhat Muppet-lite, focusing too much on the literary source material and not enough on the Muppets (103). Davis is correct in suggesting that the film asks its audience to accept the Muppets as actors; however, while the film may *ask* the audience to forget they are watching Muppets, it ultimately makes it impossible for the audience to fully suspend disbelief. Unlike human actors, the Muppets bring their lives and histories with them, and an already classic tale receives a unique spin that no strictly human production could provide.

Director Brian Henson and screenwriter Jerry Juhl take special pains at the film's beginning to establish the Muppets as actors. The opening credits cast list states, "Starring Kermit the Frog as Bob Cratchit, Miss Piggy as Emily Cratchit, The Great Gonzo as Charles Dickens, Rizzo the Rat as Himself, Fozzie Bear as Fozziwig." Only then, after introducing the principal Muppet characters, does the cast list include "and Michael Caine as Scrooge." This is important for several reasons. First, it establishes that the Muppets are actors; they are playing characters other than themselves. The list places the Muppets on the same level as the human actor, equating their performances with his. Furthermore, the Muppets are listed first — before the actor playing Ebenezer Scrooge. Traditionally, film versions of *A Christmas Carol* are identified by the person who plays Scrooge, such as George C. Scott (1984), Alastair Sim (1951), or Patrick Stewart (1999). Not here. Here, the actor playing Scrooge, though an extremely well-known and respected actor himself, is relegated to the end of the principal cast list, and he follows cast members whose roles are far less significant than his own, both in terms of screen time and importance to Dickens' original story. Likewise, on the cover of the Kermit's 50th Anniversary Edition DVD, the image in the foreground is of the same principal Muppets (and Robin as Tiny Tim). Michael Caine appears only in the background, and his image is much less distinct than that of the others.

In addition, the filmmakers continue to emphasize this dynamic in the film's opening scene, which includes this exchange between Gonzo and Rizzo. After identifying himself, not as Gonzo, but as Charles Dickens, Gonzo refuses to acknowledge Rizzo's skepticism of "a blue furry Charles Dickens who hangs out with a rat?" This scene establishes both the roles that Gonzo and Rizzo will play throughout the film and the dual-layered performance at work. Unlike on *The Muppet Show* and in some of the other movies, Gonzo is not playing himself; when the film opens, he has already assumed his role as Charles Dickens, and in that role, he addresses the audience. Gonzo, the actor, plays Charles Dickens. His role is one of many concessions the Muppets make to the original Dickens source material and the cultural expectations surrounding *A Christmas Carol*. Miss Piggy puts aside her usual diva antics to play Bob Cratchit's wife, just as Fozzie puts aside his bad jokes as Fozziwig.

Kermit's Bob Cratchit lacks many of Kermit's characteristic antics, like his exasperated scream. For the most part, the story of Scrooge's transformation is played straight, keeping close to the book.

At the same time, however, the Muppet-as-actor duality makes itself felt. The cast list, while establishing that the Muppets are playing their specific Dickensian roles, further reemphasizes their existence as Muppets. The opening credits do not list the Muppet performers; the screen does not say "Steve Whitmire as Bob Cratchit" (though the performers are credited at the end). The Kermit puppet is not simply being used as Bob Cratchit. Kermit remains, indelibly, Kermit, just as the other Muppets remain their primary characters. In the opening scene, Gonzo is still Gonzo; Rizzo sees him as blue furry Gonzo, not nineteenth-century novelist Dickens, and has to be convinced before he can accept his friend as Dickens. When Gonzo/Dickens begins telling the actual story, Rizzo both questions and comments on the "spooky" opening lines, "The Marleys were dead, to begin with." Rizzo repeatedly challenges Gonzo/Dickens's narrative knowledge, such as when he predicts Scrooge's imminent appearance. Whenever he calls Gonzo "Mr. Dickens," he says it with a tongue-in-cheek, "I'll play along" note in his voice. He asks why Gonzo/Dickens whispers and is informed that "It's for dramatic emphasis." Rizzo's constant interruptions and his observations on Gonzo/Dickens's dual role keep the audience from forgetting that Gonzo is, ultimately, only acting. Gonzo throws himself wholeheartedly into his role and tries to actually become Charles Dickens. Even when directly challenged, Gonzo/Dickens stays focused on his job. Yet, even he occasionally "forgets" and slips back into just Gonzo. When Rizzo asks if he wants some bread, Gonzo (not Gonzo/Dickens) replies, "Not while I'm working." Several of Gonzo's characteristic traits appear throughout the film as well. He enjoys flying into the past attached to Scrooge with a grappling hook, something The Great Gonzo would enjoy. He also retains his love of chickens. While attached with that grappling hook, they get dragged through some trees; Gonzo emerges with a chicken on his head, whom he introduces to Rizzo as "Louise." Later, at Fozziwig's, he ogles another chicken and exclaims, "Whoa!" For all his protestations that he is Charles Dickens, Gonzo always remains Gonzo. It could be argued that, as the narrator, Gonzo has more flexibility than the other characters because he ultimately exists outside the story; nonetheless, the other characters also retain their Muppet-ness, even when doing so requires a departure (at times a significant one) from the original Dickens novella. Muppet relationships get superimposed on top of the ones envisioned by Dickens. Besides the familiar teaming of Gonzo and Rizzo, Dr. Bunsen Honeydew and his assistant Beaker remain together, playing the two benevolent gentlemen who call on Scrooge seeking charitable donations. Their exchange with Scrooge follows that in the book quite closely (Dickens 5–6) and is one of the least Muppet-like uses of the familiar characters. Bunsen does not perform any ill-advised laboratory experiments, and Beaker does not get blown up, eaten, knocked over, or anything else. Nonetheless, they are together. Beaker retains his characteristic mode of speaking, and Bunsen retains his affable cluelessness. Also, they are the ones assigned the unenviable task (an experiment of sorts) of asking Scrooge for money.

Another familiar relationship is that between Statler and Waldorf and Fozzie Bear. For years on *The Muppet Show* and beyond, Statler and Waldorf sat up in their box and heckled Fozzie mercilessly for his bad jokes. They appear in *The Muppet Christmas Carol* (besides the reference on the sign for "Statler and Waldorf, Haberdashers") as Jacob and Robert Marley, Scrooge's old partners. This, in itself, is a Muppet accommodation, as Statler and Waldorf rarely appear apart from each other; consequently a second Marley had to be added to keep them together. That it functions simultaneously as a side reference to reggae legend Bob Marley only adds to the fun. Furthermore, as Jacob and Robert Marley, they attend Fozziwig's Christmas Party, where they sit in the balcony and listen to Fozzie/Fozziwig's speech. When it turns out to be just "Thank you all and Merry Christmas," they heckle, before deciding that they "loved" the speech because "It was short." This scene does not appear in Dickens' novella. There is no suggestion that the Marleys attended Fezziwig's annual Christmas party or that Fezziwig stopped the proceedings to make a speech (24–26). However, this scene possesses a clear *Muppet Show* pedigree and is included in the film for that reason.

The most familiar Muppet relationship in existence is probably that between Kermit and Miss Piggy. Not everyone would recognize Statler and Waldorf or Bunsen and Beaker, but anyone with even a basic familiarity with the Muppets knows that Kermit and Miss Piggy are the great romantic couple. Their relationship dates back to the very first episode of *The Muppet Show* and has developed throughout the Muppet adventures since then. At times, Kermit seems to share Piggy's feelings, while at others he seems almost repulsed by them. Occasionally, she flirts with another man to get his attention, and it always gets her attention when Kermit flirts with another woman. Therefore, when Kermit becomes Bob Cratchit, no one could even consider anyone else to play his wife. While, for the most part, their scenes together stay fairly true to the original, anyone familiar with the Muppets immediately recognizes Kermit and Miss Piggy and their pre-existing relationship. When Kermit/Bob comes home on Christmas day and Miss Piggy/Mrs. Cratchit greets him with an enormous hug, saying, "Merry Christmas, Crachy," the audience is reminded of Piggy's traditional pet name for Kermit: "Kermy." Furthermore, when the hug continues despite Kermit/Bob's (mild) protestations and eventually ends with the sound of a pinch, an "Ooh!" from Miss Piggy/Mrs. Cratchit, and Kermit/Bob's slightly embarrassed look, the moment, as tame and Victorian as it is, carries with it nearly twenty years' worth of relationship. It cannot be avoided. The viewer's knowledge of Kermit and Miss Piggy's existing relationship adds an entire subtext, perhaps even a hint of eroticism, to the Dickensian relationship intrinsic in the original text.

Nor is this limited to Muppet relationships. Just as Gonzo manages to be simultaneously himself and Charles Dickens, the other Muppet characters bring their own mannerisms and subtexts to their various roles. Some of the Muppets have roles created specifically for them by the filmmakers. Kermit/Bob's assistants in Scrooge's office do not exist in Dickens' book; Bob is Scrooge's only employee (3). However, the filmmakers cast the Muppet Rats as bookkeepers, allowing both for the Rats to perform their usual comic antics and for Kermit/Bob to have other characters with whom he can interact. When Kermit and the Rats approach Scrooge to ask for more coal, one of them says, "All of our pens have turned to ink-cicles." Another claims that their "assets have frozen." As soon as Scrooge yells at them, they immediately appear in grass skirts and start singing "Island in the Sun." Needless to say, none of this takes place in Dickens' original book, but it is all typical of the Muppets. Likewise, describing the end of the work day on Christmas Eve, Dickens writes that the "office was closed in a twinkling" (8). In the film, however, because of the presence of the Rats, the closing of the office becomes an elaborate production number featuring Kermit/Bob singing "One More Sleep 'Til Christmas" and the Rats executing an assortment of acrobatic exploits.

Likewise, the Fozziwig Christmas party looks very different than it is described in the book. For one thing, the book's character is named "Fezziwig"; his name is changed to accommodate the Muppets' Fozzie Bear. Secondly, the book never specifies what Fezziwig's business is, other than to refer to it as a "warehouse" (24); in the film, Scrooge clearly identifies it as a "rubber chicken factory." As already mentioned, Fozzie/Fozziwig plays his role straight, making none of his typical bad jokes. However, the filmmakers nonetheless make a clear reference to Fozzie's preferred style of humor in giving Fozziwig a rubber chicken factory, and indeed, the room has been decked with rubber chickens and rain boots. The party has apparently been catered by the Swedish Chef with his usual flair. Finally, the band is none other than the Muppets' own Dr. Teeth and the Electric Mayhem, composed of Dr. Teeth, Floyd, Zoot, Janice, and Animal, along with Rowlf the Dog. When the music starts, the camera focuses on Animal sitting behind his drums, but limited to merely tapping the triangle and looking disgruntled as only Animal can look. The camera moves to feature Gonzo and Rizzo with the Swedish Chef, then young Scrooge with Fozzie/Fozziwig, then switches back to Animal, who has clearly had all he can stand of the triangle and begins pounding the drums and growling in his usual fashion. Eventually, he settles back down as the band continues to play a much more upbeat version of the song they had been playing. While the latter does represent a type of music which might, conceivably have been played at an early-nineteenth-century Christmas party, the entire segment has its roots in the Muppet tradition. Dr. Teeth and the Electric Mayhem traditionally object to anything even potentially "square"; being relegated to such slow, beat-less music is unpalatable to them, so they adapt it to their own purposes, just as they often did on *The Muppet Show*. As a result of all of these changes, Dickens's Victorian Christmas party becomes a uniquely Muppet event.

Another slightly less familiar Muppet who brings his own unique character into the film is Sam the Eagle, playing the headmaster of Scrooge's childhood school. Dickens describes the headmaster as a man "who glared on Master Scrooge with a ferocious condescension, and threw him into a dreadful state of mind by shaking hands with him" (23). Dickens further implies that the headmaster is a stingy, unpleasant character overall (23). Sam makes frequent appearances on *The Muppet Show*. As a bald eagle, an American symbol, Sam often appears as the voice of American values, parodying the puritanical and uptight American image. He repeatedly called for "clean" and "tasteful" entertainment, as well as championing the more "cultural" segments of the show, and he is nearly always stymied in his quest. For example, during the show's first season, he regularly introduces the Wayne and Wanda singing team, fully endorsed by himself, but who rarely make it more than a few bars into their song before something catastrophic happens. In *The Muppet Christmas Carol*, Sam embodies Scrooge's old headmaster, bringing, once again, his own established character and history to the role. After extolling the virtues of hard work and stability, he tells young Scrooge, "You will love business. It is the American way." Gonzo/Dickens urgently whispers something in Sam's ear, prompting him to correct himself by saying, "It is the British way." The humor in this scene works without any background information. However, knowing Sam's history, both his traditional role among the Muppets as the voice of American values and his tendency to endorse things that end catastrophically, increases both the humor and the brilliance of this scene. Once again, the subtext provided by the Muppet-ness of the character deepens the experience of viewing the film.

This becomes increasingly true with a character like Miss Piggy. To be fair, Miss Piggy is largely restrained by her role as Mrs. Cratchit; she does not get to act like her usual diva self. Nonetheless, besides her aforementioned encounter with Kermit/Bob, Miss Piggy's character makes itself known in subtle ways. She primps in the mirror. She is very excited about the smell of the roasting goose. She scarfs down the chestnuts, and then when her daughter reminds her that they were supposed to save them until Kermit/Bob gets home, Piggy responds, "I wasn't eating them. I was merely checking them to see if they were not burnt. It's a chef's thing, dear." Then she gets her daughters confused, finally giving up with a "Whatever." Surely, Dickens never envisioned such things for his Mrs. Cratchit. However, when Kermit/Bob raises his glass to toast "Mr. Scrooge, the Founder of the Feast," Piggy/Mrs. Cratchit's response is almost verbatim that of Dickens' Mrs. Cratchit: "I suppose that on the blessed day of Christmas, one must drink to the health of Mr. Scrooge, even though he is odious, stingy, hard, and unfeeling" (41). Replacing only Dickens's "hard" with "wicked," Piggy/Mrs. Cratchit says exactly this. But then, she adds "and badly dressed" to her list of Scrooge's faults. This does not appear in Dickens' book, and within the film it even draws a gasp from the Cratchit daughters. Such a criticism is pure Miss Piggy. After Scrooge's transformation, when he visits the Cratchits (a scene which does not appear in the book at all) pretending to be angry, Miss Piggy comes closest to showing her true self, losing her temper with Scrooge and threatening, presumably, to "raise [him] right off the pavement" as Scrooge informs them that he's raising Bob's salary. As soon as Scrooge's words register, Miss Piggy backs down, but Scrooge does not realize how close he just came to receiving one of her characteristic karate chops. Just as the others do, she plays her role mostly straight, but Miss Piggy ultimately reminds everyone that she is, in fact, Miss Piggy, and not simply an actress playing Mrs. Cratchit.

The most significant Muppetization in the film is actually that surrounding the character of Marley, or in this case, the Marleys. In the novel, Dickens makes it abundantly and unmistakably clear that Jacob Marley's condition is one of "[i]ncessant torture of remorse" (14). Marley describes, "Oh, captive, bound, and double ironed, [...], not to know that no space of regret can make amends for one life's opportunities misused! Yet such was I!" (14). Marley and the other tormented souls who appear outside Scrooge's window make "incoherent sounds of lamentation and regret; wailings inexpressibly sorrowful and self-accusatory" (15). They walk the earth, seeing the suffering of their fellow-men and unable to do anything about it (16). It is a miserable and horrifying existence, without any redeeming factors.

In the film, the Marleys are played by Statler and Waldorf, who, as the other Muppets do, bring to their parts their own unique characteristics. Here, they assume the roles of Scrooge's partners, just as bad as he while they lived, and visiting now to warn him to change his ways or suffer their fate. However, they arrive laughing, not moaning, joking about Scrooge's age and wickedness. This is hardly indicative of repentance, and it continues. They begin their song, singing about their heartless deeds. Then they laugh. The laugh is followed by a moan and more singing about their own inhumanity, warning Scrooge that "as freedom comes from giving love, so prison comes with hate." As they continue to sing, they grow more and more tormented and spend more time wailing than laughing. But this does not erase the fact that they laughed. They laughed at their own condition; they laughed about evil deeds; they laughed about Scrooge's fate. In short, they act like Statler and Waldorf, Muppet hecklers, rather than Jacob and Robert Marley, repentant ghosts. This fits the overall film, but it does represent a significant departure from Dickens's original story. Ultimately, Statler and Waldorf remain Statler and Waldorf. Just as Gonzo and Miss Piggy and the other Muppets can only suppress their true characters somewhat, Statler and Waldorf must be who they are; they cannot change.

Finally, this fact is underscored by the casting of a human Scrooge. While it is a tradition for the Muppets to include human actors, whether as guest stars on *The Muppet Show* or in supporting roles in the films, here, the central role in the film is played, not by a Muppet, but by a human actor. There are other human actors as well, but mostly, they play roles like Scrooge's nephew Fred and his wife Clara and Scrooge's fiancée Belle — people who must be human because Scrooge is human. *A Christmas Carol* is Scrooge's story. Why not cast a Muppet as Scrooge? Simply, the nature of the Muppets does not allow for the kind of dramatic character shift that Scrooge undergoes. Clearly, no one would ever accept someone like Kermit playing Scrooge because no one would ever accept that Kermit could be that mean and heartless. Kermit is not mean and heartless, nor can he pretend to be so. At the same time, neither Statler nor Waldorf could ever be accepted as the nice and loving Scrooge because that would go entirely against their established characters. Even a new Muppet would not do. The filmmakers created some new characters for this film, most notably the Spirits of Christmas, but even they possess static characters. They do not change. In the end, only a human actor could play Scrooge because audiences are used to seeing human actors portray more fluid parts.

Since their creation, the Muppets have set themselves up as actors, playing roles other than their own. They have asked audiences to accept them as equals of the human actors they work with. Ultimately, this request is a sham. The Muppets are not human actors. Whether they play a version of themselves or a character in a classic work of literature, the Muppets bring their characters with them. Audiences know the characters and associate that knowledge with the figures on the screen. The Muppets themselves infuse whatever role they inhabit with the spirit of their Muppet character, but this is not a limitation. On the contrary, because the Muppets possess this innate duality, any project that includes them, whether it be a commercial or a literary adaptation, becomes immediately more complex and interesting, full of subtext and inside jokes. With each Muppet project, the history grows and evolves. As the Muppets move through the twenty-first century, their legend will grow and evolve as well.

Works Cited

Davis, Hugh H. "A Weirdo, a Rat, and a Humbug: The Literary Qualities of *The Muppet Christmas Carol.*" *Studies in Popular Culture* 21.3 (1999): 95–105.
Davis, Paul. *The Life and Times of Ebenezer Scrooge.* New Haven: Yale University Press, 1990.
Dickens, Charles. *A Christmas Carol.* 1843. New York: Dover, 1991.
The Muppet Christmas Carol. Dir. Brian Henson. Screenplay by Jerry Juhl. Perf. Michael Caine, Dave Goelz, Steve Whitmire, Jerry Nelson, and Frank Oz. 1992. DVD. Disney, 2005.
The Muppet Show. Season One. 1976-77. DVD. Buena Vista, 2005.
The Muppets Take Manhattan. Dir. Frank Oz. Screenplay by Frank Oz, Tom Patchett, and Jay Tarses. Perf. Jim Henson, Frank Oz, Dave Goelz, Steve Whitmire, Richard Hunt, and Jerry Nelson. 1984. DVD. Jim Henson Home Entertainment, 2001.
Norden, Martin F. "Tiny Tim on Screen: A Disability Studies Perspective." *Dickens on Screen.* Ed. John Glavin. Cambridge: Cambridge University Press, 2003.

A Rainbow for the 21st Century: *The Muppets' Wizard of Oz* and the Reimagination of American Myth

Alissa Burger

Fairy tales are told and retold, revised and reinvented over time in order to reflect the changing values and anxieties of the people and cultures that tell them. Through this process of reimagination, fairy tale discourse is instrumental in establishing American myth, expressing the themes and identities unique to its individual culture. *The Wizard of Oz*, a story first told in 1900 in L. Frank Baum's children's book *The Wonderful Wizard of Oz*, is one such distinctly American fairy tale. Chronicling the adventures of Dorothy, a young girl from Kansas picked up by a twister and dropped down in the magical land of Oz, *The Wizard of Oz* has become one of the most easily-recognizable narratives of the past hundred years, in part as a result of its adaptation by MGM Studios into the classic 1939 Technicolor film *The Wizard of Oz*. As fairy tales continue to be revised and reinvented to better suit their contemporary audiences, their narratives change as well. *The Wizard of Oz*, for example, has been adapted dozens of times, with each new revision foregrounding differences of race, gender, and contemporary context, demonstrating the active interaction of fairy tales with their surrounding culture. Jim Henson's Muppets also situate themselves in direct engagement with American culture, working to critique modern popular culture while simultaneously occupying the position of unmistakable icons. Defining characteristics of the Muppets and their critique of the surrounding culture include a spirit of playful self-reflexivity, cultural contextualization, and an explicit emphasis on performance, as well as the retelling of traditional stories and fairy tales. The Muppets occupy a privileged place within the discourse of story-telling in part because puppetry "covers almost every form of theatre, from Passion plays to Punch and Judy, from grand opera to low burlesque" (Henson Associates 3), enabling the Muppets to perform and revise cultural narratives in fantastic and intertextual ways inaccessible to other kinds of film and television. In *The Muppets' Wizard of Oz*, the charm, modernization, and spirit of self-reflexive parody characteristic of Henson's Muppets combine with the classic narrative of Baum's *The Wonderful Wizard of Oz* to create a dynamic and culturally relevant reimagination of this distinctly American myth.

Theories of myth have long been employed in critical discussions of American culture, with Henry Nash Smith defining myth as "collective representations rather than the work of a single mind" (xi), or themes that recur in the canonical works of a culture. In the case of American culture, these themes include the dichotomy of frontier and home, as well as the central significance of the hero or heroine's journey in establishing individual identity. In addition, the mythical discourse of fairy tales also plays a socialization role, championing desirable virtues and personal characteristics such as intellect, empathy, and bravery, as represented in the *Wizard of Oz* narrative by the central characters of the Scarecrow, the Tin Woodman, and the Cowardly Lion. While canonical readings of literature and culture have generally been dismissed in favor of readings which allow for a multiplicity of voices and perspectives, these established themes continue to inform cultural discourse and popular cultural representations. Situating American myth within contemporary culture, Neil Campbell and Alasdair Keen argue that myth serves the purpose of "confirming certain qualities and attributes" of a society (9). By this reading, myth adds structure and reassurance to social characteristics that are already in existence, active and under constant negotiation. The retelling of fairy tales and classic stories, such as the *Wizard of Oz* narrative, provide a productive gauge of the position of American myth in popular culture through exploration of the ways in which the story is revised over time. As John G. Cawelti argues of genre formulas, "[c]onvention and invention have quite different cultural functions. Conventions represent familiar shared images and meanings, and they assert an ongoing continuity of values; inventions confront us with a new perception or meaning which we have not realized before" (385). Therefore, by examining which values and representations fall out of use, as well as new elements which are added or substituted, revisions of traditional stories serve as indicators of shifts in cultural values, identities, and tensions.

The *Wizard of Oz* narrative got a Muppet makeover in 2005 with *The Muppets' Wizard of Oz*, a television special directed by Kirk R. Thatcher. This small screen version features singing sensation Ashanti as Dorothy Gale, Jeffrey Tambor as the Wizard, and Queen Latifah and David Alan Grier as Dorothy's Aunt Em and Uncle Henry. Kermit plays the Scarecrow looking for a brain, Gonzo is transformed into a T.I.N. (Total Intelligence Network) Thing who has lost his heart, and Fozzie Bear becomes a Cowardly Lion with stage-fright, while Miss Piggy stars as all four of Oz's witches and Pepe the King Prawn is Dorothy's loyal companion Toto. Other familiar Muppet faces pop up along the Yellow Brick Road as well, with Dr. Teeth and the Electric Mayhem headlining at the Poppyfield's nightclub, Sam the Eagle guarding the gates of the Emerald City, and Scooter working as the Wizard's personal assistant. The Muppet tradition of featured guest stars continues in *Muppets' Wizard of Oz* as well, with cameos by popular cultural icons like Kelly Osbourne and Quentin Tarantino.

Several elements of the mythic discourse underlying the *Wizard of Oz* narrative established by Baum over a century ago continue in contemporary adaptations, including *The Muppets' Wizard of Oz*, providing the continuity Cawelti refers to as convention. A theme that remains consistent throughout almost all versions of the *Wizard of Oz* story is the mythic dichotomy of the frontier and home. In addition to the continued westward expansion of which Baum's generation was a part, this period also marked the beginnings of America as a colonial force; as Michael Patrick Hearn points out in *The Annotated 'Wizard of Oz,'* at the time of Baum's writing, "[n]ow that the American Empire expanded to Hawaii and Puerto Rico and the Philippines as a consequence of the Spanish-American War of 1898, people wanted to read about foreign lands" (1). This tension between remaining safe at home and setting out for lands unknown has remained a constant concern of Oz's heroines and heroes throughout a multiplicity of adaptations, including *The Muppets' Wizard of Oz*. Another convention which has remained consistent throughout numerous adaptations of the *Wizard of Oz* story is the celebrated character traits represented by its heroes; Dorothy values family and friendship above all else, while intellect, empathy, and bravery are championed in Dorothy's companions' desire for brain, heart, and courage. These conventions make the *Wizard of Oz* narrative recognizable in its many retellings and revisions. However, as American culture has continued to develop over the past hundred years, the discourse of American myth has had to adapt to effectively address the shifting cultural context and its popular cultural representations. *The Muppets' Wizard of Oz* reimagines this American myth for modern audiences, reinventing the *Wizard of Oz* story by situating this tale within the context of contemporary American culture, emphasizing self-reflexivity by highlighting film as performative in nature through direct address of the audience and inclusion of "behind-the-scenes" material, and a representation of gender which moves Dorothy beyond the domestic space of home and family.

First, *The Muppets' Wizard of Oz* reinvents the traditional fairy tale of Oz by establishing a contemporary cultural context surrounding the Muppets' adventures along the Yellow Brick Road. With references to reality television, including an obsession with fame and celebrity, *The Muppets' Wizard of Oz* situates its characters distinctly within the social milieu of the early twenty-first century. The structure and expression of myth, including the retelling and revision of fairy tales, necessarily undergo significant changes over time in order to remain relevant to the culture that surrounds them. *The Muppets' Wizard of Oz* lifts the *Wizard of Oz* narrative out of the fantastical realm of traditional fairy tales by establishing recognizable connections to the everyday in order to situate the story within the context of twenty-first century popular culture. A key element that is added to establish this context is the discourse of reality television, including the Muppets' *American Idol*–style auditions to find a singing sensation to join them on tour, the Wicked Witch's reality show shot in her "lair of evil," and the Wizard's live broadcast as he grants the wishes of Dorothy and her friends. In an example of competition-based, talent show-format reality programming, Kermit and the Muppets take to the road to search for their next big star. However, the focus is not on the competition itself; as Kermit informs Dorothy, she is "the best singer that we've heard anywhere." Instead, the emphasis remains on ensemble performance, with Dorothy's first televised performance featuring her singing with the Muppets, complete with Miss Piggy's standard attempts to steal the spotlight. The Wicked Witch's reality program, on the other hand, plays up fame and celebrity, rather than talent. Inviting camera crews into her home, the Wicked Witch provides her "fans" with an inside glimpse of her private life, including her capture and intended execution of prisoners Dorothy and Toto. As the Wicked Witch enthusiastically chirps into the camera, "[t]oday you'll see me do my hair, take my daily bottled water bath and, as an added bonus, I'll try on some awesome footwear that will help me totally rule all of Oz"; however, this is footwear that the Wicked Witch will have to cut off Dorothy's legs to get, with the witch playing up glamour and fashion to the exclusion of individual suffering. Finally, the Wizard's live wish fulfillment for Dorothy and her companions highlights the discrepancy between illusion and reality. The Wizard "cures" the Cowardly Lion's stage fright with a shiny golden microphone, but shunts the Lion from the stage before he has a chance to test out his new courage; he gives the T.I.N. Thing a candy heart and reunites him with Camilla the chicken, though the couple's almost immediate squabbling proves that even televised, idealized romantic love is far from perfect. Finally, the Wizard also grants the Scarecrow's wish by filling his empty head with bran cereal, presenting him with "bran new brains," a gift that leaves the Scarecrow running for the nearest bathroom. Despite their obvious shortcomings, the Scarecrow, T.I.N. Thing, and Cowardly Lion are pleased with their gifts; it is Dorothy who calls the Wizard's bluff, finally realizing that she'd rather be a singer than a star, privileging talent over celebrity and choosing the reality of hard work and dedication over the illusion of fame offered by the Wizard. As Dorothy tells her friends, "this Wizard hasn't given you anything you didn't already have.... Wizard or no Wizard, you were already brave and kind and smart." Everyone wins, except for the Wizard, whose powers are revealed as clever posturing, and Dorothy returns to Kansas to succeed or fail on her own, keeping the cultural obsession with celebrity for celebrity's sake in check.

However, the context of reality television has a more sordid, exploitative side as well; this darker side of reality television and instant celebrity is most dramatically demonstrated early in the Muppets' talent search, when Kermit laments the difficulty of finding "an all–American girl with talent," to which Rizzo responds with the question "How do the producers of *Girls Gone Wild* do it?" An exceedingly mature cultural reference for a Muppet audience made up largely of young children, this aside is in keeping with the Muppets' long-standing refusal to shy away from controversy and cultural taboos. Consider, for example, a UK spot musical performance in Season Two of *The Muppet Show*, featuring Miss Piggy as a very pregnant bride stood up at the altar. As Piggy sings from Henry E. Pether and Fred W. Leigh's "Waiting at the Church," on receiving a message from her beau,

> Here's the very note
> This is what he wrote:
> I cannot get away to marry you today
> My wife won't let me [*TMS*, "John Cleese"].

An admittedly risqué segment for its time, this musical number also slyly highlighted the shifting gender roles of the late 1970s, the uncertainty of traditional relationship structures, and the myriad of tensions and anxieties underlying the whole upheaval. Henson Associates have expressed dissatisfaction with recent infantilizing of the Muppet characters and noted that *The Muppets' Wizard of Oz*, as the first televised special since Disney acquired rights to the Muppets, has been viewed as an artistic turning point. As Henson Company co–CEO Lisa Henson comments, "[Disney] was clear that they are interested in going back to that adult humor that kids also like.... In recent years, we felt market pressure to age down the Muppets, and it became a self-fulfilling prophecy" (Fonseca 66). References to contemporary popular culture, including exploitative reality television and obsession with celebrity, as well as Miss Piggy's continually aggressive pursuit of Kermit, mature humor, and their retelling of a slightly fractured fairy tale situate the Muppets within the twenty-first century context and for better or worse, return the Muppets to their edgy and culturally-reflexive roots.

Second, *The Muppets' Wizard of Oz* engages with traditional cultural narratives and reinvents American myth by foregrounding its filmic structure as performative. This emphasis of performativity is achieved through direct address of the film audience and the featuring of supposedly "behind-the-scenes" or "making-of" segments embedded in the film itself, traditions that have been a part of the discourse surrounding Jim Henson's Muppets since *The Muppet Show*. This emphasis on the performativity of film and popular culture is achieved through two significant techniques: establishing the position of *The Muppets' Wizard of Oz* in the context of the larger mythic narrative and foregrounding "behind-the-scenes" moments, such as Quentin Tarantino's studio pitch for the fight scene between Dorothy and the Wicked Witch of the West. First, *The Muppets' Wizard of Oz* repeatedly positions itself in direct and interactive discourse with previous versions of the *Oz* narrative. Moments after Dorothy lands in Oz, the concrete conventions of the story are established, much in the spirit of "ground rules" for the adventure to come. As Cawelti defines conventions, these characteristics "are elements which are known to both the creator and his audience beforehand — they consist of things like favorite plots, stereotyped characters, accepted ideas, commonly known metaphors and other linguistic devices" (385). The Muppet reimagination of the *Oz* narrative, like all revisions and adaptations, brings many of its own unique inventions to the story as well, but these conventions are intended to spark recognition in the minds of viewers of this Muppet film as an Oz story, with all of its implied contexts. Miss Piggy's Tattypoo lays out the significance of the magic shoes for Dorothy, succinctly summing up "how things work in enchanted lands" and providing the ideological and fantastical parameters of the story. Toto instructs viewers, through a direct address of the television audience, "[f]or those of you who have *Dark Side of the Moon*, press play ... now," acknowledging an entire set of beliefs and practices established around MGM's 1939 film and synonymous with *The Wizard of Oz* in some popular music circles. Finally, with a parade of rats starring as Munchkins, Rizzo explicitly unites convention and invention, presenting a book titled *Oz For Dummies*, from which he provides the following definition:

> *Rat: a long-tailed rodent, especially one of the genus rattus*
> *Munchkin: a cuddly, cute, and clean creature who resides in the land of Oz*

Rizzo's definition establishes two fundamental realities surrounding the *Wizard of Oz* myth and its attendant discourse. First, there are certain recognizable traditions, including characterizations, which do not need questioning; for example, Munchkins are friendly and helpful. This convention and others like it — magic shoes, the importance of friends and family — demonstrate the connection of *The Muppets' Wizard of Oz* as part of the larger *Wizard of Oz* myth. Second, Rizzo's definition begins to outline the parameters of invention in this Muppet reimagining, signaling this version's departure from the traditional narrative: rats are Munchkins, magical shoes are not always comfortable, and Dorothy wants to be a famous singer, rather than being returned to Kansas. By combining convention and invention, *The Muppets' Wizard of Oz* uses an emphasis on performativity to establish itself within the context of the larger *Wizard of Oz* mythic discourse.

This emphasis on performativity in *The Muppets' Wizard of Oz* also provides a "behind-the-scenes" peek at the making of the movie, as well as the constructed nature of cinematic formulas. Moments of dramatic climax, in particular, are revealed as significantly coded for the big and small screens. When Dorothy misses her audition, the caretaker of the East Delta Hall wields a giant paddle fan, blowing a lone tumbleweed past Dorothy, in an attempt to "make the moment more dramatic." A similar climactic moment is signaled at the Wicked Witch of the West's castle with Sal's ominous intonation of "da da dah..." as the witch prepares to send the Flying Monkeys after Dorothy. Both of these formulaic constructions are revealed as illusion, with Dorothy scoffing at the fan-waving caretaker and Sal's sound effect met with exasperated dismissal. The revelation of these dramatic codes as tired clichés which fail to effectively carry any narrative significance works in tandem with the film's other elements to establish a sharp contrast between reality and illusion. The dissonance between appearance and truth is a common convention in almost every version of the *Wizard of Oz* myth: the Wizard is not a wizard, and Dorothy's friends have always had the characteristics for which they are searching. The narrative inventions added to this discourse by *The Muppets' Wizard of Oz* highlight and heighten this original theme in their contextualization of reality television, as well as their criticism and dismissal of largely defunct cinematic conventions, like ominous sound effects and lonely, blowing tumbleweeds.

While negotiations of cinematic formulas situate *The Muppets' Wizard of Oz* within the larger context of film and television conventions, it is the incorporation of "making-of" and "behind-the-scenes" content within the film itself that establishes its position in the tradition of the Muppets in general and *The Muppet Show* specifically. Focused on the production of a weekly variety program, *The Muppet Show* featured both the on-stage performances of the Muppets and their guest stars, as well as the backstage work that went into preparing for the show. This dual perspective blurred the line between on-stage and off-stage, performance and production; as the Henson Associates reminisce in *The Art of the Muppets*, "The television *was* their stage" (6, emphasis original). This tradition of "behind-the-scenes" material has continued through Muppet features such as *The Muppet Movie*, and this custom is evident in *The Muppets' Wizard of Oz* as well. Cult director Quentin Tarantino's studio pitch is the most significant "making-of" segment in *The Muppets' Wizard of Oz*, and one of the most controversial and debated asides in the Muppet repertoire, with many fans finding this particular guest appearance incongruous or simply confusing. A consultant for the big fight scene between Dorothy and the Wicked Witch of the West, Tarantino proposes ideas for the scene to a studio executive played by Kermit the Frog. Beginning with an elaborate samurai sword-fighting scenario surrounded by fiery explosions, Tarantino runs through a litany of decreasingly convoluted scenarios for the fight scene, before settling on a simpler and less violent alternative in which Dorothy kicks the Wicked Witch into a bathtub. The negotiations between Kermit and Tarantino are reminiscent of Kermit's backstage *Muppet Show* haggling with various characters about their skits and on-stage time or his compromises with Scooter for more money or creative control. Admittedly, Tarantino's pitch is much more high-tech Hollywood than Kermit's *Muppet Show* struggles, but the tone of give-and-take negotiation remains largely the same. Kermit's role in this discussion is largely to pull Tarantino back, with repeated reminders of the audience and context of the film that the television audience is watching simultaneously with this "behind-the-scenes" break. As Tarantino initially proposes, "I'm talking Oz in flames! Burn, baby, burn! You digging it?" Kermit uncomfortably responds that this first pitch "sounds a bit violent for a family film." Tarantino reconsiders, coming up with a morphing scenario, "done in the classic Japanese anime style — you know, for the kids." But while the audience is a bit more clearly defined here, the Muppet film context is lost on the director, to whom Kermit responds with the constructive criticism that this second pitch "sounds expensive." After continued discussion and negotiation, Kermit and Tarantino are able to reach a compromise, in which the Wicked Witch is kicked into a bathtub, where she melts. Talking Tarantino out of a scene of decadent violence echoes Kermit's negotiations with Miss Piggy's attempts to be in every scene and the demands of Scooter's Uncle, who owns the theatre, regarding creative control of *The Muppet Show*; this glimpse of a fictional "making-of" dilemma, updated to fit the twenty-first century cinematic context, works to foreground the performativity inherent in *The Muppets' Wizard of Oz* and continues a long-standing tradition that began with *The Muppet Show*.

Finally, *The Muppets' Wizard of Oz* reimagines the structure of American myth underlying the *Wizard of Oz* narrative by providing a gender representation of Dorothy which takes her permanently beyond the domestic space of home and family. Baum's original *Wonderful Wizard of Oz* established Dorothy Gale as one of the first independent female heroines, with Baum's work "almost universally acknowledged to be the earliest truly feminist children's book, because of spunky and tenacious Dorothy ... [who] refreshingly goes out and solves her problem herself rather than waiting patiently like a beautiful heroine in a European fairy tale for someone else, whether prince or commoner, to put things right" (Hearn 13). However, upon closer exploration, Dorothy is not quite the independent, liberated action heroine Hearn describes. While Baum's Dorothy leads her friends down the Yellow Brick Road, overcoming many obstacles as they search for the Wizard of Oz, her main objective in going to see the Wizard is to find a way to get back to Kansas and the domestic sphere of home and family. As Bonnie Friedman points out, "[t]he boy's coming-of-age story is about leaving home to save the world. The girl's coming-of-age story is about relinquishing the world beyond home. It is about finding a way to sacrifice one's yearning for the big world, the world of experience, and to be happy about it" (9). Dorothy's companions are actively seeking to improve themselves, to address some perceived personal lack, and speculate about how their lives will be different — and better — when they can think, feel, and face danger without fear. On the other hand, Dorothy does not want to change anything about herself or her life; she just wants to get back home and pick up where she left off, her identity and happiness invested in her role as the dutiful niece of her Aunt Em and Uncle Henry. This unwavering dedication to home and family situate Dorothy unquestioningly as the "good girl" of the story, following a tradition of dichotomously-represented gender roles that have typified fairy tales for centuries. On one side of this divide are the good girls: beautiful princesses, protective fairy godmothers, and others of their saccharinely sweet sisterhood. Dorothy is one of these good girls, as is the Witch of the North, who bestows a magic kiss on Dorothy's head to protect the girl on her journey (Baum 50). In direct contrast to these good girls are, predictably, bad girls, whose vanity, wickedness, and desire for power know no bounds: evil queens, cruel stepmothers, and terrifying witches, like the witches of the East and West, whom Dorothy must kill before being able to return to Kansas. The results of the fairy tale discourse and structure underlying Baum's *Wonderful Wizard of Oz* are that even through Dorothy is an auspiciously proactive and independent heroine for the early twentieth-century, her power and agency are circumscribed by her all-consuming dedication to home and family, as well as the dichotomous nature of gender representation common in fairy tales, including Baum's stories of Oz.

As fairy tales are revised and reinvented to better suit their shifting cultural contexts, the characters that populate these tales undergo important changes as well. The development of female characters is particularly significant in exploring the process of reimagination of American myth. As Jack Zipes argues, "[o]ne of the qualitatively distinguishing features of the fairy tale in America during the last decades of the twentieth century has been the manner in which it has questioned gender roles and critiqued the patriarchal code that has been so dominant in both folk and fairy tales until the 1960s" (142). Ashanti drops into Muppet Munchkinland as a distinctly twenty-first century Dorothy. Skeptical of the Munchkins, Dorothy tries to rescue the wicked witch her house has fallen on and refuses the good witch Tattypoo's offer of the magical silver shoes. Tattypoo, one of the many witches played by Miss Piggy, attempts to give Dorothy a crash course in fairy tale reasoning, snapping, "Listen, high pockets! Here's how things work in enchanted lands: Shoes have magical powers. If you get the shoes, you get the powers. But if you're going to question every little detail, the whole thing's gonna fall apart and we might as well call it a day, okay?" Dorothy is unconvinced by fairy tale logic, though; it is commercialism that finally wins her over ("They're Manolos..."), and she gladly takes the offered footwear. However, the most significant change between Baum's Dorothy and the heroine of this Muppet reimagination of Oz is the young girl's wish. Baum's Dorothy only wants to find a way to get back to Kansas; in contrast, when Ashanti's Dorothy lands in Muppet Munchkinland, her request is not to be sent home, but to become a famous singer, and it is this desire for fame and fortune which leads Dorothy and her friends down the Yellow Brick Road to find the Wizard. Momentarily distracted by a desire to return home, Dorothy has second thoughts, describing Kansas as "flat, boring, and gray," and chooses fame and fortune over going home. However, the fame offered by the Wizard is revealed as a fraud, image with no substance, and Dorothy finds her victory empty and meaningless. As her companions have shown Dorothy, nothing is more important than being with friends and family, and Dorothy recapitulates and asks to be sent back to Kansas. Upon returning home again to Aunt Em and Uncle Henry, Dorothy's adventure takes another turn away from the domestic sphere, with Kermit's offer of a spot touring and performing with the Muppets. Dorothy wavers, reluctant to leave home again so soon when she has only just found where she belongs. Aunt Em redefines home, however, telling Dorothy "you'll always be home with us, no matter where you are." Aunt Em sends Dorothy out into the world with a blessing rather than a struggle, giving the girl's coming-of-age story, as discussed by Friedman, an entirely new dimension. As Friedman theorizes the adolescent girl's struggle, "[t]he drama of the daughter's journey is: who will control her. Will she capitulate to the Wicked Witch or will she make it home?" (24). Aunt Em and *The Muppets' Wizard of Oz* offers a third option: Dorothy controls herself and her own destiny, able to follow her dreams without sacrificing her privileged place within her family.

In addition, *The Muppets' Wizard of Oz* also disrupts the dichotomous representations of gender which typified earlier fairy tales, including Baum's *Wonderful Wizard of Oz*. In earlier versions, Dorothy is scripted as a good girl because she helps those around her, misses her family, and wants to go home; on the other hand, the Wicked Witch is bad because she is "a woman who wants" (Friedman 23), obsessed with accumulating power and possessing the shoes. *The Muppets' Wizard of Oz* adds another dimension to this desire, with the Wicked Witch wanting to be famous as well, pioneering her own reality television show and carefully cultivating her public image. As Friedman argues, the figure of the woman who wants is "a nightmare vision of feminine power, a grotesque of female appetite — as if to say that to be a woman who wants is to be a woman who can only want, whose wants are by definition out of control.... The suppressed has surfaced, and, volcanic, might blot out the world" (24). But there is a twist here: Dorothy has the same desires. She wants to be a famous singer, and she won't give up the shoes. The only difference between these two women — the good girl and the bad girl — is the way they treat those around them; while the Wicked Witch encircles herself with servants and groupies, Dorothy is surrounded by friends and family, people who care about her and want her to succeed. This reimagining of legitimate femininity to include desire opens up a whole other way for Dorothy to be a good girl; she does not have to sacrifice herself or her wants, she can follow her own dreams and self-interest to success. As long as she loves those around her and is loved by them in return, she will be a good girl, defined by her reciprocal relationships, rather than relationships based on power and control. Dorothy can be good without losing herself; she can have personal success and rewarding relationships with others without having to subsume her desire or her identity to the wishes of others. The disruption of dichotomous representations of gender common in fairy tales allows Dorothy to become a more complex and independent heroine in *The Muppets' Wizard of Oz*, opening up a new world of possibilities for Dorothy to express herself and establish her identity as a young woman.

The Muppets' Wizard of Oz has failed to win the approval of life-long Muppet fans, in large part as a result of the contextual revisions situating the fairy tale within contemporary popular culture, with the film criticized as being risqué, mildly offensive, and "a tad too hip" (Kelleher 39). From this perspective, the Muppets have lost a sense of sweetness and innocence remembered from childhood; however, as Miss Piggy's aforementioned tongue-in-cheek rendition of "Waiting at the Church" suggests, this innocence may be largely attributed to a sense of nostalgia and longing for a fantastical utopian vision, rather than the works of the Muppets themselves. As Zipes argues of the fairy tale tradition, it has at its heart a "utopian purpose ... the fairy tale has always projected the wish and possibility for human autonomy and eros and proposed means to alter the world" (142). Fairy tales, from this perspective, should point the way to an idealized world, in which good triumphs over evil and, presumably, everyone lives happily ever after. *The Muppets' Wizard of Oz* meets most of these requirements: friends and family are of central importance, whether in Oz or Kansas; positive personal characteristics such as intelligence, kindness, and bravery are celebrated; the Wicked Witches of Oz are both destroyed; Dorothy returns to Kansas but doesn't have to give up her dream of singing. That's about as close to "happily ever after" as it gets. However, the small details of contemporary life, like reality television, celebrity obsession, and emphasis on performance, shatter the utopian vision of the classic fairy tale. Ironically, these very idiosyncrasies have characterized the Muppets since *The Muppet Show*, with their "behind-the-scenes" performance format and weekly celebrity guest stars. In these same details, *The Muppets' Wizard of Oz* crosses into the discourse of American myth. Rather than simply restating canonical representations of American identity and values, contemporary American myth must be viewed as active and revisionist, combining Cawelti's theory of convention and invention to better meet the context and reality of contemporary American culture. Many of the characteristics and touchstones of identity expressed in the *Wizard of Oz* myth have remained constant through repeated adaptations, including *The Muppets' Wizard of Oz*; however, the manner in which the story is told must change with the times and the shifting framework of American myth, including the fluctuating "qualities and attributes" (Campbell and Kean 9) of that culture. In *Fairy Tale as Myth/Myth as Fairy Tale*, Jack Zipes points out the importance of the revisionist process of myth and contemporary fairy tale, highlighting the interactive nature of this discourse. In terms of the retelling and reimagination of fairy tales, one notable process of establishing these tales for a twenty-first century audience is the creation of "[p]arodies and revisions of the classical fairy tale in various forms—TV commercials, films, literature—to provide entertainment, to question convention, and to signal something new through a familiar signifier" (160). These parodies and revisions have had a good deal of success in contemporary popular culture, including James Finn Garner's series of *Politically Correct Bedtime Stories*, films such as Paul Bolger and Yvette Kaplan's *Happily Never After*, and perhaps most notably, Dreamworks' animated *Shrek* trilogy. The *Wizard of Oz* narrative has had its own share of parodies and revisions as well, including Sidney Lumet's *The Wiz*, Gregory Maguire's novel *Wicked: The Life and Times of the Wicked Witch of the West*, and the adaptation of Maguire's work for the Broadway stage by Stephen Schwartz and Winnie Holzman. These works turn the structure and assumptions of classic fairy tales on their head, question traditional gender roles and narrative forms, and highlight the interactive process of storytelling and American myth.

The Muppets' Wizard of Oz actively negotiates the boundaries of classic fairy tales and engages with the revisionist process of American myth through the establishment of a contemporary cultural context, emphasis on performance, and alternative gender representations, resulting in a dramatic revision of the discourse of American myth underlying the traditional *Wizard of Oz* tale. The result is the *Wizard of Oz* narrative reimagined in a way only the Muppets could achieve, bringing their spirit of self-reflexive parody and contemporary cultural relevance from the stage of *The Muppet Show* into a Kansas twister and down the Yellow Brick Road to *The Muppets' Wizard of Oz*. Many of the mythic themes informing the Wizard of Oz narrative have remained constant over the past one hundred years, since Baum's first writing. Family and friends still occupy a privileged position in the hearts and lives of many, there's still no place quite like home, and intelligence, kindness, and bravery continue to be personal characteristics both sought after and rewarded. However, American culture and the mythic structure which underlies it has changed drastically since the dawn of the twentieth century; fascination with the frontier has given way to obsession with fame and celebrity, while personal achievement often overshadows community and solidarity. As Kermit, Miss Piggy, and the rest of the Muppets remind their viewers with *The Muppets' Wizard of Oz*, while the myths and fairy tales of American culture are indispensable in understanding national identity and character, these stories must be occasionally reimagined to better suit the contemporary context, as well as to maintain personal and cultural relevance for a new generation of viewers.

Works Cited

Baum, L. Frank. *The Annotated Wizard of Oz*, Centennial Edition. Notes by Michael Patrick Hearn. New York: W.W. Norton, 2000.
Campbell, Neil, and Alasdair Keen. *American Culture Studies: An Introduction to American Culture*. New York: Routledge, 1997.
Cawelti, John G. "The Concept of Formula in the Study of Popular Literature." *Journal of Popular Culture* III: 3 (1969): 381–390.
Fonseca, Nicholas. "Wizard of Frog." *Entertainment Weekly* (20 May 2005): 66.
Friedman, Bonnie. "Relinquishing Oz: Every Girl's Anti-Adventure Story." *Michigan Quarterly Review* Winter 1996: 9–28.
Hearn, Michael Patrick. *The Annotated Wizard of Oz*, Centennial Edition. New York: W.W. Norton, 2000.
Henson Associates. *The Art of the Muppets: A Retrospective Look at Twenty-Five Years of Muppet Magic*. New York: A Muppet Press/Bantam Book, 1980.
"John Cleese." *The Muppet Show Season Two Special Edition*. Prod. The Muppets Holding Company. DVD. Buena Vista Entertainment, 2007.
Kelleher, Tony. "The Muppets' Wizard of Oz." *People* (23 May 2005): 39.
The Muppets' Wizard of Oz. Dir. Kirk R. Thatcher. Perf. Jim Henson's Muppets, Ashanti, Jeffrey Tambor, Queen Latifah, David Alan Grier, Quentin Tarantino. 20th Century–Fox, 2005.
Smith, Henry Nash. *Virgin Land: The American West as Symbol and Myth*. Cambridge: Harvard University Press, 1950.
Zipes, Jack. *Fairy Tale as Myth/Myth as Fairy Tale*. Lexington: University Press of Kentucky, 1994.

Gonzo, (the Great) Cultural Critic
Jennifer C. Garlen

"Art! Art! Art!"
The Great Gonzo, *The Muppet Show*

As a prime time network television series whose original intended audience was equally made up of adults and children, *The Muppet Show*, unlike most other puppet-based programs either before or since, was not primarily or avowedly created as an educational program of any kind. Instead, it attempts to amuse a diverse audience by mixing many different kinds of entertainment together in its variety show format. Most of the material used on the show occupies a middle space in the traditional cultural hierarchy, probably because Jim Henson and the show's other creators, necessarily mindful of the need for good ratings and regular viewers, imagined that this kind of material would appeal to the broadest possible audience. This general focus on "middlebrow" entertainment leads to the prevalence of certain types of guest stars on *The Muppet Show*, like popular singers and Broadway stars, as well as notable film and television actors of the day, because those celebrities are recognizable to both adults and children, and their performances are generally pieces that broad audiences instantly know and easily appreciate.

No material, however, is really beyond *The Muppet Show's* grasp, and on many memorable occasions the program's sketches dip below and reach above the realm of middle class amusement, often at the same time. Although the appearances of guests like the experimental puppetry troupe Mummenschanz, ballet superstar Rudolf Nureyev, flautist Jean-Pierre Rampal and opera diva Beverly Sills certainly all demonstrate the show's willingness to break out of the middle ground, *The Muppet Show* also has its own in house agitator for thinking outside the bourgeois cultural box. The Great Gonzo, that vaguely avian performance artist *cum* daredevil, specializes in sketches that simultaneously present both "high" and "low" culture, thus leading him to introduce his performances with his trademark phrase, "while, and at the same time." Gonzo's sketches are particularly interesting because of their conflation of the two extreme ends of the conventional cultural hierarchy; his performances simultaneously educate the audience about traditional, canonical Art yet subvert its claims to superiority or special status by yoking it to bizarre, flamboyant stuntmanship. Throughout *The Muppet Show's* five season run, Gonzo functions as one of the show's primary advocates for capitalized "Art and Culture" even as he undermines the traditional notion of what those terms mean, and, as a result, his performances and similar sketches on the program, as well as his appearances in later Muppet productions, subtly work to shape a new perception of different levels of culture and their respective values.

Gonzo is frequently referred to as a "performance artist," which gives a general idea of the kind of act that he brings to *The Muppet Show* stage. Performance art seeks to challenge conventional notions about Art through its avant-garde transformation of the unexpected and/or the mundane into Art. As such, it often attracts skepticism or open hostility from more conservative critics and audiences. For example, the public notoriety of performance artists as a group reached its peak in 1990 when the National Endowment for the Arts revoked grant funding from four controversial performance artists, the "NEA Four," because of their material; this incident formed one of the most publicized battles of the ongoing culture wars between liberals and conservatives (Lewis 31). As a performance artist, Gonzo enthusiastically challenges his audience (both Muppet and human) about what constitutes Art. Although he seldom seems to have much success with the Muppet audience in the theater, and they do sometimes boo him, they don't seem to harbor the same antipathy for him that they do for Fozzie Bear, whose more traditional comedy act almost always falls flat. Perhaps the sheer spectacle of Gonzo's performances makes him more watchable than Fozzie, especially since Gonzo's idea of performance art frequently involves the risk of death and dismemberment. His penchant for extremity has led Christopher Finch to describe Gonzo as an "overambitious hybrid of Harry Houdini and Evel Knievel;" Finch also speculates that Gonzo might in fact be a masochist, an idea borne out by Gonzo's enjoyment of being tortured in *Muppet Treasure Island* (104–105). Perhaps because of these qualities, Gonzo appears to be a perennial favorite with the Muppets' human audience; his role on the original series increased over time, and his appearances in later productions indicate how central to the Muppet cast he has become, even to the point of being the protagonist of *Muppets from Space* and eclipsing the roles of other major characters with his parts in *The Muppet Christmas Carol* and *Muppet Trea-*

sure Island. Thus, while the middlebrow tastes of the Muppet Theater audience might not always be satisfied by Gonzo's performance art, the human audience has clearly been won over to admire the challenging and unusual nature of his work.

The hierarchical perspective of culture that Gonzo resists through his performance art has its own significant history, and it might be useful to review the background and development of terms like "high" and "low" in relation to art and culture. Lawrence W. Levine offers a history of these concepts in *Highbrow/Lowbrow: The Emergence of Cultural Hierarchy in America*, in which he argues that twentieth-century notions of cultural hierarchy were developed over the course of the late nineteenth century. Levine traces the ways in which public attitudes towards Shakespeare and opera, for example, changed over the course of the nineteenth century, becoming increasingly elitist and privileged rather than popular. Eventually, self-appointed arbiters of Culture would deem these kinds of productions "high" culture, and therefore more valuable, more edifying and more worthy of attention, than "low" culture, which basically included everything else. However, these categories have always been subject to change, so that what one generation regards as "low" might be regarded by the next as "high," or vice versa (Levine). The stakes of this debate might seem rather abstract until one realizes that the ongoing "culture wars" that began in the United States in the 1960s are waged over exactly this kind of argument regarding what is worth knowing about and what isn't. Gonzo's acts of cultural conflation take on a greater significance when we connect his performances with this protracted public debate, which carries serious political ramifications for both conservative and progressive culture warriors. Refusing even to acknowledge the hierarchical divide that supposedly severs "high" and "low" art, Gonzo merges all artistic acts into a single category of "Art" or "Culture," thus positioning himself at the far left end of the progressive view of culture. Like Herbert J. Gans in his classic study, *Popular Culture & High Culture*, Gonzo rejects the idea that highbrow culture is inherently better than middlebrow and lowbrow culture, and his acts become lively demonstrations of Gans' assertion that "all taste cultures are of equal worth" (Gans xv). Gonzo embodies the type of cultural consumer Gans refers to as an "omnivore," someone who accepts and internalizes culture from many different taste levels (Gans 9–12). From this perspective, Gonzo's acts of cultural conflation become charged performances, not merely entertainment but striking political statements about the very natures of Art and Culture and what they mean.

Many of Gonzo's most memorable sketches provide striking examples of this cultural conflation. Gonzo's debut on the very first regular episode of *The Muppet Show* reveals his early commitment to his revolutionary cultural project. In this episode, which stars dancer Juliet Prowse, Gonzo performs a stunt in which he eats a rubber tire to the tune of *Flight of the Bumblebee*. The operatic orchestral piece by the Russian composer Nikolai Rimsky-Korsakov provides a strikingly "high" culture backdrop to Gonzo's bizarre tire-eating stunt, an act which connects Gonzo to the circus sideshow performers who popularized the term "geek" in the early twentieth century and were known for biting the heads off of chickens and snakes or devouring other ostensibly inedible objects. In this first performance, then, we see what is regarded as the highest level of culture, represented by the classical opera piece, already being yoked together with the lowest level, represented by Gonzo's circus freak stunt.

Later episodes present similarly strange combinations of "high" and "low" cultural elements, thus confirming Gonzo's role as the show's chief purveyor of Art viewed askew. Not surprisingly, given the show's musical emphasis, classical music most frequently represents traditional Art in Gonzo's performances, but other artistic forms, including poetry and dance, also show up as the highbrow elements of Gonzo's sketches. The wide variety of highbrow performances and lowbrow stunts attests to an incredible diversity of talent on Gonzo's part, since he demonstrates a new set of unusual skills in almost every sketch. In the Season Two episode featuring Julie Andrews, for example, Gonzo plays Mozart's *Eine Kleine Nachtmusik* on the bagpipes while sitting on a tall wooden pole that is being chewed through by a beaver. Season Three has Gonzo return to Rimsky-Korsakov with a yodeling performance undertaken while riding a motorized pogo-stick. In Season Four, the episode starring Dudley Moore includes a particularly memorable sketch in which Gonzo recites Percy Bysshe Shelley's "To a Sky-Lark" while attempting to defuse a huge, high explosive bomb. Season Five features a segment in which Gonzo conducts Rowlf and a violinist playing Franz Liszt's *Liebesträume* No. 3 while dueling a crab. Other Gonzo performances merge the bizarre with more contemporary, generally "middlebrow" examples of Art, as do Gonzo's rendition of "Top Hat" while dancing in a vat of oatmeal in Season Four and his attempts to outdo Paul Simon as a songwriter in Season Five. Of course, Gonzo also performs straight musical numbers and more conventional stunts on the show, from singing "Jamboree" to catching cannon balls in his bare hands, but his over-the-top performance pieces form some of the most memorable and unusual segments of *The Muppet Show*, and they are ultimately the defining sketches for Gonzo's character.

A closer look at one of these key Gonzo moments sheds more light on what exactly is going on with Gonzo's interpretation of Art. In the Season Two episode starring Peter Sellers, Gonzo appears in a backstage segment in which Sellers proposes to perform a very Gonzo-esque act on the show, a piece in which Sellers recites the soliloquy from *Richard III* "whilst, and at the same time" playing a pair of tuned chickens. Sellers' appearance in this scene is itself a demonstration of a very conflated sense of Art; the British actor sits at a dressing room table in a Viking helmet complete with horns, a single boxing glove, a corset and a fake beard with matching long red hair. These items range all over the cultural map, with the Viking helmet suggesting highbrow opera, the corset hinting at middlebrow morality and melodrama, and the boxing glove evoking the lowbrow blood sport. Sellers explains the outfit to Kermit by saying, "It was to have been, my dear Kermit, it was to have been a grand impersonation of her late majesty Queen Victoria, whilst on vacation at Bognor Regis in the year 1888." When Kermit asks what happened, Sellers replies that he "couldn't remember what she looked like!" Of course, dressing as Queen Victoria certainly has cultural resonance, both highbrow and middlebrow, since playing the queen implies a certain BBC/PBS upper crust sort of entertainment, while Victoria herself was a quintessentially middlebrow sort of person, stodgy and narrow-mindedly moral. Moreover, Sellers' version of Victoria is clearly a drag queen, a figure of transgressive cultural significance, as well as a circus sideshow's "bearded lady," and all of these elements have their own peculiar ties back to Gonzo's character. Still dressed in this strange costume, Sellers goes on to perform his *Richard III* piece for Kermit; the tuned chickens conclude the soliloquy with a round of "Shave and a Haircut." Throwing in Shakespeare returns us to highbrow entertainment, of course, especially since the piece in question is a celebrated soliloquy from a very "serious" history play, but ending it with singing chickens and the comically cartoony musical bit sends the whole thing racing back down into the very lowest of lowbrow amusements. After the soliloquy ends, Kermit admires the act but says that Sellers cannot do it on the show. When Sellers demands to know why, Kermit answers that "Gonzo just did it last month." Gonzo then appears and, his eyes wide with shock, declares, "And it died, Peter!" We don't actually see Gonzo perform the *Richard III* soliloquy, but we know that he did perform it at an earlier point, and it is precisely the kind of act that Gonzo generally does present on the series. Furthermore, it allows Gonzo an opportunity to have an actual conversation about his performance pieces with another person, in this case Peter Sellers, who, like Gonzo himself, is an actor chiefly known for his penchant for the bizarre.

Gonzo's complaint to Peter Sellers at the end of this sketch, that "people have no taste around here," demonstrates Gonzo's sense of himself as a proponent of a valuable kind of culture, not merely a sideshow purveyor of a bread and circuses sort of amusement. Gonzo's vision of himself as a legitimate artist is another core element of his character. *The Muppet Show's* dialogue repeatedly and persistently connects Gonzo to his ruling passions of art and culture, making the link between the two hard to miss by any observant viewer. On the original Juliet Prowse episode, Kermit introduces Gonzo as the show's "resident artist." After his tire-eating routine is booed off the stage, Gonzo mutters, "Yokels! What do they know about art?" In the Season One episode featuring Charles Aznavour, Gonzo tries out a backstage act in which he pounds a rock with a mallet while shouting, "Art! Art! Art!" and later declares that the answer to the question, "What is man's role in the universe?" is "art and culture." Gonzo's bomb-defusing stunt on the Dudley Moore episode is introduced by Kermit as "a real treat for all you fear and culture lovers." The words "art" and "culture" appear over and over again, and on *The Muppet Show* their use is almost always connected to Gonzo in some way. Clearly, the show's creators intend for us to associate Gonzo and his performances with these concepts.

Of course, Gonzo's inherent weirdness is also a given element of his character, since his whole personality is so "outside the box" that nobody even knows what he actually is, at least until *Muppets from Space* identified him as an alien in 1999. With his hooked beak, blue feathers, and heavy-lidded eyes, Gonzo is sometimes associated with turkeys, which would partly explain his amorous pursuit of chickens, but he is more frequently identified as a "weirdo," a "thing," or a "whatever." His role as sideshow "geek" again connects him to the chickens and emphasizes the bizarre nature of his character. His name connects him to Hunter S. Thompson's edgy "gonzo journalism," a term coined in the first part of the 1970s, early enough to have been a direct inspiration for the Muppet's name and personality. Gonzo journalism, like the Muppet character, conflates different levels of culture through its intermingling of subjective, street-level material with traditional, objective reporting. The word has since passed into the popular lexicon, where it now means "bizarre" and "unconventional," although its current usage may well have as much to do with the Muppet himself as it does with Thompson. In his person, then, as well as in his acts, Gonzo represents something beyond conventional culture. Even when he performs strictly middlebrow numbers, like "Memory Lane," "Jamboree," and "Act Naturally," his appearance and delivery bring a weirdness to them only rivaled on the show by Marvin Suggs and His Muppaphones and Bobby Benson's Baby Band. Although it's true that any number performed by Muppets becomes suffused with a certain amount of weirdness, Gonzo is the most visible Muppet to be defined by his weirdness in a consistent manner, through his appearance, his name and his penchant for extreme cultural conflation.

Gonzo's weirdness and his conflated sense of culture have their critics, even among the other Muppets on the show, particularly Sam the Eagle. Sam is essentially Gonzo's ideological opposite concerning the nature of art and culture. Although Sam is, ironically, also a blue, avian character, his values and personality are in direct conflict with those of Gonzo. Jordan Schildcrout accurately describes Sam as "a cross between Uncle Sam and America's national bird with a dash of Richard Nixon, [who] represents a conservative, nationalist Puritanism that makes him both a snob and a prude" (832). Constantly complaining about "weirdos" and "freaks" on the program — terms that are also frequently applied to Gonzo specifically — Sam espouses a definition of culture that is extremely narrow and that fits with his jingoistic, dogmatic character. Sam despises Gonzo in particular and most of the other Muppets as well for their heterodox views of entertainment and art; his ire often falls on Dr. Teeth and The Electric Mayhem because their long-haired, rock and roll sensibility directly clashes with his insistence on conformity and "decency." Sam's idea of culture is embodied by the "Wayne and Wanda" sketches that he usually introduces throughout the first season, often with glowing praise for their perceived qualities of normalcy and decency. In one typical introduction, Sam assures the audience that not only are Wayne and Wanda "tremendous singers, they're church people." Of course, the Wayne and Wanda numbers turn out to be painfully pedestrian renditions of songbook standards in the style of *The Lawrence Welk Show*, redeemed for the real audience of *The Muppet Show* only by their inevitably violent endings. It says something about the program's attitude toward Sam's definition of culture that his beloved Wayne and Wanda never actually manage to finish a performance. Their performances disappear completely later in the series, suggesting that the numbers are too flat-footed and banal, even as jokes, to be kept around indefinitely. While their songs clearly reflect middle class culture, as do most of the show's other numbers and performers, the guest stars and the majority of the show's sketches and songs are presented by *The Muppet Show* as popular and fun, while the Wayne and Wanda numbers are depicted as stiff, outdated, and hopelessly square, much like Sam himself.

Sam's adoration of Wayne and Wanda reveals that his natural tastes are squarely middlebrow, but he yearns to be recognized as an advocate for and expert on highbrow culture, as well. In his efforts to appear aesthetically refined, he loudly decries anything that he perceives as lowbrow culture, especially rock music and the numbers performed by Gonzo. He constantly badgers Kermit to include more culturally respectable acts on the show, although he also actively discourages guest stars whom he admires from going out on stage, since he feels that it would be a disgrace for them to be associated with the "weird, sick show" that the Muppets produce. As a cultural conservative, Sam desires to educate the audience with "real" Art because he is deeply concerned about the moral value of the entertainment being offered. His lectern sketches on the show reinforce his conservative agenda, as he rails against immoral practices like nudity and suspect liberal concerns like environmentalism, although, ironically, the joke always ends up being on Sam, as he himself is naked and is a representative of a species endangered by poor environmental stewardship.

The show further undermines Sam's authority as cultural arbiter by having him fail to recognize traditional high culture even when it literally appears right in front of him, as it does when Rudolf Nureyev shows up for his guest star appearance and is immediately thrown out of the theater by Sam, who mistakes him for yet another "weirdo." As he pushes Nureyev out the door, Sam shouts, "Get out of here, you freak, you hippie! You weirdo! Get out — move, move! Get a haircut! Who do these punk kids think they are?" The haircut comment is priceless; it solidly pegs Sam's character as patriarchal, authoritarian, conservative and seriously uncool. Despite this initial gaffe, Sam is thrilled to have a guest who fits his definition of culture finally appear on the show. "At last!" he gloats to Kermit, "To have a man of dignity, a man of culture, on this weird, sick show of yours!" Of course, we then find out that Sam believes Nureyev to be an opera singer, which again undermines his reliability as a judge of true culture. Later sketches reinforce our doubts about Sam's representation of himself as an expert on culture and Art. In the Season Three episode starring Lynn Redgrave, Sam again betrays his ignorance by mistaking a slick looking Muppet for the "real" William Shakespeare, whom Sam believes to be the author of "Robin Hood" as well as *The Sound of Music*. Sam's pretensions to highbrow status are merely that, without real knowledge or taste to back them up. If Sam were in fact knowledgeable about traditional highbrow culture, he would also recognize it when it appears in Gonzo's acts, albeit blended with lowbrow amusement.

When informed of his mistake about Rudolf Nureyev's identity, Sam covers by replying, "Culture is culture," a statement which means a lot more than Sam intends in the larger context of the show, since the series as a whole equalizes many different levels and types of culture through the performances of Gonzo the Great, the other Muppets, and the show's many guest stars. In the Nureyev episode alone, Nureyev himself performs a porcine version of *Swan Lake* with a giant lady pig, the Electric Mayhem plays a rocked out version of Bach's Minuet in G Major, the Veterinarian's Hospital regulars perform a Shakespearean version of their usual sketch, and Miss Piggy and Link Hogthrob stage a very confused operatic number, in which they sing Mozart's *Don Giovanni* but are dressed in Wagnerian costumes. Despite the show's preference for middlebrow performances in general, we see this kind of conflation play out in many other episodes throughout the series. Mark Hamill and Angus McGonagall the Argyle Gargoyle gargle Gershwin, while Gilda Radner performs a medley of songs from *The Pirates of Penzance* with a seven foot tall talking carrot and Miss Piggy recites Wordsworth's "Daffodils" only to be sneezed off stage. Thus, it is Gonzo's conflated vision of culture that the show ultimately advocates, while Sam's strictly hierarchical, judgmental view is derided and undermined.

One sketch that particularly highlights the ideological opposition of

Gonzo and Sam occurs in the Beverly Sills episode in Season Four. Backstage, Gonzo excitedly announces to the opera star that he has "created a new art form ... [which] will rank with the creation of the first opera. It's a cultural breakthrough!" Gonzo's new art form turns out to be spoon hanging, which he and Sills then engage in, much to the dismay of Sam, who enters the room to worship the traditional High Art star just in time to see her and Gonzo with spoons hanging from their noses. "What's the matter?" Sills asks the dumbstruck Sam, "Don't you like art?" Sam runs screaming from the dressing room, while Sills looks to Gonzo (and the television audience beyond him) and says, "Poor fellow, he's obviously a lowbrow." All of the key elements that define Gonzo and Sam's characters appear in this brief sketch: Gonzo associates himself with "art" and "culture" but understands those terms very differently from Sam, who also believes himself to be an advocate of "art" and "culture," but whose limited definitions are undermined by Gonzo's artistic experimentalism, Sills' willingness to endorse Gonzo's views and the audience's participation in the joke between Gonzo and Sills at Sam's expense. Furthermore, the presence of a watchword like "lowbrow" indicates just how conscious of all this material *The Muppet Show* writers are; they know perfectly well that they are using these characters and sketches to take sides in the culture wars and advance a particular attitude toward art and culture in their viewers.

Gonzo's work as a unifier of different kinds of art and culture has not appeared as extensively in the Muppet films, where the original show's aesthetic sense and ideological values have been repackaged for new generations of viewers. Most of the Muppet films, beginning with *The Muppet Movie*, emphasize Gonzo's weirdness as his defining characteristic. He is presented as strange and difficult to identify, and he retains his daredevil proclivities, but he does not appear specifically or persistently in his role as cultural critic in any of the first three Muppet films or in the majority of more recent productions. Even though Gonzo appears as a major character in *Muppet Treasure Island* and even as the protagonist in *Muppets from Space*, these films prioritize his strangeness and generally fail to develop his identification with art and culture. This missing element might be explained by the different audience expectations for the films or because of the requirements associated with a sustained narrative as opposed to a variety show format, but it diminishes a full understanding of the character's function and significance. However, this important element of his character does get some notable development in *The Muppet Christmas Carol* (1992), in which Gonzo impersonates Charles Dickens and narrates the events of the film. Dickens certainly qualifies as an exemplar of canonical literary art, and Gonzo's portrayal of him reflects a certain reverence for the writer and his work, even as Gonzo's daredevil enthusiasms are somewhat retained, albeit in very muted form, in elements like his hitching a wild ride with Scrooge and the Ghost of Christmas Past with the help of a grappling hook. As the teller and authority figure for the film's story, Gonzo enjoys an especially highlighted opportunity to encourage the audience to embrace Art, this time in the form of Dickens' beloved tale. If anything, *The Muppet Christmas Carol* overcompensates for the general absence of this facet of Gonzo's character in the other Muppet films; none of the later Muppet productions has offered quite the balance between geek and *artiste* that the original show demonstrates so effectively.

This blended approach to Gonzo's character needs to be recognized by Muppet Studios' current and future creative forces because it speaks so palpably to the cultural attitudes that are increasingly prevalent in modern society. Encouragingly, television and internet productions of the last few years have demonstrated a returning sense of the importance of Gonzo's identity as performance artist and cultural arbiter. The 2002 NBC Christmas special, *It's a Very Merry Muppet Christmas*, was the first glimmer of a return to this approach to the character. In the special, Gonzo stays mostly in the background of the plot, but his few key scenes highlight his connections to art and culture. We see him designing a bizarre Cirque du Soleil performance piece with an insane Frenchman (played by Matthew Lillard); later he appears as a homeless entertainer with a sign identifying him as a "performance *artiste*" clearly displayed. The best, although most subtle, use of Gonzo in the special is certainly his role as Toulouse-Lautrec in the manic *Moulin Rouge!* parody. The casting choice connects Gonzo with art and weirdness all at once; it is absolutely perfect. The 2008 YouTube videos released by Disney to promote the Muppets also present a return to this effective take on Gonzo's character and purpose. In the video titled "Classical Chicken," Gonzo conducts a flock of "tuned chickens" who perform *The Blue Danube Waltz*. The short sketch returns Gonzo to his *Muppet Show* roots; in his signature purple tuxedo, Gonzo appears on the screen and announces, "Greetings, culture lovers and citizens of the World Wide Web!" He then proceeds to direct an increasingly energetic group of chickens, led by Camilla, of course, as they cluck their way through Strauss's classical piece. Purportedly posted by Gonzo himself under the pseudonym "weirdowhatever," the YouTube video and member page present the character with a full sense of his role as cultural arbiter, performance artist, and daredevil. Whether Disney will continue to realize the full potential of the character remains to be seen, but at least the viral marketing campaign demonstrates that the clever humor and cultural sophistication of Gonzo and his fellow Muppets have not been lost entirely.

Ultimately, the significance of Gonzo's ideological position on art can be seen in its effects. Generation X grew up on *The Muppet Show*, and the program's conflated sense of culture has penetrated deep into its collective consciousness. Along with other popular entertainments like the Bugs Bunny cartoons and Monty Python, *The Muppet Show's* egalitarian mix-up of different levels of culture challenges traditional views about what kinds of art and culture are valuable or appropriate for specific audiences. A television show can be entertaining to children, while, and at the same time, entertaining to adults, as well. It can be both subversively didactic and overtly amusing. It can familiarize viewers with traditional high culture while simultaneously challenging its privileged position as "better" than other forms. Gen Xers and the generations that have followed have absorbed all of these messages from *The Muppet Show*, and the intellectual distance between high and low culture has been significantly shortened. Today, our sense of culture is broader and more diverse than ever before; we are willing to call a lot of things "art" that our parents and grandparents might deride as "trash." Our generational conflict with our more culturally conservative forebears has already been played out for us between Gonzo and Sam, and we have clearly decided that weirdos have a better sense of art and culture than straight-laced squares. Comic books, rock music, and puppet television shows can be discussed with equal artistic seriousness as novels, operas, and plays. Now, more than ever before, "culture is culture," and it's an attitude that Gonzo the Great, cultural critic, would enthusiastically endorse.

Works Cited

"Beverly Sills." *The Best of The Muppet Show Featuring Tony Randall, Beverly Sills and Pearl Bailey*. DVD. Time Life and Jim Henson Home Entertainment, 2002.
"Classical Chicken." YouTube. December 10, 2008 <http://www.youtube.com/watch?v=Ob6TTU1knUM>
"Dudley Moore." *The Best of The Muppet Show Featuring Peter Sellers, John Cleese and Dudley Moore*. DVD. Time Life and Jim Henson Home Entertainment, 2001.
Gans, Herbert J. *Popular Culture & High Culture: An Analysis and Evaluation of Taste*. Revised & Updated Edition. New York: Basic Books, 1999.
Finch, Christopher. *Jim Henson: The Works*. New York: Random House, 1993.
It's a Very Merry Muppet Christmas Movie. Dir. Kirk R. Thatcher. Perf. Steve Whitmire, Dave Goelz, Bill Barretta, Eric Jacobson, David Arquette, Joan Cusack. NBC. 2002. DVD. MGM Home Entertainment, 2003.
Levine, Lawrence W. *Highbrow/Lowbrow: The Emergence of Cultural Hierarchy in America*. Cambridge: Harvard University Press, 1990.
Lewis, Michael J. "After the Art Wars." *Commentary* 125.1 (Jan. 2008): 31–36. *Academic Search Premier*. EBSCO. University of Alabama in Huntsville, Huntsville, AL. 22 Aug. 2008 <http://search.ebscohost.com/login.aspx?direct=true&db=aph&AN=28084159&site=ehost-live>.
The Muppet Show Season One Special Edition. Prod. The Muppets Holding Company. DVD. Buena Vista Home Entertainment, 2005.
The Muppet Show Season Two Special Edition. Prod. The Muppets Holding Company. DVD. Buena Vista Home Entertainment, 2007.
The Muppet Show Season Three Special Edition. Prod. The Muppets Holding Company. DVD. Walt Disney Company, 2008.
Schildcrout, Jordan. "The Performance of Nonconformity on *The Muppet Show*— or, How Kermit Made Me Queer." *The Journal of Popular Culture* 41.5 (October 2008): 823–835.

Part Three

Theories and Strategies

The American Journey Narrative in the Muppets Movies
Tara K. Parmiter

"Ah, a bear in his natural habitat.... A Studebaker."
Fozzie Bear, *The Muppet Movie*

When the Muppets made the move from television to the movie theaters in the late 1970s, their adventures naturally broadened to fit the demands and possibilities of the larger screen. As Jim Henson explained about *The Muppet Movie*, he and his team sought to create a film that was "the reverse of 'The Muppet Show'.... On the television show we'd invite one guest into the world of the Muppets. In the movie, we are taking the Muppets out into the real world" (qtd. in Culhane 53). Henson specifically perceived this change from small screen to big screen as a movement outward, so perhaps it is not surprising that the Muppets' forays into the "real world" are so often cast as journey narratives. No longer limited to short sketches in the immediate confines of Sesame Street or the Muppet Theater, in their movies the Muppets take to the open road, "moving right along" as they sing in one of their most memorable songs.

But more than just being an endearing Muppets tune, "Movin' Right Along" speaks to the wanderlust that has shaped American culture from our earliest explorations of the howling wilderness to our contemporary cross country road trips. In the montage that accompanies this song from *The Muppet Movie*, the scene shifts back and forth between intimate views of Kermit and Fozzie in the front seat of their Studebaker and expansive helicopter shots of the antique car winding through rolling hillsides and fertile farmland, emphasizing the beauty and richness of the American landscape. This sequence truly shows a "bear and a frog seeing America," in Fozzie's words; whether they "hitchhike, bus, or yellow cab-it" on their travels from the Southern swamps to the glitter of Hollywood, Kermit and Fozzie find joy in passing through each new region and picking up a new traveler, a new insight, or a new sense of purpose along the way. When Kermit sings, "Getting there is half the fun, come share it with me," he voices a philosophy that seems essential not only to this movie, but also to countless tales of quests, journeys, and travels that have always been a staple of our fictions, our Muppets movies in particular. As "Movin' Right Along" suggests, although our dreams about our destinations set us going, often times the real adventures happen when we're on the road.

In *The Art of Travel*, philosopher Alain de Botton observes, "If our lives are dominated by a search for happiness, then perhaps few activities reveal as much about the dynamics of this quest—in all its ardour and paradoxes—than our travels" (9). Although Kermit and Fozzie are fictional creations, in movie after movie their search for happiness sets them in motion through uncharted territory, and their travels reveal a striking desire to share their adventures with their fellow wayfarers. *Muppet Treasure Island* (1996) and *The Muppets' Wizard of Oz* (2005) offer two classic literary journeys with a Muppets twist; *Muppets from Space* (1999) plays with intergalactic travel, as Gonzo strives to find his brethren from another galaxy; even *The Muppet Christmas Carol* (1992) revolves around time travel, as Gonzo and Rizzo the Rat act as our tour guides to Ebenezer Scrooge's holiday journey of self-discovery. In this essay, however, I focus on the first three Muppets films—*The Muppet Movie* (1977), *The Great Muppet Caper* (1981), and *The Muppets Take Manhattan* (1984)—in part because these films were completed during Jim Henson's lifetime and in part because of the specific ways these films embrace and re-interpret the classic American journey narrative.

Travel and journeying have always been at the heart of American fictional narratives, whether in literature or film. As travel writer William Least Heat-Moon argues, travel narratives are "typically American" for "every American is a descendant of travelers from the eastern hemisphere.... From the time of the first crossing over the Bering land bridge, mobility has been one of the elemental qualities of the American experience" (20). Not only has mobility been essential to our everyday lives, but many thinkers claim it has been essential to our character development as well: according to historian Frederick Jackson Turner, for example, Americans developed their love of freedom, Yankee inventiveness, and rugged individualism through the unique experience of traveling across an ever-moving frontier. It's no wonder, then, that some of the most quintessential American classics—from *Moby-Dick* and *Huckleberry Finn* to *Easy Rider* and *Star Wars*—revolve around the adventures of wandering heroes, testing their mettle against a wild landscape.

However, although the classic American journey narrative typically focuses on an individual, or perhaps a pair of individuals, seeking their fortune on the road, the Muppets recast this journey as one of accumulation: as Kermit travels to Hollywood, London, or Broadway, he not only learns more about his unique identity but he picks up friends along the way who help him understand himself as a member of a diverse and delightfully bizarre community. And although each journey starts out with a traditional quest towards a specific destination, along the way the Muppets realize that "getting there is half the fun": the important thing is not whether they make a movie or solve a mystery or perform on the Great White Way, but that whatever it is, they share the experience together.

The quests that propel the Muppets forward in these movies fall into three familiar patterns: the road trip, the European trip, and the trip to the big city. Although these journeys have several distinct similarities, each one serves a slightly different function, both in American culture and in the Muppets' movies. For example, as a road film, *The Muppet Movie* draws on the tradition of the westward trek across the frontier towards the promise of the American dream. Bringing the Muppets together behind the wheel of a car, Jim Henson and his team tap into the power of the road as an American icon. David Laderman, in *Driving Visions: Exploring the Road Movie*, describes the road as "an essential element of the American society and history, but also a universal symbol of the course of life, the movement of desire, and the lure of both freedom and destiny" (2). Similarly, in *Romance of the Road*, Ronald Primeau reminds us, "For most of this century, Americans have treated the highway as sacred space. Roads and cars have long gone beyond simple transportation to become places of exhilarating motion, speed, and solitude. Getting away is a chance at a new start, a special time to discover self and country, glide through vast empty space and then come home to write or sing about the adventures" (1). Metaphorically, as these theorists suggest, the road offers a place not just of discovery but of self-discovery; following our dreams, we have a chance to start anew, to see the world through fresh eyes, to find ourselves as we move along. Our road trips, in other words, not only take us out into the world, but allow us to journey inwards as well.

Indeed, from the opening sequence in the swamp, where Kermit shares his dreams about finding the "Rainbow Connection," *The Muppet Movie* links travel and movement explicitly with the search for self. As Kermit sits strumming his banjo and singing on a log, a frantic Hollywood agent approaches in a row boat, crying out, "Help! I have lost my sense of direction!" "Have you tried Hare Krishna?" Kermit quips in return. The pun, conflating directions on the map with a sense of purpose in life, sets the stage for the ensuing adventure: charmed by Kermit's quick wit, the agent encourages Kermit to answer an open audition in Hollywood for "Frogs wanting to become Rich and Famous." The agent literally becomes the agent of change for Kermit, issuing what mythologist Joseph Campbell refers to as the "call to adventure" and providing the push that starts Kermit's westward movement (51). He also sets the Hare Krishna joke in motion, which we encounter later as a critique of Fozzie's dismal performance as a stand-up comedian — "This guy's lost." "Maybe he should try Hare Krishna?" — and on the bulletin board outside the Electric Mayhem's coffee-house/church — "Lost? Have you tried Rev. Harry Krishna?" Even the jokes in this movie, or "running gags," as Kermit calls them, travel!

More profoundly, though, Kermit's trek across the country allows him to confront his own dreams. As a lone frog in a swamp, Kermit sings about finding a "rainbow connection" with "lovers" and "dreamers," but the only one to join him in the song is his reflection on the water's surface. Through the angles of the film it almost appears that Kermit is singing in call-and-response with a second frog, but he's clearly alone. Later in the film, however, when it seems that Kermit may have failed in his quest for fame, he has a heart to heart with himself, and on screen, we see this heart-to-heart as a troubled Kermit talking with a physical manifestation of his inner self. The second Kermit speaks encouragingly to our froggy protagonist, offering the sage advice that Kermit often provides others:

> KERMIT: I brought 'em all out here to the middle of nowhere. It's all my fault.
> KERMIT 2: Still, whether you promised them something or not, you gotta remember, they wanted to come.
> KERMIT : But, that's because they believed in me.
> KERMIT 2: No, they believed in the dream.
> KERMIT : Well, so do I, but...
> KERMIT 2: You do?
> KERMIT : Yeah, of course I do!
> KERMIT 2: Well then?
> KERMIT : Well then, I guess I was wrong when I said I never promised anyone. I promised me.

In the back and forth of this little Socratic dialogue, Kermit's mind gently leads him to the realization that his dreams of Hollywood are too important to let slip away. Kermit had been so focused on his concerns for his friends that he hadn't confronted his own doubts and desires. Only when he realizes that "I promised me" does he merge back into one frog, suggesting that he has come to a stronger understanding of who he is through his travels.

The Great Muppet Caper's European trip is similarly concerned with questions of identity, for American journey narratives to foreign countries often center on the culture shock of travelers comparing new customs and places to the familiar sights of home. Indeed, as many travelers will recognize from their own adventures abroad, sometimes it's not until we find ourselves immersed in a foreign culture that we truly recognize ourselves as "Americans." Since most early Americans emigrated from Europe, European journeys have held a particularly prominent place in our fictions and our travels. As Janis P. Stout puts it in *The Journey Narrative in American Literature*, "Europe has been the necessary destination, the place where the American or American imagination has had to go in order to define itself by reference to an other" (68). Whether in fiction by Henry James and the writers of the Lost Generation or in 20th century films such as *Roman Holiday* or *National Lampoon's European Vacation*, the European trip transforms Americans into weirdos in a weird land, forcing them to confront and often to reassess their identities while abroad.

This confrontation is made explicit in many ways in *The Great Muppet Caper*, for as a whodunit, this film is rife with identity confusion. Although Kermit and the gang are primarily trying to track down a jewel thief who has been hounding Lady Holiday, a glamorous fashion designer played by Diana Rigg, they also have to sort out their own identities along the way. One of the great running gags of this movie is that Kermit and Fozzie are identical twin brothers even though, as their boss points out, they "don't look anything alike." Apparently, the resemblance is only clear to others when both "twins" wear their hats and don a broad Muppet grin, but those cues don't help Fozzie, who can't even remember who is who when he's looking right into Kermit's green face. For instance, when flying to England in the cargo hold of a plane, crated in boxes and distinctly labeled "Frog" and "Bear," Kermit complains of the cold, and Fozzie tells him "You're lucky — you have fur." "No, no, no," Kermit responds, "You're the one with the fur. Turn on your light and see for yourself." Light suddenly shines through the bars of the crate marked "Bear," and we hear Fozzie exclaim, "Oh yeah — I keep mixing us up." Later, as Kermit and Fozzie stand together before a mirror in their hotel room, Fozzie has to ask, "Which one am I?" "You're the one on the right!" Kermit responds in exasperation. The joke runs full circle when Kermit sits alone on a park bench and overhears a teenage girl cry, "Look dad, there's a bear." "No Christine, that's a frog," her dad explains. "Bears wear hats." Though these moments can easily be overlooked as simple gags, in the context of journey narratives, they keep reminding us of the importance of seeking our identities and distinguishing ourselves from those around us. If Fozzie can't recognize his own physical appearance, how likely is he to understand his own individuality?

Although Kermit and Fozzie's roles as unidentical identical twins provides the opportunity for plenty of Muppets silliness, Miss Piggy's situation as a young American in London, hoping to break into the modeling business, reveals the deeper confusions that can occur when we leave home for unfamiliar territory. Confusion abounds after Miss Piggy seeks a job as a high fashion model and is hired as a receptionist by Lady Holiday. When Kermit soon after enters the office to interview the real Lady Holiday, he instead finds Piggy, and a bit love struck he mistakes her for her boss. That initial mistake leads to a lively night of dining and dancing, but when Lady Holiday arrives at the same club and is robbed again, Miss Piggy's cover is blown. She flees the scene, leaving behind not only a glass slipper — the classic footwear of a woman in disguise — but also mounting suspicions about her involvement in the heist. Later, the real thieves manage to frame Miss Piggy, in part because Piggy is so willing to take someone else's place as a model in Holiday's fashion show, thereby granting the thieves a chance to plant the evidence on her. Unlike Kermit and Fozzie's twin gag, Piggy's identity confusions are not comic relief — they're serious and potentially life threatening, ultimately sending her to jail. In the context of the European tour, Miss Piggy demonstrates the temptation to use travel to reinvent ourselves as someone else: longing to be a model, she seeks to re-model herself into someone she's not. As Miss Piggy's situation suggests, we may be tempted to present a false face when we travel abroad, hoping to be perceived as more daring or alluring than we are at home, but although there's incredible freedom in taking on this new identity, we also risk losing ourselves in the performance.

This threat of losing ourselves while traveling is further emphasized in *The Muppets Take Manhattan*, in which the gang makes the traditional trek to the big city to try their luck on Broadway. In both *The Muppet Movie* and *The Great Muppet Caper*, the journey motif allows the Muppets to find each other and to coalesce as a group; *The Muppets Take Manhattan*, on the other hand, opens with the Muppets already in a tightly knit group, and it is their journey to New York that actually tears them apart. On one level, this change reflects the specific scenario of the plot: in this third movie, the Muppets play recent college graduates, poised on the threshold of adulthood and not yet ready to part from the friends who had helped them through their formative years. Rather than going their separate ways, the Muppets head off to New York City together, determined to take their senior play, *Manhattan Melodies*, and turn it into a Broadway hit. As a result, their trip to New York isn't truly the journey of the movie; their arrival in the big city is just the start of the adventure. Their transitional state is emphasized by the comic touch of their accommodations: for a quarter a day, each Muppet rents a locker in the bus station rather than a more traditional hotel room. The scene of all the Muppets in their individual lockers has a charmingly *Laugh-In*-like visual appeal, but more seriously, it reminds us that they are living in a transitional space, a place that travelers pass through, but not one in which to plant roots. This liminal space becomes a necessary jumping off point for their adventures inside and outside of New York.

But New York City itself offers another reason for the reversed narrative movement of *The Muppets Take Manhattan*: although New York dazzles and glows from afar, when we follow our dreams to the city we risk getting lost in the crowd. The size and scope of New York remind us that we are small tadpoles in a big pond, that millions of others have also come to the city to pursue similar dreams. It's a place of perpetual movement, the city that doesn't sleep, a city where you're as likely to lose your sense of self as you are to find it. Novelist and essayist E. B. White may sum it up best when he writes, "On any person who desires such queer prizes, New York will bestow the gift of loneliness and the gift of privacy" (148). In traveling to New York, Kermit and his gang have to face these stark gifts, most notably when Kermit first loses all his friends, who leave him alone in the city while they seek their fortunes elsewhere, and then loses his own memory after being struck by a taxi cab. Though he is diagnosed with amnesia, Kermit is truly suffering from a loss of identity: his friends had left town when they failed to sell their show, and Kermit had depended on the wacky vitality of his band of "dogs and bears and chickens and stuff" to define who he was. Without his friends, he "loses his sense of direction," and winds up working at an ad agency with a group of frogs who are virtually indistinguishable from each other. Gil, Bill, and Jill, along with Kermit, who in his amnesic state goes by "Phil," all share the same mannerisms and the same tone of voice. The similarity in their names, their clothes, and their nasal intonation suggests that these frogs are interchangeable, with nothing to make them stand out in the crowd. Left on his own, Kermit faces the anonymity of the city, almost fading away into generic frogness.

Across each of these films, the journey opens up questions about individual identity, whether that identity is discovered through travel or threatened by it. How do we find our "sense of direction" or the path to the "rainbow connection"? How do we figure out where we "fit right in" when we are immersed in a strange culture far from home? How can we sing "look at me, here I am, right where I belong" when lost in the overwhelming crowds of the city? But what's most notable about the Muppets' movies is that their journeys are not only about the quest of the individuals but about the whole group. For the Muppets, it's not enough to discover oneself on the road; the larger goal is to find one's place in the community.

For example, in *The Muppet Movie*, although Kermit sets off to pursue his dream and to seek his identity on the road, he does not follow the path of the solitary wanderer, the American loner, like Huck Finn, who "lights out into the territory" to escape the limits of civilization; nor does Kermit adhere to the general pattern of road films, in which a pair of individuals sets out to see the country or just as often to rebel against it (see Cohan and Hark 8). Although typical road movies such as *Bonnie and Clyde* or *Thelma and Louise* present their protagonists as outsiders, raging against the confinements of society, *The Muppet Movie* tempers that rage with humor, showing that outsiders are just out there waiting to get together. "We've picked up a *weirdo*," Fozzie remarks when Gonzo first joins their group, but one of the most enduring messages of this film is that weirdos like us are everywhere, and we can find them if we just start looking. Each town in the movie seems to have one resident Muppet, one fuzzy odd-ball who may fit in by playing the piano at the local bar or by winning beauty contests at the county fair, but who still seems unlike the other members of that community. With every new outsider they invite to join in the journey, the gang coalesces and takes shape, no longer single Muppets in otherwise generic communities but a vibrant and diverse company of weirdos.

This emphasis on community building can be seen in the modes of transportation Kermit adopts along his journey. After the Hollywood agent informs Kermit of the promises out west in Hollywood, Kermit appears riding a bicycle down the road, a solitary conveyance for a solitary frog. But after his bicycle is crushed by a steamroller, he next joins Fozzie Bear in his uncle's Studebaker, a cozy car for two, though not designed for a large crowd. Therefore, when the Studebaker collides with Gonzo's clunky plumber's truck, the gang next picks up a larger station wagon with room for a frog, a bear, a dog, a pig, a chicken, and a whatever, as Gonzo is generally classified. Ultimately, after this vehicle breaks down in the desert, the whole gang careens into Hollywood in the Electric Mayhem's bus, a motley crew of hopefuls who collectively storm the studio head's office, even though the casting call only requested "frogs." Like Dorothy in *The Wizard of Oz*, Kermit finds a group of uniquely flawed yet endearing companions during his travels and invites them to join him on his pilgrimage. But whereas Dorothy accumulates fellow travelers only to leave them behind when it's time to return home, Kermit instead finds his home on the road among this new circle of friends.

Kermit similarly finds a welcoming crew of strange friends on his trip to London, and as Americans in a foreign country, these friends not only help establish Kermit's sense of community but also his sense of national identity. The Happiness Hotel, listed glibly in the guidebook as a "place to park your carcass," seems to be the center of the expatriate Muppets community in London. The Electric Mayhem makes it their home in between gigs ("which makes it what, five years now?" Floyd speculates); Rizzo the Rat heads a group of red-uniformed rat bellhops; a lively jug band, classic characters from old *Muppet Show* skits, play their banjos in the lobby; even Sam the Eagle has an upstairs room, from which he can glare down on the crowd, spurning them from his lofty perch with a stinging, "You are all weirdos." With this blanket indictment, Sam presumes to speak as the voice of American ideals and values, and he consciously separates himself from his fellow hotel guests. Yet the hotel community focuses explicitly on American ideals of life, liberty, and the pursuit of happiness as they welcome their new friends into the fold.

For instance, in a classic Muppet-style punch line, Fozzie and Gonzo sing about what at first appears to be the horrendous conditions of the hotel — "You've got every kind of critter, / You've got every kind of pest" — as if they were planning to slap the hotel with a health violation. Yet without missing a beat, Pops, the old man working at the front desk, completes the lyric with "But we treat them all like equals, just like any other guest." This line is both a joke and a remarkably democratic sentiment: in the Muppets' world, "critters" and "pests" are considered just as worthy of attention as anyone else, equally likely to "fit right in" with the rest of the gang. The Happiness Hotel caters to an eclectic clientele, and even though they have a Union Jack hanging noticeably to establish the British location, their sensibilities and their sympathies are distinctly American.

Indeed, although they are on location in London and encounter several British actors in cameo roles, much of the humor in *The Great Muppet Caper* arises from the overt Americanness of the Muppets in an English setting. Besides the clearly American roots of the Happiness Hotel, Miss Piggy converses with a fellow American trucker in CB radio-lingo as she races from the British police, and with typical Muppet absurdity, the gang manages to thwart the theft of the fabulous Baseball Diamond by calling on America's favorite pastime, playing an actual game baseball with the giant gem. And although Sam the Eagle initially criticizes the weirdness of the hotel inhabitants, by the end of the movie we know even the symbol of America has given the Muppets his seal of approval. When the entire gang is faced with fighting the jewel robbers, Fozzie rouses their spirits with a motivational speech, reminding them that they are "in this thing together." "I'm just as scared as you are," he assures the crowd, "but this has to be done. We don't want the bad guys to win. We gotta to do this for justice, for freedom, for honesty." As he speaks, inspirational music swells in background, with chords similar to the closing "from sea to shining sea" of "America the Beautiful." As the group declares their dedication to the mission, Sam pokes his head into their room and proclaims, "At times like these, I am proud to be an American." While the viewers may often laugh at Sam's conservative views, in this instance we can't help agreeing with him; having journeyed across the ocean to find a missing jewel, the Muppets have found instead an affirmation of some of our most cherished American ideals.

With *The Muppets Take Manhattan*, the community focus is less on Americanness and more on the diversity and multiculturalism of the metropolis. As mentioned earlier, one of the most despairing moments of Kermit's journey is when he loses all his friends; when the Muppets realize their plans may not come to fruition as soon as they hoped, they all go their separate ways, leaving Kermit behind. As they sing to each other that "Somehow I know, we'll meet again, / Don't know just how and I don't know just when," the gang disperses across the country. Miss Piggy departs in a classic Hollywood train station scene, with Kermit standing forlornly on the platform and catching the handkerchief she throws him; Scooter rides off on a bicycle; Gonzo and Camilla steal a ride in the back of a farm truck; Rowlf heads out in a bus (with the clever joke that the dog takes the Greyhound!); the Electric Mayhem stand by the side of the road hitching for a ride (we can just imagine the kind of *On the Road* adventures they might experience); and Fozzie leaves in an empty boxcar. Each Muppet takes a different mode of transportation, emphasizing that they are heading out alone, no longer buoyed by each other's support; unlike *The Muppet Movie* in which the gang consolidates into one vehicle, here their separate departures emphasize the crumbling of their community. As the song ends and all the Muppets appear together to sing a final "it's time for saying goodbye," the picture fades from the group to a lonely Kermit, walking down an empty New York street at night, looking crestfallen. Even though he still has a dream, the most important part of that dream — his circle of friends — is gone.

Whereas Kermit is left in New York to face his identity alone, the rest of the gang seeks their fortune elsewhere, sending Kermit postcards about their adventures. Fozzie, for example, returns to his roots to explore one of the quintessential rituals of bear culture: hibernation. Settling into a quiet cave with several other bears who are nothing more than sleeping mounds, he seems painfully out of place in his "own" community. "How do they do it?" he marvels as he looks around. "I've been trying to sleep for days. Anybody got some warm milk?" The other bears want to sleep, but Fozzie has difficulty conforming. His postcard to Kermit may blithely claim, "I love it out here in the woods; it's where a bear should be," but we viewers can see that he's suffering there without his friends, his music, his comedy. Rowlf's situation is perhaps worse than Fozzie's: instead of returning home to a community of dogs, he gets a job at a dog kennel, where he essentially serves as jailer to his fellow canines. When his charges start howling, explaining that "we want to go home," Rowlf can only raise his head and join them in their cries.

The problem for Fozzie in the cave and Rowlf at the pound, likewise for Kermit at the frog-run ad agency, is that rather than finding the vibrant diversity promised by the big city, they've been limited to a narrow, homogenous community. The Muppets have always thrived as diverse group; whenever Kermit describes his friends, he has to ramble out a list of "frogs and dogs and bears and chickens and whatever." As such, they're a perfect match for New York City, a place where different people and voices merge into a sometimes cacophonous, sometimes melodious madness. New York attracts artists and writers and performers; those who feel out of place in their small towns often find large groups of like-minded, creative individuals in the diverse landscape of the city. Although it's easy to feel lonely in the crowd, E. B. White also assures us that the diverse groups of people give the city its "passion." Describing these folks who come to New York "in quest of something," he writes, "Whether it is a farmer arriving from Italy to set up a small grocery store in a slum, or a young girl arriving from a small town in Mississippi to escape the indignity of being observed by her neighbors, or a boy arriving from the Corn Belt with a manuscript in his suitcase and a pain in his heart, it makes no difference: each embraces New York with the intense excitement of first love, each absorbs New York with the fresh eyes of an adventurer" (152). This variety of people gives New York its spark; Kermit would call them the "lovers" and "dreamers," and he recognizes that their power multiplies as more people share in the adventure. When he and the gang finally get the chance to put on their show, what makes it work is their lively cast of "*more* frogs and bears and chickens and whatever": all the homogenous communities come together on the New York stage into a zany, heterogeneous collective. When Kermit looks into his cast members' eyes and sings, "look at me, here I am, right where I belong," we recognize he has reached his destination at last.

This sense of belonging highlights one of the most important philosophies of all the Muppets movies: we will find our selves when we find our home, and that search for home is the true purpose of our travels. At heart, the first three movies are all origin stories, imagining how the delightful group of Muppets came together to form their wacky extended family. This search for home separates the Muppets movies from many American journey narratives, for home has traditionally been perceived as the place from which to escape, or at least to "get away" from for a spell. It's also in this search for home that the Muppets' movies most differ from Joseph Campbell's description of the heroic quest, which generally follows the shape of a rite of passage: "A hero ventures forth from the world of common day into a region of supernatural wonder: fabulous forces are there encountered and a decisive victory is won: the hero comes back from this mysterious adventure with the power to bestow boons on his fellow man" (30). Kermit may leave the swamp, face difficult hardships, and triumph over evil forces, but he does not return home; he creates a home.

In *The Muppet Movie*, for example, Kermit and the gang arguably find home, not in Hollywood, which was the destination of their journey, but in each other's company on the open highway. When Fozzie first looks out the car window at the passing landscape and declares, "Ah, a bear in his natural habitat," we assume he is referring to the great outdoors; instead, he closes with the punch line, "A Studebaker," suggesting that he feels most at home on the road. The delightful absurdity of the line hits us at once: of course a car is not a bear's natural habitat, but why shouldn't it be? Why can't a bear, or a frog or pig or chicken or even one of us watching the film, define home not as a set spot on a map but wherever we feel like we belong? Fozzie is not rooted by place but is completely mobile, free to travel the country to gather up the group that will become his family and truly define his "natural habitat."

Kermit voices this realization more explicitly in his showdown with the movie's villain. Many road films, such as *Bonnie and Clyde* or *Thelma and Louise*, are compelled forward by the protagonists' run from the law; in these outlaw road films the road offers freedom and escape, a space to critique the dominant culture and to push or even cross boundaries (see Laderman and Cohan & Hark). In *The Muppet Movie*, the gang is chased not by the law but by corporate America: a regional fast-food giant, Doc Hopper, is determined to make Kermit the spokesfrog for his French Fried Frog's Legs restaurants. In a way, Hopper offers Kermit a shortcut to his dream: doing all the TV commercials for the restaurant would make Kermit rich and famous, but it would also make him complicit in a commercial enterprise that literally eats up Kermit's kind. In refusing to work for Hopper, Kermit makes a case for which dreams are most worth pursuing, and which companions are most worth inviting on our journeys. As he explains to Hopper, "Yeah, well I've got a dream too. But it's about singing and dancing and making people happy. That's the kind of dream that gets better the more people you share it with. And, well, I've found a whole bunch of friends who have the same dream. And that kind of makes us like a family." This family spirit is highlighted at the closing of each film as the Muppets gather together all their friends and cohorts for the final parting shot. Whether collecting a crowd of monsters and *Muppet Show* regulars on the sound stage at the end of *The Muppet Movie*, or sending Muppets parachuting through the air at the end of *The Great Muppet Caper*, or gathering with the whole Sesame Street gang for a wedding at the end of *The Muppets Take Manhattan*, each film culminates with the extended Muppet family "together again."

Considering Fozzie's claim that his Studebaker on the highway is his natural habitat, it's worth asking, what *is* a Muppet's "natural habitat"? And by extension, what are *our* natural habitats? In an increasingly mobile world, where even our puppets take to the open road, Jim Henson and company remind us that home need not be centered in place but can be found in community. We often assume that the mobility of modernity and the rootedness of home are binary forces, but the Muppets assure us that our journeys need not keep us away from those we love. At journey's end, the Muppets always know that they have not *returned* home, but have *found* it. As Kermit puts it in the last line of *The Muppets Take Manhattan*, "What better way could anything end? / Hand in hand with a friend."

What better way *could* the journey end?

Works Cited

Campbell, Joseph. *The Hero with a Thousand Faces*. Princeton, NJ: Princeton University Press, 1949.
Cohan, Steven, and Ina Rae Hark, eds. *The Road Movie Book*. New York: Routledge, 1997.
Culhane, John. "The Muppets in Movieland." *The New York Times Magazine*. June 10, 1979.
De Botton, Alain. *The Art of Travel*. New York: Random House, 2002.
Laderman, David. *Driving Visions: Exploring the Road Movie*. Austin: University of Texas Press, 2002.
Least Heat-Moon, William. "Journeys into Kansas." *Temperamental Journeys: Essays on the Modern Literature of Travel*. Ed. Michael Kowalewski. Athens: University of Georgia Press, 1992. 19–24.
Primeau, Ronald. *Romance of the Road: The Literature of the American Highway*. Bowling Green, OH: Bowling Green State University Popular Press, 1996.
Stout, Janis P. *The Journey Narrative in American Literature: Patterns and Departures*. Westwood, CT: Greenwood Press, 1983.
Turner, Frederick Jackson. *The Frontier in American History*. 1920. Tucson: University of Arizona Press, 1986.
White, E. B. "Here Is New York." *Essays of E. B. White*. New York: HarperCollins, 1999. 148–168.

It's Time to Get Together for Some Sex and Violence on *The Muppet Show*?

Kathleen E. Kennedy

Unlike the eponymous *Sesame Street*, *The Muppet Show* was aimed squarely at adults and engaged the hoary themes of sex and violence fearlessly, at least initially. As *The Muppet Show* struggled to gain a foothold in American TV, sex and violence seemed to be emphasized, beginning with a pilot facetiously subtitled "The End of Sex and Violence on Television." In Season One, human guest stars struggled with violent Muppets and sometimes enacted sketches featuring, and occasionally even fetishizing, sexualized violence. Season One's progressive politics highlighted the issues of women's rights and racial equality and questioned unexamined responses to violence and sexualized violence. Yet in subsequent seasons, the developers of *The Muppet Show* shifted the way they portrayed sexual or violent material. After the first season, most violent acts occurred between Muppets, and any violence the human stars faced was undercut by revealing the play-acting of the guest stars in their role of victim or of the Muppets as perpetrators. These later renderings of violence produced simpler and more cartoon-like aggression than the violent and sexual sketches that had been featured in Season One, and by Season Three much of the violence was simply condemned. While the sketches of Season One of *The Muppet Show* provided material that encouraged audience members to question their assumptions about gender, race, sex, and violence in complex ways, in following seasons, while feminist causes continued to be promoted, violence was depicted more simply.

The Pre-Show Mayhem

Crucial to development of *The Muppet Show* sketches was the Muppets' appearance on *The Ed Sullivan Show* from 1966 to 1970. Although lacking much interaction with humans, these sketches establish the kind of political, adult humor that interested Henson on the eve of *Sesame Street*'s 1969 launch. Of the twenty sketches included in the *Muppets Magic from the Ed Sullivan Show* DVD, nearly half include some violent element, and these violent sketches often convey social or political messages.[1] For example, "The Computer Dinner" (reprised in the George Burns episode on *The Muppet Show*) features a Cookie-Monster prototype devouring a "computer," but only the expensive components. In the end, ProtoCookie discovers that the device remains functional when it announces, from his stomach, that it is a bomb. When the bomb detonates, bits of fur mix with the smoke in the air, visually suggesting the reality of the event. Demonstrating remarkable visual economy, the sketch suggests both the frightening financial and political power of the military complex, and the self-defeating nature of rampant consumerism.

The lip-synced "I've Grown Accustomed to Your Face" is one of the few of these early pieces to suggest sexualized violence. In it, Kermit sits in drag, lip-syncing the lyrics to a face that is eaten by Yorick, who has been hiding under the face, or hiding as the face. (Yorick's antics were familiar to audiences from his appearances on Henson's earlier *Sam and Friends* show) (Finch, *Henson* 19). Then Yorick pursues Kermit silently back and forth across the stage, eventually revealing his intent: to eat Kermit. While the studio audience howls audibly in laughter at this pursuit, the claustrophobic, blank stage enhances the fearfulness of the situation, as does Kermit's soundless mouthing of the words to the song, while simultaneously trying to avoid and then fight off Yorick. Kermit shivers in fear, hits at, and later kicks at, his pursuer. The song finishes just as Yorick manages to begin devouring Kermit's leg, and drags his prey offstage, while Kermit appears to scream silently. The uncomfortable sketch concludes with no rescue in sight for the hapless drag queen frog.

Certainly, if Kermit has "grown accustomed to [this] face," then the sketch serves as a dire warning about how little we can really know about what is going on in other peoples' minds, and illustrates it with the literalism only available in a puppet theater. The sketch insists that assault can be perpetrated by those we know best, as more recently available statistics document is often the case. In addition, this radical sketch demands that the audience recognize that not only "bad girls" can be victimized, but "good girls" (and perhaps queer girls) as well: here Kermit wears that traditional symbol of correctly-performed femininity, a pearl necklace. Indeed, this highly disturbing sketch deserves more lengthy consideration than I have room for here, in light of postmodern feminist and queer criticism of rape and violence directed at drag queens, drag kings, and transsexuals, and the transgendered. In the end, "I've Grown Accustomed to Your Face" is as sexually violent as the Muppets ever got.

Given his already-developed popularity with adult audiences, and following *Sesame Street*'s successful debut, Henson desired an outlet for more adult humor, lest the Muppets become synonymous with children's programming. Despite *Sesame Street*'s popularity since its 1969 reception, *The Muppet Show* took a long time to arrive, and it was not until changes in FCC policy made a prime-time slot available in 1975 that *The Muppet Show* was picked up for syndication by a British production company (Brown D37).

Season One: "You want a high heel in your hamhock?" — Tiffany Gonzales ("Rita Moreno")

Season One of *The Muppet Show* showcased sex and violence in ways that encouraged adult audiences to think about these issues in progressive ways. A number of episodes feature problems of particular importance to contemporary feminists fighting for the Equal Rights Amendment. Other episodes engaged the topic of race and racial stereotypes: topics rarely dealt with in complex ways on television even today. In a simple example that raises consciousness of domestic abuse, one first season episode features Ruth Buzzi in a knock-down fight with Sweetums, all the while they sing the romantic duet "Can't Take My Eyes Off of You" to each other. In another example, Candice Bergen, an outspoken celebrity feminist, ended a sketch in which her character was overwhelmed by traditional wifely tasks by rebelling, ripping off her pioneer-style dress to reveal a t-shirt with a feminist logo and pants underneath (*TMS* "Candice Bergen"). Unlike other sketches we shall examine, no harm to human or Muppet takes place in the episode, but Bergen and *The Muppet Show* suggest strongly that one-sided domestic power relations are not respectful of women, and, indeed, make men look like ignorant puppets.

Consider the episode starring Sandy Duncan, which opens with a fraught number that illustrates classic Second Wave, 1970s-style feminism: a female character takes over a male song, and male space (a bar, being drunk) and triumphs. Duncan's number emphasizes gender immediately, when she sings a Manilow tune and changes the lyrics of "What's a Nice Boy Like Me (Doing in a Place that Never Closes)?" to "nice girl." Sex and violence move from a rather soft-core subtext of the original lyrics, to a frighteningly hard-core possibility in the regendered lyrics. While the original lyrics may question the singer's judgment, the issue of safety does not arise in the same way with a male voice. When the singer is a woman, however, the audience fears that this behavior could lead to physical harm and sexual threat, and the choreography encourages this fear. As Duncan's character pounds "rows of whiskey sours" performers in human-sized Muppet-costumes manhandle her, even pointedly ripping off her skirt. This sexualized threat is nowhere evident in the original song, but neither is the triumphant conclusion. At the close of the song, surrounded by monsters, Duncan exhales on each threatening monster. As she does so they all fall to the floor, apparently stunned by the alcohol in her breath. Duncan's "nice girl" character drinks her potential attackers under the table "like a man," as understood by Second Wave feminist tenets. A twenty-first-century, Third Wave feminist audience might note that she triumphs both with and without her skirt: she persists in being a "nice girl" while in a bar, while drinking, wearing her skirt or stripped of it. While some guest-stars flirt with violence in a single sketch, some made it a theme throughout their appearance, and one such episode can stand as an example for the ways in which sex and violence were showcased and linked throughout so much of Season One. Rita Moreno's guest appearance is a dense example of these conflicts and was recognized as excellent at the time, earning her an Emmy for her performance in 1977.[2]

In Moreno's first sketch on *The Muppet Show*, she dances to a tango with a tangled past. Originally "Adios Muchachos" by Lenny Sanders, Sanders and later lyricist Dorcas Cochran released it again with a different set of lyrics as "I Get Ideas" in 1951, and it was a hit song for years afterwards. While the score alone is used in the sketch, any audience member familiar with the song would recall that the tone of the new lyrics echoes that of the dance, beginning with: "When we are dancing and you're dangerously near me/ I get ideas." Both Moreno's character and her dance partner seem to get "dangerously close" to each other at times during this sketch: each shoves, hits, and eventually throws the other through a wall. Moreno's character relishes the spectacle she's created of herself and gives the European knuckles-out wave to her appreciative audience upon her apparent victory, like a matador. Nevertheless, the star's aggression is not rewarded, and her dance partner catches her from behind during her wave and tosses her through the same hole she pitched him through moments earlier.

Later in the episode, the "Panel Discussion" sketch again exposes Moreno in another stereotypical character, but one who stands up for her abilities as a woman and as a Puerto Rican. It appears that here, while introduced as "Tiffany Gonzales," the character is based on Moreno's character Googie Gomez, from the 1975 Broadway show *The Ritz*. Reviews called Gomez a "torrid, slightly ravaged Latin chanteuse," a "tawdry cabaret queen of queens, who almost speaks English, can nearly sing, and will tear out the eye of Cyclops for a main chance," and a "Puerto Rican chanteuse ... with raven hair and a raven's throat" (Considine 79; Barnes, 34; Kerr X5). On *The Muppet Show*, Gonzales speaks with a strong Puerto Rican accent, is aggressive, and covered in loud gold clothing and jewelry. While the most physically violent Gonzales gets is to hold Kermit's mouth shut, she engages in a loud argument across the panel table with Miss Piggy. When Miss Piggy derides Gonzales' accent, Gonzales refuses to accept her Caribbean-English as anything less valid than the Standard American English spoken by Piggy: "I speakah as gooda Englishchas the next guy!" Indeed, Moreno reports that she suffered this sort of prejudice herself in the entertainment industry, regardless of the type of English she used (Considine 84). Gonzales uses her bilingualism as a weapon, claiming that she's quoting a helpful local saying when she says in Spanish: "When dealing with a foolish little sow what you want to do is to threaten to kill her [*Cuando uno trabaja con una cochinita majadera lo que hay que 'cer es que darle la amenaza de posibilidad de asesinarla*]."[3] Gonzales translates the expression for her Anglophone panelists very freely: "one more crack from chou and you are one dead enchilada." Clearly an aggressive speech directed at Piggy, the discussion ends in loud arguing from all, with Kermit hopelessly introducing the topic of the next Panel Discussion as "Improving U.S.-Latin American Relations."

The "Talk Spot" also features violence and positions Moreno as the victim. When Moreno begs Kermit to drop the script and just ad lib a chat with her, Kermit passes off his discomfort with this idea onto another: "the guy holding the cue-cards." The "guy holding the cue-cards" turns out to be Sweetums, and when she suggests to Sweetums that he "can hold anything [he] want[s]," he tosses the cue-cards immediately, grabs Moreno under his arm, and walks off camera, ignoring her muffled protests. Kermit quips with aplomb that the trouble with their guests is that they so often get "carried away;" however, the gentle humor attempts to explain away an abduction that, while harmless in the circumstances, is not one of Moreno's choosing. Violent to others in previous sketches, here, Moreno herself experiences a lack of agency.

Moreno's closing act has her battling against mistreatment when she attempts to sing "Fever" while Animal follows his own tune instead of playing background drums. Attempting to save her number, Moreno confronts Animal towards the end of the sketch, threatening in Spanish: "Listen, buddy. All I wanna tell you is that you shouldn't do that. It's not nice, you understand? Look at me when I'm talking to you. This is my number, and if you bother me any more I'm gonna hit you so hard, it's gonna leave you stupid. Cool it." Saying this in Spanish without the partial translation given in the "Talk Spot" reminds the audience of the bilingualism on *Sesame Street*; however, code-switching on *The Muppet Show* accomplishes different things and can be deployed aggressively. Identifying Moreno's position as a polyglot, in command of multiple languages, it also allows her to castigate a cast member in a language many members of her audience may not understand. Anyone familiar with the Muppets might not be expecting Animal to understand Spanish, but it seems that he does, and even verbally questions Moreno's harangue as she steps back around the drum kit to her mark. Needless to say, Animal's drumming gets no better.

Demonstrating control over her material, Moreno ends the song before the stanza on Captain Smith and Pocahontas: by 1976, Moreno's days of playing "Mexican senoritas and Indian princesses" were over, as greater ethnic and racial sensitivity began slowly to be exercised in Hollywood (Moreno ATA). She further exercises control over the scene, when she walks back behind the drums, pulls enormous cymbals from behind the drum kit, and smashes Animal's head between them. Reminding us that sex and violence are never too far from the surface in *The Muppet Show* in Season One, Animal gurgles as he passes out "that's my kind of woman!" Consonant with Second Wave feminism, Moreno comes across as talented and strong, and Animal as a less-articulate show boater, who can manage to think about sex even with his ears ringing.

The violence in Moreno's episode extends all the way to the curtain call, where the star appears with her Muppet dance partner from her opening sketch, and dramatically throws him offstage. When Kermit expresses some shock, she insists that: "that's okay. He loves it. I had lunch with him today. It's okay." Moreno's American Television Academy interview reminds us that she attempted to get to know fellow actors, often over lunch, and here the suggestion is that the violence of these maneuvers were topics of discussion between herself and the other dancer. Sometimes a full body Muppet performer, sometimes an empty shell, this dance partner's hybrid physiology complicates the violence, however, and demands the audience answer whether violence to a human is the same as violence done to the figure of a human. This moment, at the close of *The Muppet Show*, denies the audience a simple reading of the connection between sex and violence on the episode.

Seasons Two and Three: Violence Lite

The degree to which Moreno's episode concerned itself with matters of sex and violence was not to be often repeated. Seasons Two and Three of *The Muppet Show* continued to include an interest in sex and violence, but for the most part, toned down their representations of both and demonstrated a preference for comical, implied violence, over the political commentary of Season One. Violence was often limited to the short, cold opening, as Scooter alerted the star to the curtain's imminent rise. In these short sketches, for example, Zero Mostel is eaten by a monster, Crazy Harry causes an explosion in Harry Belafonte's dressing room, and Marisa Berensen's "alligator luggage" threatens to eat her. Few of these violent beginnings signal significant violence elsewhere in the episode, however. Whereas Season One featured

Muppets being violent to guests, in Season Two, the guests are more often violent towards the Muppets, and no one is truly afraid or harmed in the sketches. While Season Three is far more violent than Season Two, the violence is primarily between Muppets and is not put to the political use it was in Season One.

In Season Two, violence in sketches is often simply alluded to, or otherwise discussed as part of the act. Jaye P. Morgan suffers particularly from mayhem perpetrated by Animal and Crazy Harry (*TMS* "Jaye P. Morgan"). She admits in the "Talk Spot" that she "is starting to feel like a moving target." In this sketch, however, the magician reveals the trick, and the teeth are pulled from the violence that seems to have Morgan so rattled. In order to demonstrate how harmless the explosions really are, Kermit explodes into a cloud of smoke, only to walk back onstage past Morgan's elbow. Each disappears from the stage by "exploding."[4] During the curtain call, Morgan admits the essential harmlessness of this violence: "I've been blown up, beaten up, insulted: everything's happened to me, but I've had a great time. I mean it." In the next episode, after narrowly missing a bomb explosion that manages to mangle Kermit offstage, Peter Sellers goes on-stage as one of his Goons characters, an accented, mustache-sporting physical therapist and tortures the Muppet Link Hogthrob (*TMS* "Peter Sellers"). Link is "massaged" into a variety of impossible positions and expresses pain, but verbally assures Sellers that he is fine. In his appearances on the sketch "Pigs in Space," Link is such a boor (boar?) that the audience could easily be pleased to see Link's ego finally cause him the pain he deserves. Link ends this sketch unable to move from the table, as Seller's character shuffles offstage, abandoning Link to cry plaintively for help. The sharpness of the rebuke to Link's ego in this sketch is undercut immediately following it, however, when Link appears backstage, apparently mobile and comfortable, asserting that it "was the best massage of [his] life," despite Kermit and Fozzie's concerns to the contrary.

The episode featuring Dom DeLuise proves exemplary of Season Two in its treatment of violence. The cold opening features DeLuise's head on a platter: the joke is a sight-gag, and never referred to again during the episode. DeLuise's opening number, a scientific expedition to Koozebane, further demonstrates the harmlessness of the violence in Season Two. DeLuise's character stumbles upon a warren of Koozbanian creatures, who steal his hammer and radio. When he tries to regain these items, the Koozebanians hit him on the head with the hammer. At the end of the sketch, DeLuise falls into one of the holes and pops back up in the hole dressed as a Koozebanian, uttering "merdlidop" just like the Koozebanians do. While apparent alien assimilation could be portrayed as frightening, here DeLuise and the Koozebanians laugh as the scene closes: this is all for fun. Other instances of violence in the episode seem to be explained by a sort of "tough love." In the "Shepard's

Institute of Animal Protection," DeLuise plays a shelter worker filming an advertisement for the shelter's fund drive. As he highlights a number of the fine creatures in need of adoption (all large monsters), the monsters become increasingly demanding of DeLuise, until the sketch ends with the guest star being mobbed by irritable monsters, one of whom eats DeLuise's lab coat. While clearly potential threats, the shelter worker insists, even in the face of contrary evidence, that these monsters can make wonderful, loving household pets, until the very end, when mauled by a monster, DeLuise asks for "help, I mean really, help!" Later in the episode, Miss Piggy and DeLuise trade insults, a sparring match which ends when Piggy beats up DeLuise. This seems like a significant rift until the closing number, "We Got Us," when DeLuise sings a song about friendship to Piggy. Despite their serious argument, by the end of the episode, they have reaffirmed their friendship. While violence is portrayed throughout the episode, it never has serious consequences for DeLuise or for any of the Muppets. Opportunities for social critique in such setups as these are few and not developed.

Jean Stapleton's episode in Season Three provides a nice parallel to DeLuise's, and demonstrates how Season Three evolves from Season Two in its treatment of violence (*TMS* "Jean Stapleton"). The comical violence begins in the cold opening, as Stapleton appears to have three hands, one of which attempts to choke her. As with many violent cold openings, there is not much more violence in the episode. Even the finale conveys the theatricality of violence, at least for the guest star. Against Kermit's cautions, Stapleton insists on doing her closing number, "I'm Just Wild about Harry" with Crazy Harry, accompanied by his unique instrument, the Explodaphone. Kermit appears to be seriously concerned, warning Stapleton: "but you could get killed," and introducing her act as "taking her life into her own hands ... and throwing it away." Nevertheless, Stapleton reassures Kermit that "[she's] not new to this business." The guest star's expertise is here a protection from Crazy Harry's explosives, explosives dangerous to other Muppets. Indeed, as Harry creates a series of explosions throughout the song, Stapleton ducks, squeals, and startles, but smiles and enjoy the entire performance unharmed. Here, the threat of Harry's explosions is apparently real, but only insofar as they are "scary": Stapleton knows she will not be harmed. In Season Three, violence can be terrible, but it is only harmful to Muppets.

Rather than frightening, as we see in the Muppets threatening Sandy Duncan, or troublesome enough to have violence done to them, as Animal experienced in the Rita Moreno episode, in Season Two, male Muppets appear ineffectual or simply annoying to male guest stars. We have already considered the example of Sellers' character mangling Link Hogthrob. However John Cleese and Sylvester Stallone perform in sketches where Muppets are powerless against the human star's greater physical power. Cleese is called upon to "fix" Gonzo's accidentally super-elongated arm (*TMS* "John Cleese"). He does so by simply pulling on Gonzo's other arm, and then his legs, to lengthen each remaining limb accordingly. No stranger to pain, the sounds Gonzo makes indicate that he is not comfortable during this process, but has no ability to escape Cleese's grasp, and once the operation is completed, no ability to leave the table on which he is seated, elongated legs dangling, useless. Later, in retaliation for making Cleese take part in a song against his will, Cleese closes the number by throttling Kermit. Likewise, Sylvester Stallone faces a talking punching bag who would very much like to be hit by an action hero like Stallone (*TMS* "Sylvester Stallone"). Stallone is puzzled by this apparent masochism, but complies with the bag's wishes. Indeed, the tendency for Muppets to be seen as weak next to the guest stars is exemplified when Stallone faces a lion in a gladiator fight, only to end up singing "Let's Call the Whole Thing Off" when the lion doesn't really want to fight him.

In contrast, violence between Muppets can be devastatingly effective, as demonstrated to its extreme by Miss Piggy. While Miss Piggy is treated at length elsewhere in this volume, no article about sex and violence on *The Muppet Show* would be complete without a nod to Piggy's volatile temperament and comfort with her own sexuality. While Frank Oz could describe Piggy in 1978 as "lusty," he also had more politically inflected comments: "She's had her consciousness raised, but she still likes diamonds. She's a very '50s lady, and that's part of the problem" (Skow). Feminists in the early twenty-first century might argue that a feminist who likes sex and diamonds could fit comfortably in Third Wave feminism (and that it is perhaps unfortunate for Piggy that it did not exist yet). While Piggy's rise from chorus pig to star took place in Season One, her violence increases measurably in Season Three, often related to scuffles with Kermit over his lack of interest in her. Indeed, the domestic violence that haunted Season One between Muppets and guest stars is by Season Three almost exclusively a feature of Piggy and Kermit's tempestuous (non)relationship, an excellent example of the larger trend towards increasing violence between Muppets examined in this article.

Characteristic of Season Three is the episode featuring Lesley Ann Warren. In it, characters act in feminist ways, and violence by Muppets towards Muppets is rejected as acceptable social behavior. As is typical of Season Two, the cold opening finds Warren startled by a large monster in her dressing room but quickly becoming charmed by him. The violence in the episode begins with Dr. Teeth singing "Mack the Knife," against Sam the Eagle's objections that it represented "an appalling song of gore and violence." An instructive comparison to this sketch is Dr. Teeth's song, "Love Ya to Death," performed by the Electric Mayhem in one of *The Muppet Show*'s pilot episodes, and again in shortened form in the Harvey Korman episode. The lyrics concentrate on domestic violence: for example, "I'll break down your resistance with every trick I got/ I know I'm gonna make you happy baby, whether you like it or not." In the pilot and the later episode, "Love Ya to Death" is performed without comment. In contrast, while "Mack the Knife" is no less horrific, noting the murders, arson, and rape perpetrated by the titular character, Sam argues strenuously against including such terrible topics on the show. Unlike in the pilot and Season One, by Season Three, Dr. Teeth must resort to subterfuge to complete his song.

In another sketch illustrating the kind of explicit criticism of violence seen throughout Season Three, Warren reacts in disgust when she discovers that her accompanist for "Just the Way You Are" is to be Marvin Suggs and the Muppaphone. In an earlier episode with Raquel Welch, Marvin and the Muppaphones are interviewed in the "Talk Spot," and Marvin's sadism is revealed. The truth of Suggs' insistence that he and the Muppaphones share "mutual love and respect" is exploded by his silencing their murmured protests by shouting at them and hitting them with his mallet. Suggs alludes to a horrible fate for the Muppaphone members; every two or three months the members are replaced, as they "go flat ... like little pancakes." Suggs will not reveal to Kermit what happens to the retired Muppaphone members then, but says, "I don't think you want to know." Indeed, being a Muppaphone is viewed by some characters as torture: in the Gilda Radner episode, Marvin breaks his promise to the Witch Doctor, who transforms him into a Muppaphone as punishment. Here we see a theme developed throughout the season: Suggs is being cruel and causing real harm to his fellow performers. By the time Lesley Ann Warren appears on the show, he must resort to deceit to gain access to the stage: in this case, by locking Rowlf in his dressing room and going on in the kind dog's place. The reality of Sugg's violence towards other Muppets is suggested by its results, and Suggs is punished explicitly (by the Witch Doctor) and implicitly (by being hustled off-stage when Rowlf escapes).

In the finale of the episode, Warren's character attempts facetiously to seduce Link Hogthrob in a disco club. "Aren't you Link Hogthrob?" she squeals, and Link avers that he is, and that "perhaps [Warren has] admired me from afar." At this point the camera delivers a close up as Warren breaks the fourth wall and winks at the audience. Warren will be in control here, the wink insists. From here, Warren begins aggressively trying to get Link to dance with her, and Link becomes intensely uncomfortable. This provides Warren's lead-in to "The Last Dance," which she sings and to which she dances. During the performance, Warren literally pulls Link around, as he struggles to flee, and when she places his hands on her suggestively, Link turns away.

Turning traditional gender expectations on their heads, here, as in Sandy Duncan's "What's a Nice Girl Like Me" sketch, the woman is in charge of herself in a location where she is traditionally supposed to be passive. On one hand, this simple reversal is classically Second Wave. On another, it strikes me that in this sketch, Warren's character fits Oz's description of Piggy: Warren's character too has had her consciousness raised and still likes diamonds. The wink in particular reads as an ironic invitation to the audience voyeuristically to watch Warren control the scene, and this action can be read by a contemporary audience as very Third Wave. Far from a *Girls Gone Wild* sketch featuring a woman exhibiting herself to the male gaze, this disco scene is being arranged by the woman involved to reveal something about Link, whose hesitancy, no less than the small scarf knotted around his neck, suggests, may not be as overly heterosexual as the Swine Trek Captain might wish to appear.

The Muppet Show launched in an effort to remind audiences that Muppets were adults, too, and not just the children and child-safe adults of *Sesame Street*. Beginning as a vaudeville program inflected by late 1970s progressive politics, Season One is thick with sex, violence, and complex issues of race and gender that could not be performed on *Sesame Street*'s family-friendly stage. *The Muppet Show*'s immediate popularity in England, and eventual popularity in the U.S., provided the show's developers the security to construct a special mode of adult entertainment, capitalizing on the unique possibilities of a cast of Muppets interacting with a human guest star. Nevertheless, the edginess of Season One was curtailed. Season Two finds the cast engaging the stars in less extreme ways, until in Season Three sex and violence are dealt with in a restricted fashion only. In Season Three, while feminist politics continued to be promoted, violence is expressed between Muppets only, and condemned by Muppets and guest stars alike.

Notes

1. The titles of the following sketches are those given by the scene index of the DVD (*Muppets Magic*). The 20 episodes form a representative sample, as the Muppets appeared on *Ed Sullivan* a total of twenty-five times. The Muppets were also featured in numerous commercials, and these appear to be oftentimes violent as well. See the Purina commercials added to the third season's DVD-extras for examples.

2. Moreno's sketches suggest elements of her own life, including her penchant for lunching with guest stars, her later frustration with cue-cards while working on *The Electric Company*, and her role in *The Ritz*. This parallelism suggests that Moreno had some influence on the material of this episode, which was not always the case with guest stars (Finch, *Muppets*, 96, 101). Material about Moreno's life mentioned in the following paragraphs was drawn from her interview with the American Television Academy in 2001.

3. My thanks to Marta Rivera Paczynska at Tufts University: her experience with Puerto Rican idiom made these translations of Spanish possible.

4. Ironically, a viewer watching closely after the top of Morgan's hat "explodes" will note that the hat caught fire in reality (or the materials used to make the smoke failed to burn out), and as the "Talk Spot" ends, the fire appears to spread steadily across the top of the hat.

Works Cited

Barnes, Clive. "Making the Most of 'Ritz' Steam Bath." *New York Times*, Jan. 21, 1975. 34.
Brown, Les. "'The Muppet Show,' Veddy Much at Home Abroad, Thank You," *New York Times*, Jan. 8, 1978. D29, D37.
Considine, Shaun. "A Latin from Manhattan Stars at Last." *New York Times*, March 30, 1975. 79, 84.
Finch, Christopher. *Jim Henson: The Art, the Magic, the Imagination*. Random House: New York, 1993.
_____. *Of Muppets and Men: The Making of the Muppet Show*. Alfred A. Knopf: New York, 1981.
Kerr, Walter. "Albee's Unwritten Part: McNally's Missing Joke." *New York Times*, Feb. 2, 1975. X5.
Moreno, Rita. Interview. American Television Academy. 2001. January 15, 2007. <http://www.emmys.org/foundation/archive/interviews.php>.
Muppets Magic from the Ed Sullivan Show. DVD. Good Times Entertainment, 2003.
The Muppet Show Season One. Jim Henson, DVD. Buena Vista Home Entertainment, 2005.
The Muppet Show Season Two. Jim Henson, DVD. Buena Vista Home Entertainment, 2007.
The Muppet Show Season Three. Jim Henson. DVD. Buena Vista Home Entertainment, 2008.
Skow, John. "Those Marvelous Muppets." *Time*, Monday, Dec. 25, 1978, 4 July, 2008 <http://www.time.com/time/magazine/article/0,9171,948400,00.html>.

"British to a Fang, British to a Whisker": Reconsidering *The Muppet Show*'s National Identity

Rayna Denison

> Listening to these fine entertainers you may think they are American but no, they're not, not at all, they are British to a fang, British to a whisker.... Indeed, all The Muppet Shows were made here at Elstree so they're British all right, we've bagged them, and as the shows have been sold to more than 100 countries they are worth having.
>
> McGill 1977

On the surface, *The Muppet Show* (1976–1981) is an unambiguously American television show. Viewed from a production standpoint, creator Jim Henson, an American, infused the show with many American cultural tropes, besides which the show's star characters had, in large part, been developed for pre-existing American television shows from *Sam and Friends* (1955–1961) to *Sesame Street* (1969–). From an exhibition point of view, *The Muppet Show* was generally shown first in the USA, giving America a proprietary claim to it. Corporately too, Disney's purchase of the franchise has afforded the Muppets with a seemingly unassailable American association.

While all this is true for the Muppets, it is, however, also true that *The Muppet Show* was British.[1] Produced and made in the UK for (Lord) Lew Grade's Associated Television (ATV) company at Elstree Studios in England, it will be argued here that *The Muppet Show* was, in several important ways, also a British show.

Recognition of *The Muppet Show*'s Britishness has been a hit and miss affair. At the time of its initial broadcasts, *The Muppet Show*'s Britishness appears to have been a significant factor in newspaper comment on the show within the UK, and hence this is the primary subject of this chapter. However, outside Britain, and indeed over time, memories of *The Muppet Show*'s Britishness appear to have faded. Despite this apparent forgetfulness, the Britishness of *The Muppet Show* has once again become part of its commercial discourse in recent years with DVD re-releases of the show working in a variety of ways to remind viewers of *The Muppet Show*'s multiple national origins. This chapter will work to demonstrate that Britishness, whether overt, covert or melded into internationalism, remains a substantial aspect of *The Muppet Show*'s history and culture.

Accessing debates about *The Muppet Show*'s national identity requires the demarcation of a field of study. This chapter focuses on two aspects of the show, its texts and its British review context, taking them as the basis for analysis. Using a mixed reception studies methodology that looks at both the show and its reception in the British press (following the work of Janet Staiger and Barbara Klinger) the British past of *The Muppet Show* will be analysed in order to examine its national identity. This investigation will then be embellished with a consideration of the Britishness evident in the recent release of the first two seasons of *The Muppet Show* on DVD. In so doing, it is hoped that this chapter will be able to weigh the relative importance of national identity to *The Muppet Show* and to gauge the ways in which such debates have worked to shape long term understandings of the show.

Opening up discourse around the national identity of *The Muppet Show* makes a further set of debates apparent. These revolve around the authorship of the television show. British reviewers and commentators on *The Muppet Show* in the late 1970s and early 1980s frequently mobilised personalities from its production as authors in order to bolster their claims about the show's nationality. Unlike film studies, where authorship has long been a hotly contested area of study (for a précis of debates see Gerstner and Staiger), in television studies it would seem that the authorship debate has not raged quite so hotly (Thompson and Burns' edited collection provides a good overview of the reasons for such differences). Therefore, while authorship debates in television studies, as elsewhere, do tend to focus on production personnel, unlike film studies, the range of production roles played by the television author goes far beyond the role of "director."

While film studies has remained concerned with the director as author, works regularly appear in television studies and the popular presses that cite the producer, the "creator," the star, or the writer as the individual responsible for bringing the show to air. Producers like David E Kelly, channel and network executives like Michael Grade in the UK, stars like Sarah Jessica

Parker and those undertaking multiple roles, such as Joss Whedon, all feature in work on the authorship of the television text. Despite the variability in the assignment of authorship, however, in television studies, as with film, the notion of collaborative authorship remains under-scrutinized (a concept outlined neatly by VF Perkins). Cathy A. Sandeen and Ronald J. Compesi provide an exception, declaring that "[t]he task of interpreting creative processes of any form involves identifying cooperating production personnel and the mechanisms which help govern routine behavior" (162). They conceptualize such behavior as the formation of authorship networks, saying that "television programs are made possible through the integration and coordination of a myriad of professional roles" (162). This is a useful way to begin thinking through the complex relationships behind the scenes that helped to inform the national identity of *The Muppet Show*. Put another way, in arguing for a reconsideration of *The Muppet Show*'s national identity, it is useful to broaden out claims for its authorship, to move beyond the figure of its creator Jim Henson and to think through who was deemed important at the time of its creation. Finding the key personnel of *The Muppet Show* and delineating its national identity more thoroughly enables a better evaluation of whether, as McGill claims, *The Muppet Show* is really something "worth having" and why.

The Muppet Shows — *Locating and Remembering National Identity*

Part of the difficulty in attempting to outline the nationality of *The Muppet Show* rests in the fact that there was not one version but many versions of the show available throughout the world. Press reports from the late 1970s state that the show was available in over 100 nations worldwide and viewed by almost as many millions weekly (Last). *The Muppet Show* was, therefore, an internationally available show that had no "authentic" or singular textual existence. Rather, it was cut, recut, dubbed and otherwise altered dependent on where it was being screened. The text's variability supplies one of the central reasons for its appreciation now as an American product. It would seem that audiences and commentators alike tend to pick up on those elements that are least changed and therefore most easily recognizable when assigning both nationality and authorship to texts. However, returning to those initial texts and working through the changes that were made, and the effects such changes may have had, means that we become better able to speak with authority about its identity and authorship. In doing so, it is not my intention to imply that there was a single version of *The Muppet Show*, but rather that the competing versions available have impacted on how the show has been understood. By thinking through the British aspects of the show and the ways the show was altered for its British broadcasting, the importance of Britishness to *The Muppet Show* begins to become apparent.

In describing the ways in which *The Muppet Show* was made, the show's sole Season One director, Peter Harris, outlined the weekly schedule saying that the bulk of production took place Mondays to Thursdays, but "Friday, we re-edit the previous week's American show to get the British version. Ours is two minutes longer, with only one break, not three, so Jim does extra material that we have to work in" (Fiddick). Harris works here to differentiate and create production hierarchies in relation to the different versions of the show. His own British nationality is worked into the discussion in order to prioritize the show's British version ("our" version) while the preceding American version is presented as more disrupted and less complete. This commentary is then compounded when Peter Fiddick's article continues: "The effort has paid off. Jim Henson thinks the style and speed of the humor have helped make it a bigger hit in Britain than anywhere else" (Fiddick). In this description of the show and its working practices, even its American creator apparently places the British version higher in the hierarchy of *Muppet Show*s than its American counterpart. While these comments appear in a British newspaper, and therefore may well be expected to present a pro-British reading of the show, there is ample justification here to perform a reading of the "British" extra materials added to Seasons One and Two as these should indicate what relationship these textual elements had to national identity.

The texts of *The Muppet Show* contain a variety of references to the show's British roots, from British stars appearing as guests, to British cultural references in sketches, to the discrete segments added to the show to meet the demands of its longer and less interrupted broadcasting. These latter discrete textual elements were widely varied, with some making direct reference to British culture while others made none at all. Moreover, these segments also varied widely in their format and content, most frequently containing songs, but also occasionally being comprised of comedic sketches. The most commonly recurring sketch type sees Rowlf the Dog at a piano in the centre of a simple set, performing a song. Examples of this in the first season can be seen in the episodes starring Ruth Buzzi, Jim Nabors, Florence Henderson, Sandy Duncan, Candice Bergen, Avery Schreiber, Ben Vereen, Twiggy and, with Sam the Eagle, Valerie Harper. In fact, these were the primary sketches that featured Rowlf, who, with the exception of his appearances in "Veterinarian's Hospital" sketches, was otherwise a relatively minor figure within *The Muppet Show*'s early narratives.

The list accounts for almost half the first season, and there is a noticeable difference in quality between these skits and those in the rest of *The Muppet Show*. The sketches tend not to be introduced by another Muppet character, but are, rather, inserted without comment near the middle of the show.

Rowlf's sets tend to be very simple in these song numbers, frequently containing little more than Rowlf sitting at a piano in front of a painted backdrop. Moreover, the camerawork tends to be simple, for example, two camera set ups and the use of slow zooms, with character movement and editing creating the majority of the "movement" within the shots. When performing the song "Cottleston Pie" in the Florence Henderson episode, for example, we are provided with a profile shot of Rowlf at the piano (performed by Jim Henson, singing as Rowlf's body and head, while a trained pianist performed Rowlf's hands). In the background, a beige back wall with a painted motif is the only remaining detail of the set. The song begins with a zoom out from a tight shot of Rowlf playing, coming to rest in a medium shot. The camera then remains static, but a second shot of Rowlf's hands playing the piano is inserted just once, to emphasize the "real" performance being undertaken by the puppeteers (for more on Muppets and performance see Denison and Tillis). From this example, it should be clear that there was little of the stylized camera work (which often included complex lenses and trick photography), editing and multi-level staging and multiple camera set-ups that became hallmarks of the rest of *The Muppet Show*. While there are obvious reasons for this simplicity, from the guest star's departure, to the need to be able to add the sequences in relatively short spaces of time, this scaled-back series of songs also implies that the British aspects of the show were not a high priority.

However, there were notable exceptions to this rule. In the Vincent Price episode from Season One, for example, the horror movie theme of the show is continued in a special British spot that sees ghost Muppets superimposed on the shot while they sing "I'm Looking through You." In another, and perhaps more significant exception, in the Joel Grey episode, a Sherlock Holmes spoof titled "Sherlock Holmes and the Case of the Disappearing Clues" is staged, featuring Rowlf as Holmes, with another dog Muppet named Baskerville playing Watson. The sketch is not musical and takes place in a drawing room as a human sized monster, playing the butler, proceeds to eat all the evidence of the murder he committed, including an early version of Miss Piggy, playing the maid. This sketch is culturally interesting as it parodies the well-known British murder mystery series by Sir Arthur Conan Doyle and is also exceptional due to its elaborate staging, multiple Muppet characters, and violent content. As the variety in the segments should indicate, while the British portions of *The Muppet Show* were not necessarily integral to the overall narrative arcs of each episode, they were nevertheless important to the integrity of the show overall. It would seem even from these few examples that, in fact, these British segments became both a showcase for one of the most memorable Muppet characters, Rowlf the Dog, and that they presented (albeit scaled back) opportunities to foreground the performative aspects of the Muppets' puppetry.

These segments also had commercial significance. "Cottleston Pie" was one of a number of songs performed for the British version of *The Muppet Show* that later made their way onto "*The Muppet Show* Album," a record produced in 1977 (by Arista Records). While such famous songs seen by American and UK audiences as "Mahna Mahna" appeared on the album, so did a number of songs unknown outside of *The Muppet Show*'s Britain incarnation. One example, taken from the Valerie Harper episode, featured Sam the Eagle and Rowlf performing "Tit Willow." Rowlf proclaims the "cultural" value of the song in order to get Sam to perform its chorus, which he does, reading the title of the song in a monotone. The deadpan verbal humor derived from the performance translates well to the non-visual record medium, providing an insight into the forward thinking of Henson and Frank Oz, who perform the song sketch. Given the album's international availability, it would be fair to posit that the British version of *The Muppet Show* played a vital part in the wider intertext of the show, adding significantly to its profits and not just to its cultural transferability.

A further textual element of the show's Britishness, or lack thereof, which created comment in the 1970s, was its use of guest stars. An *Evening Standard* article from 1979 claimed that the British Independent Broadcast Authority (IBA) had cited *The Muppet Show* as a "British" program featuring "too many foreign names" ("Muppets—Too many foreigners"). Indeed, Season One of *The Muppet Show* featured a heavily American (and other non–British stars like Charles Aznavour) set of guest stars, with only a few British names, whereas Season Two found an almost 50–50 balance (Last). British stars from Season One included Twiggy and Bruce Forsyth, while, once the popularity of the show had been cemented, the second Season featured a wider variety and higher profile set of British star names from Peter Sellers to Elton John. On the surface this trend might indicate a growing recognition of the Britishness of *The Muppet Show* across its first two seasons, and a recognition of the domestic industry and audiences that supported it in Britain. However, a closer look at some examples will challenge this view and will demonstrate that the accents and presences of guest stars were not necessarily any more nationally fixed than was the case for the show itself.

In an early episode from Season One, British model and star Twiggy guest starred on *The Muppet Show*, performing in a range of sketches. In particular she performed several musical numbers, one of which sees her dressed as an American country girl and performing with an American accent. Peter Ustinov and Peter Sellers likewise performed a variety of comedic sketches in their episodes wherein the focus was on their virtuosity of accented performance. In one sketch from the Ustinov episode, for instance, he appears with Bunsen Honeydew as a mimic robot that can do a variety of national accents belonging to world leaders, performing everything from a Russian

Premiere to a British Prime Minister and an American President before devolving into a mixed language rant in languages and accents from Chinese to Italian in the space of a couple of minutes. Sellers performed more throughout his episode as divergently inflected national character types. He opens the episode, for example, performing as a Traveller or gypsy and in a later sketch performs as a physical therapist who is uncomfortably close to Adolf Hitler in accent and tone. As these examples should imply, the British national identity of British stars on *The Muppet Show* was not always emphasized and, indeed, their international or transnational performance-based personae may well have worked to mask their British origins.

One interesting exception to this is presented in the Season One Bruce Forsyth episode. Kermit's introduction to Forsyth is interesting as it actually emphasizes the comedian and emcee's British stardom, overtly attempting to explain Forsyth's star persona for a non–British audience:

> Hello, hello, hello. And if I sound a little British tonight it's because our special guest star is one of England's truly great performers, Mr. Bruce Forsyth. He sings, dances, plays the piano, tells jokes, in fact he's a one man variety show and we're really pleased to have him with us.

Similar introductions can be found for other guest stars whose star personae were not well established, or not based, in America. Introducing Charles Aznavour, for example, Kermit says, "Bonsoir, bonsoir, Mesdames et Messieurs. Ah, that's 'ladies and gentlemen.' You'll notice a little French sneaking into my speech." Here we can see how the Frenchman's national identity becomes an excuse for *The Muppet Show* characters to explore alternative national identities, accenting the whole of the episode. Therefore, accent in *The Muppet Show* worked in two basic directions, on the one path reinforcing the normalized American accent of the show and its characters, while occasionally on another working to obfuscate alternative nationalities or even, on rare occasions, to celebrate it.

British Reception of The Muppet Show: *Authors Everywhere*

If the accent of the show was normally American, then this was mainly the result of the American puppeteers who worked on *The Muppet Show*, behind (and indeed under) the scenes. However, an examination of *The Muppet Show*'s British reception reveals perhaps unexpected patterns of Britishness appearing in conjunction not just with the show's guest stars, but also amongst its hidden human cast. Three examples are worth exploring in some depth here, as they work to counter the notion that *The Muppet Show* was solely the product and creation of Jim Henson: Frank Oz, Lew Grade and Louise Gold.

In a set of articles that appeared in the British Press following Open Days at the Elstree Studios in 1977 and 1981, Frank Oz was consistently mobilised as one of the central creative personae behind *The Muppet Show*. In the first instance, Peter Fiddick, writing in 1977, ambivalently comments: "I found myself in a cluster of people, most of whom also looked old enough to know better, round this slim six foot, chicly balding, all–American guy squeaking like a lady pig" (Fiddick). In this article, Fiddick's focus is on the "identity problems" suffered by Oz, and it is Oz's relationship with his performance object, Miss Piggy, that becomes the locus of the article. However, in amongst the discussion of Oz's identity crisis, a star persona begins to be wrought for him. As the previous passage indicates, physical characteristics that mismatch with his on-screen puppet characters are emphasized, particularly around gender. Just as significantly, however, a concurrent discourse around his American national identity also emerges in the cliché of the "all American guy." Just four years later, at another Open Day at Elstree, Byron Rogers wrote a second in-depth exposé of the making of *The Muppet Show*. Rogers begins by asserting the ambivalent relationship between Kermit ("a public figure") and Jim Henson ("only begetter of the Muppets") (Rogers). The primacy of both Henson and his most famous character seem assured here, until the journalist abruptly segues into a much more lengthy discussion and interview with Frank Oz. Oz is described as the "chief puppeteer" of *The Muppet Show* and also as "probably the most accomplished puppeteer in the world." After asserting these credentials, Rogers then moves on to appropriate Oz for the British: "He was born in England, where his parents paused on their eastward exodus out of Poland, and was brought up in California" (29). Here, Rogers carefully inserts a modicum of British national identity in the broader authorial discourse he works to create around Oz, and while it is only a small part of that persona, it nonetheless challenges the hitherto unproblematically American identity of *The Muppet Show*'s behind the scenes personnel.

In a similar move, British identity is compounded by repeated reference to producer Lew Grade (head of the ATV production company that made *The Muppet Show*). In his role as the producer of *The Muppet Show*, Grade is commonly cited in relation to industrial discourses, rather than creative discourses, circulating around the show. For example, in 1979, the *Sunday Mirror* ran a short article titled "Miss Piggy Sees Red" discussing *The Muppet Show*'s potential broadcast in Russia. Here, Grade (by this point Lord Lew Grade) is the only member of the production team mentioned, and in relation to a recent meeting with the Pope he is quoted as saying, "No, I did not leave His Holiness a cassette of the Muppets" (*Sunday Mirror*). Grade's political power and high profile are emphasized by these remarks, but his relationship with *The Muppet Show* is problematized by the wary tone of his comments.

In a second series of articles, also from 1979, another industry-led Grade-centred discourse emerged when it was claimed that the "Muppets Face Exile" (Pratt). Five weeks into a strike by the Independent Television Network's (ITV) workers (under the auspices of the ACTT union), reportedly over pay and the use of new technologies, Grade announced that "[t]here is a danger that England will lose the Muppets" (*Morning Star*). Citing the need to produce half a series of *The Muppet Show* in time for international export, Grade claimed to be considering offers from France and Germany to shift production to the Continent (Pratt). Here, the proposed move is discussed by journalists as "exile" (Pratt) and deportation (*Morning Star*). In the first case, the national implication is one of Britishness, with the show being forced to leave its country of origin, but in the latter, there is a sense of tenuous or uncertain national connection. As if to accent this point, the industry discourse around Grade is extended to the show in the *Morning Star*, which asserts that "the popular Muppets TV series were yesterday threatened with export from Britain by Lord Grade" (*Morning Star*). "Export" positions the show as a product, and Grade as the businessman responsible for it; however, the sense of a loss to Britain, rather than any inherent Britishness is the key term in which *The Muppet Show*'s relationship to Britishness is mobilized here. The layering of industry discourses around Lew Grade would seem, therefore, to consistently relate to the show's relationship to national identity, rather than to Grade's status as a British producer. Moreover, the distance between the show's textuality and Lew Grade's involvement with it is repeatedly emphasized, thereby implicating the producer with the show's circulation and distribution more than with its creative production. Therefore, while Grade is consistently presented as a key figure in the discourses of *The Muppet Show*, his apparent distance from its creative personnel and textuality would seem to deny his role as an author of the text.

Jim Henson, on the other hand, was presented as central to the definition of *The Muppet Show*'s national identity. In most cases where he is mentioned, Henson is referred to as, or discussed in relation to, the show's American national identity. However, Henson can also be seen to have been searching for British talent from very early in the show's existence. For example, shortly before winning the Golden Rose of Montreaux prize in 1977, Ken Irwin wrote that Henson and company were "looking for a couple of British actresses to train as puppeteers to join them in the new series—to play the girly roles beneath those strange characters" (Irwin "Muppetmania!"). Shortly thereafter, in another articles, Irwin writes that "now Henson has just signed up 21-year-old actress Louise Gold. *She now spends hours every day practising hand movements in front of a huge mirror ... surrounded by 200 puppets*" (Irwin

"Muppetmania makes a million!," emphasis in original). This latter quotation occurs at the very end of a relatively long article on the success of *The Muppet Show*. It gives Gold's employment the final word in the discourse around the show, implying its increasingly British composition as well as her importance to its continuing success. However, Gold's junior role in the show (her training and, in later reports, her performance of a new character rather than as one of the established Muppet characters, see Ewbank) also offers an understanding of her position as subordinate to the show's original American performers and her additional Britishness as subordinate to an otherwise overwhelming Americanness. Similarly, Gold's hiring for the show is authorized by Henson, who legitimates her presence through intensive training; a training system originated by Henson himself. In this way, Gold's employment brings with it a muted Britishness constrained by American authors.

The British press, through these discussions can be seen to have been negotiating *The Muppet Show*'s national identity; to have been highlighting Britishness where it was only marginal, or where it was subordinated, while also working to create alternative readings of the show's production, with creativity couched in Americanness and business in Britishness. These negotiations were an important method by which the show's authorship was extended beyond its "only begetter," into discussions of the increasingly internationalized Anglo-American identity of *The Muppet Show*. While the Muppets may have started out American, the transportation of the show to Britain and the various production personnel added to the Muppets in order to create *The Muppet Show* produced a series of challenges to any simplistic reading of the show as "American." The next and final section of this chapter is intended to complicate this reading of *The Muppet Show*'s ambiguous national identity even further, discussing the ways in which the "lost" British past of the show is being rediscovered through its relationship with new technologies.

The Expandable Text and the Rediscovery of Britishness in The Muppet Show

The British aspects of *The Muppet Show* were fragmented and lost in the same fashion as the texts were fragmented and altered depending on their multi-national (re-)broadcast contexts. Moreover, once *The Muppet Show* finished its initial cycle of broadcasting, much of the nuanced national identity fought for by British journalists seems to have passed out of mind, particularly in light of subsequent *Muppet Show* film and cartoon spin-offs. These spin offs increased the levels of fragmentation, sometimes recounting the show's Britishness (as in *The Great Muppet Caper*, which was set in England) and sometimes eliding it. The *Muppet Babies* (1984–1991) animated series was more overtly American in content (for analysis of the cartoon, see Kinder 62–71). British national identity decreased in importance over time, then, as the show ceased its British production and attention shifted to ancillary and more temporally discontinuous texts. However, since the growth of DVD, a new market and new audiences for the original *Muppet Show* texts have appeared. Furthermore, due to the nature of the release of *The Muppet Show* on DVD, a growing recognition of the show's British past is being disseminated to these new audiences. Whether for the purposes of nostalgia, or in the name of creating an ever more "complete" understanding of *The Muppet Show*, DVD has become a crucial factor in remembering the British past of the Muppets.

Barbara Klinger has been instrumental in opening up discussions around DVD and film collecting cultures and in recognizing that these cultures are in turn affecting the texts being produced. In a discussion around the range in DVD texts produced for consumers and the importance of special edition DVDs produced to encourage specialized film collection, Klinger asserts that

> In their ability to "remake" a film, successive special editions enable the kind of product differentiation so important to the repurposing, that is, to the strategy of reselling the same titles. In the process, through shifting supplemental materials, the feature film has an instant built-in and changeable intertextual surround that enters into its meaning and significance for viewers.... Given that films today are often shot with the idea of saving certain footage for DVD release, the notion of the expandable text has become an intimate part of the production process [Klinger 72].

Much the same can be said for the way television shows are now being produced on DVD for the home market. There tend, however, to be fewer "special edition" DVDs for television shows, perhaps because television texts tend to be much longer and therefore more resource intensive to produce and more expensive to purchase. Many series now run at 20 or more episodes per season, requiring between four and six DVDs on average whereas films only *require* a single disc. Special edition film DVDs now tend to be multi-disc affairs, with usually one disc containing the film and additional discs containing extra special features. Television shows, on the other hand, tend to be already packaged as multi-disc sets, and therefore when special features are included, they tend to be attached to either individual episodes or provided as a part of the final disc for the season. Television's special features therefore tend to act on the individual episode texts as well as on the overall meanings of the shows, indicating perhaps a greater level of expandability than is the case for the film text. Moreover, as was the case with *The Muppet Show*, DVD is also being used in more experimental ways in relation to television than is the case for film, resulting in potentially greater shifting textual and intertextual meanings.

Though it was not shot with the intention to "save" portions of footage for DVD productions, *The Muppet Show*'s releases on DVD exemplify the nature of textual experimentation and repackaging taking place in relation to the television DVD. Like some other popular series, for example, *Buffy the Vampire Slayer* (1997–2003) and *Family Guy* (1999–), when *The Muppet Show* was initially released on DVD, it was done so piecemeal in fragmented collections titled *The Very Best of The Muppet Show*.[2] Instead of providing complete seasons, these "*Very Best of*" DVDs contained the episodes from the show that were most likely to attract cross-over audiences, for example the Mark Hamill *Star Wars* themed episode and the Sylvester Stallone episode. In addition to these full episodes, these single disc releases contained "50-minute edited compilation[s] of the funniest sketches from various shows" (DVD back cover, *The Very Best of The Muppet Show, Vol. 1* (2002), a refrain repeated on the back of each volume describing similarly edited fragments from each season). These edited compilations repackaged *The Muppet Show*, condensing whole seasons into short, fragmented sketches containing the most famous guest stars, historically popular sketches, and the most memorable song numbers from the show. The effect of these compilations was to largely elide *The Muppet Show*'s episodic narratives, to delete from the show's history any potentially "weak" or unpopular sketches, and to highlight sketches redolent with intertextual pop culture references, like the sketch that starred Miss Piggy as the Wonder Woman-inspired "Wonder Pig." Though these DVDs essentially eviscerated the original show, they did have the benefit of making *The Muppet Show* available for repeatable home viewing for the first time since their initial broadcasts (home video recording notwithstanding). As the first legitimate way in which to re-view and collect *The Muppet Show*, these DVDs acted to whet the appetite of television DVD collectors while, at the same time, providing a largely de-contextualized re-envisioning of the show.

It was not until release of *The Muppet Show Series One Special Edition Four-Disc Box Set* in its entirety in 2004, that *The Muppet Show*'s British past once again began to be embraced and remembered by its industrial owners. In the first place, this was the first time that *The Muppet Show* was released in its entirety in Britain. In the second, this release was the first time that special features really began to insist on the cultural importance of Britain to *The Muppet Show*. Although *The Very Best of The Muppet Show*'s various volumes contained "making of" featurettes that cited the British locale of *The Muppet Show*'s creation, in this special edition box-set for Season One, repeated attention can be drawn to the complete and British nature of DVD texts, via the "Muppet Morsels" special feature. The "Muppet Morsels" are described in the packaging as a "special PLAY mode filled with fun facts about the Muppets." Actually, the "Muppet Morsels" function might be better thought of as intended for (adult) fans, focused as they are on the details of the show's production ranging from the dates that the shows were recorded and aired, to descriptions of how the shows sketches were constructed, to drawing attention to which scenes were added for the British versions of each episode. Referred to as "UK spots" in the "Muppet Morsels," the singling out of each UK spot in each episode enhances perceptions of the discs as high quality versions of the text and raises up the British version as the most complete, and therefore most desirable, version of *The Muppet Show*.

Conclusions

>JANICE (to Zoot): "You know, just once I'd like to stand next to Queen Elizabeth."
>ZOOT: "Ah, I'd rather sit in with Count Basey" ["Peter Ustinov," Season One].

The second of *The Muppet Show* seasons has, at the time of writing, just been released on DVD (2007). Unlike the first, it does not provide the "Muppet Morsels" that emphasized the Muppet's (rediscovered) Britishness. However, the season does contain the near 50–50 split in guest stars previously discussed, so it is not unreasonable to assume that the British orientation of the show is more overt in the newer series, and therefore that it may require less explanation. Or, equally, the more stream-lined and less expansively intertextual approach to the Season Two DVDs may indicate instead a return to assumptions about and recognitions of *The Muppet Show* as American. In this respect, at least, *The Muppet Show*'s release on DVD reflects a similar pattern to its initial broadcast cycle, perpetuating the show's complex relationship to its national origins. Moreover, the DVD texts are both new and old at the same time, providing newcomers to the franchise with their first opportunities to read the show, while at the same time serving a set of audiences who watched it the first time around. The perceptions of these two groups are liable to be very different, and more research would be needed before any definitive statements could be made about whether or not Britishness is important to the global audiences for the show.

Nonetheless, this does not alter the fact that Britishness pervades *The Muppet Show*. It is in the show's texts: in the quotation above, Janice makes reference to the British monarchy, wistfully wishing to be able to interact with the Queen. In other examples we can see Fozzie Bear ambiguously claiming that he's "good enough to play the Palace," without being clear if he means Buckingham or an unknown theatre. In yet another example, performing a British song and dance number in Season Two, Kermit, Fozzie and a variety of other characters appear in stereotypical, old-fashioned British costumes ("Don Knotts," "Burlington Bertie"). From dialogue to costuming to the stars and extra sketches, *The Muppet Show* was filled with overt and covert references to British culture.

The Britishness of *The Muppet Show* goes further than its texts, as meanings were accrued to the show through its reception. The show's authorship was expanded beyond Jim Henson, at least in Britain, and even its most seemingly American aspects were probed for British connections. That Frank Oz, a very American accented performer, was cited as a potentially British aspect of the show's creation indicates how deep the search for British meaning in *The Muppet Show* went in the late 1970s and early 1980s. Consequently, as a diverse range of British aspects of the show came to be discussed in the press, it becomes more and more possible to read the show as a British property. In so doing, it is not my intention to argue that *The Muppet Show* was not American but rather to open up discussions of its potential meanings at differing historically significant moments, in order to be able to better discern how *The Muppet Show*'s meanings have changed over time and what it meant to specific people in those historically significant moments. By not treating *The Muppet Show* as a monolithic and unchanging entity, rich nuances can be discerned in both its texts and the texts that circulated around it.

DVDs have broadened the scope of such arguments even further. In the case of the Season One special edition of *The Muppet Show*, DVD is both a forward and backward looking technology. The "Muppet Morsels" for instance, work to create a "traffic in trivia" (Klinger 74) that helps to foster Muppet fandom, inasmuch as the trivia could be viewed as providing access to, and explanation of, a now historically distant production process and phenomenon.

The Muppet Show is therefore no different from any other media text in that understanding its meanings requires engagement with the text in context. The contexts investigated here have produced a set of readings that show how contested, changeable and uncertain national identity can be. For *The Muppet Show*, being "British to a fang, British to a whisker" means that the show was embraced by a review culture that sought to make it its own; that its phenomenal status was such that the British press negotiated with its American aspects to create a British identity that legitimated its regular and wildly popular appearances on British television screens. To put this in its context, Angua McGill, writing for the *Evening Standard* claims, in March 1977, that

> On the stroke of 5.15, I happened to be walking through the radio and television department of Harrods and there, on a third of the television sets in the place was Kermit, waving his green arms about.
>
> Everybody, customers and assistants alike, paused and edged towards him. The other sets were all busy with The Pink Panther and some ducks but no one paid them heed.
>
> All eyes were on Fozzie Bear's duet with Peter Ustinov. Thank goodness the show finished at 5.45 or they'd never have got the store shut [McGill].

The compulsive, hypnotic viewing conditions described by McGill reveal the phenomenal proportions of *The Muppet Show*'s British success and, indeed, many of the reasons behind attempts to mark the show as belonging to "us" in Britain. So, perhaps in a denial of the earlier quote from McGill's article, it is not the fact that *The Muppet Show* was sold across the world that made it worth having. Perhaps instead, we could reconsider that it was "worth having" because it was so much a part of British culture.

Notes

1. When referring to "British" nationality, the term is intended to cover the very English production of *The Muppet Show* as well as its broadcast and reception throughout the British Isles.
2. Fragmentations of television shows, and their repackaging in order to extend the franchise or brand of the show, have taken a variety of forms. For example, for *Buffy the Vampire Slayer*, character based discs were produced in addition to the box-sets for each season of the show, providing highlighted episodes from multiple seasons. For *Family Guy*, and other animated shows like *Spongebob Squarepants* (1999–), seasonal episodes have been collected onto special holiday-oriented DVD releases.

Works Cited

Denison, Rayna. "*The Muppet Show*: 'Sex and Violence': Confusion around the Muppet Body." *Intensities Journal* 4 (Winter 2007). <http://intensities.org/Issues/Intensities_Four.htm> (last accessed 08/02/08).
Gerstner, David A., and Janet Staiger. *Authorship and Film*. New York: Routledge, 2003.
Kinder, Marsha. *Playing with Power in Movies, Television and Video Games: From Muppet Babies to Teenage Mutant Ninja Turtles*. Berkeley: University of California Press, 1991.
Klinger, Barbara. *Beyond the Multiplex: Cinema, New Technologies, and the Home*. Berkeley: University of California Press, 2006.
_____. "The Contemporary Cinephile: Film Collecting in the Post-video Era." *Hollywood Spectatorship: Changing Perspectives of Cinema Audiences*. Ed. Richard Maltby and Melvyn Stokes. London: British Film Institute, 2001. 132–151.
_____. *Melodrama and Meaning: History, Culture and the Films of Douglas Sirk*. Bloomington: Indiana University Press, 1994.
Making Television: Authorship and the Production Process. Ed. Robert J. Thompson and Gary Burns. New York: Praeger, 1990. 161–174.
Perkins, VF. "Film Authorship — The Premature Burial." *CineAction!* 21–22 (November 1990): 57–64.
Sandeen, Cathy A., and Ronald J. Compesi. "Television Production as Collective Action."
Staiger, Janet. *Interpreting Films: Studies in the Historical Reception of American Cinema* Princeton, NJ: Princeton University Press, 1992.
_____. *Media Reception Studies*. New York: New York University Press, 2005.
Thompson, Robert J., and Gary Burns. *Making Television: Authorship and the Production Process*. New York: Praeger, 1990.
Tillis, Steve. "The Actor Occluded: Puppet Theatre and Acting Theory," *Theatre Topics*. 6.2 (1996):109–119.

British Film Institute Newspaper Clippings Collection

Davies, Russell. "Civilisation and its Contents." *Sunday Times*, 22 Aug. 1981.
Ewbank, Tim. "Bad news for Miss Piggy!" *Sun*, 04 Mar. 1978.
Fiddick, Peter. "All hands on deck." *Guardian*, 23 May 1977.
Ingrams, Richard. "*The Muppet Show*." *Spectator*, 07 Jan. 1978.
Irwin, Ken. "Muppetmania!" *Daily Mirror*, 14 May 1977.
_____. "Muppetmania makes a million!" *Daily Mirror* 17 Aug. 1977.
Last, Richard. "£280,000-an-hour to run Muppets." *Daily Telegraph* 27 Aug. 1977.
Lewin, David. "The Muppet file." *Sunday Mirror* 09 Sep. 1979.
McGill, Angua. "Never Mind that Frog Ms Piggy—I Love You!" *Evening Standard*, 16 Mar. 1977.
"Muppets—Too many foreigners." *Evening Standard*, 07 Mar. 1979.
North, Richard. "Under the tables with Kermit." *Observer*, 08 Oct. 1977: 47–50.
"Oh no! Muppets may go!" *Sun*, 14 Sep. 1979.
Pratt, Tony. "Muppets Face Exile." *Daily Mirror*, 14 Sep. 1979.
Rogers, Byron. "Puppet Love." *Daily Mail Weekend*, 02 Apr. 1994: 6–8.
_____. "Puppet Love." *Sunday Telegraph*, 26 Jul. 1981: 29.

The Muppet Show as Educational Critique
Julie G. Maudlin

Perhaps the most memorable sketch that comes to mind when one thinks about *The Muppet Show* and education is that of Alice Cooper and the hairy, full-bodied Muppet monsters performing "School's Out" in the closing number of a third season episode that aired on November 2, 1978. Cooper is accompanied by his own backup band, the Vile Bunch, a motley crew of curious creatures and, during the mayhem, Muppet-monster Thog appears and sets off an explosion with a firecracker. A dark, haunted-house like school stands in a shadowed back-drop, and, as he dances among the brightly-colored, misshapen monsters dressed as students, Cooper rips off his black graduation attire to reveal a red devil suit, complete with tail. The performance ends with a final explosion, flinging paper and plaster all over the stage as a gleeful Cooper gnaws on a giant bone.

Aside from that one unforgettable sketch, there are virtually no distinct references to school, students, or anything that could be directly interpreted as "educational" in any of the later episodes of *The Muppet Show*. Why, then, is it worthwhile to consider the show as a form of educational critique? On a personal level, the desire to ponder the educational insights offered by this cultural phenomenon stems from a position as a teacher-educator, a student and fan of popular culture, and a child of the late 1970s whose early identity development was largely influenced by Jim Henson's wacky characters. From the perspective of curriculum theory, a field that employs both historical and philosophical approaches to critically analyzing educational curriculum and policy decisions, it is worthwhile to examine forms of popular media, particularly iconic and personally relevant ones, as "texts" to be read and analyzed. Utilizing this theoretical lens, texts such as *The Muppet Show* can be examined as forms of "critical pedagogy," which have been most recognizably defined by Ira Shor as "habits of thought, reading, writing, and speaking" that go beyond "surface meaning, first impressions, dominant myths, official pronouncements, traditional clichés, received wisdom, and mere opinions" and allow us to discover the deep meaning of "any action, event, object, process, organization, experience, text, subject matter, policy, mass media, or discourse" (129).

In examining *The Muppet Show* as a way of thinking and acting that holds insight for educators, the insights of curriculum scholars can provide some context for critical analysis. As Daspit and Weaver note, "When critical theories offer their reading of popular culture texts, they often emphasize the ways in which the texts re-inscribe or resist the hegemonic status of power blocs" (xxvi.) While this tradition of critical reading should continue, it is also important to recognize "how popular culture texts contain their own pedagogical messages that share in our vision as critical theorists" (xxvi). Thus, the question remains, what pedagogical messages does *The Muppet Show* hold for its viewers? *The Muppet Show* is not exactly what one might consider an "educational" show. Therefore, the pedagogical insights of *The Muppet Show* are not readily apparent and thus require some interpretative digging. In order to speak in terms of "educational" value, it is necessary to first establish what *The Muppet Show* is *not*, which is its public television predecessor, *Sesame Street*.

Years before Jim Henson's Muppets segued into prime time, they made a huge impact on children's programming with the introduction of *Sesame Street*, which premiered on November 10, 1969, on the National Educational Television (NET) network, and moved the following year to that network's replacement, the Public Broadcasting Service. It is fitting that *Sesame Street* appeared on television in the closing weeks of 1969, because it signaled the beginning of a new era during which public views on education and the impact of the media were heavily influenced by societal changes.

As society and culture underwent the rapid transformation of the baby boomer coming of age, the post–Sputnik concern for the future of American education continued to grow. As Louis J. Rubin, who was working as a curriculum consultant at the time, notes, "We began comparing the achievement of American youths, along with the status of our culture and our scientific progress, with the communist block. The argument was that if we took a page out of their book, we could create better scientists" (qtd. in Marshall et al. 41). As a result, the Progressive child and society-centered ideals and the democratic aims of education that had been the focus of educational developments in the early part of the century became overshadowed by more scientific approaches that looked to behavioral and cognitive psychology, as well as discipline specialists, to enhance the rigor of American curriculum. The interests and life experiences of students, which had been the focus of the work of Progressive theorists like the prolific John Dewey, soon took a backseat to subject matter, and teachers were expected to become human conduits for the transmission of essential knowledge.

The burgeoning idealism of Progressive education, with its humanistic focus on personal experience, appealed to the liberal ideals of those whose desires for morality and justice had been awakened by the Civil Rights struggle, and the conflicts between an old guard that sought to reestablish the supremacy of science and a new generation that wanted to escape parents' controlling grasp erupted in the decade of political turmoil and change that was the 1960s. It was during this decade of dissent and transformation that concerns about the potential detrimental effects of mass media, particularly movies and television, were a subject of widespread debate, especially in light of newly developing trends toward flamboyant excess and liberal attitudes toward sex and experimentation with illegal substances. As the influence of cognitive science grew, so did the interest in how Americans, particularly children, were being impacted by the explosion of visual mass media. These concerns were brought to light when, at the 1961 meeting of the National Association of Broadcasters, Newton Minow, the head of the FCC, launched an attack on television, declaring that it was a "vast wasteland" (Baughman 61). He claimed that television consisted of nothing more than a deplorable cycle of "game shows, violence, audience participation shows, formula comedies about totally unbelievable families, blood and thunder, mayhem, violence, sadism, murder, Western bad men, Western good men, private eyes, gangsters, more violence, screaming, cajoling and offending" (Baughman 61). Minow's speech led in part to the formation of the Carnegie Commission on Educational Television, and in 1967, President Lyndon Johnson accepted the Commission's recommendations to enact legislation that would formalize the role of commercial television as producing "low culture programs" while establishing the production of "high culture" programs as the goal of public television (Spring 395). This legislation not only recognized the mass educational and social reform potential of television, but it also formally established a binary between commercial and educational programming. The commission's proposal also bestowed on children's educational television the role of preparing preschool children for formal education, establishing a model in which the television (like the teacher in the subject-matter model) becomes the vessel by which young children, especially disadvantaged preschoolers who might not otherwise have access to early preparation, could be indoctrinated through government-approved curricula. Utilizing federal funds, the commission spearheaded the creation of the Children's Television Workshop to produce a children's series, and the success of the commission was evidenced in the almost-immediate success of *Sesame Street*. In fact, during the first year the show was broadcast, it was estimated that nearly half of the preschool-age audience watched the program, and in certain low-income sections of New York City, the audience increased to over 90 percent of at-home children (Lesser).

Unlike *The Muppet Show*, *Sesame Street* had a very distinct didactic approach, as its primary goal was to teach children basic academic, life, and social skills. The show was formatted as a series of short commercial-like segments that varied among live-action, animation, and Muppet vignettes. The skills were taught to viewers through repetition, along with colorful and engaging visuals to accompany the concepts being addressed. The Muppet and human characters also explicitly taught academic content and introduced life and social skills (such as safety, sharing, etc.) through "real-life" situations. In spite of subtle adult humor, like parodies of typical "high culture" shows, designed to entice parents to watch the show alongside their children, the show became widely known for its appeal to the young, and Henson's Muppets were deemed by network executives as children's entertainment (Finch 81).

The overwhelming popularity of *Sesame Street* established the value of television as an educational tool and signaled the beginning of a passive "video" curriculum that would soon become commonplace in America's schools and continues to influence curriculum today. What is more significant here, however, is the fact that Jim Henson's Muppets, the primary characters of *Sesame Street*, were employed in an educational campaign that was cultivated by fear. Certainly, the desire of government officials to exercise more control over television might have stemmed from the growing conflicts that characterized the late 1960s and early 1970s. Divisiveness seemed to loom at every turn, in the conflicts between communism and capitalism, the glaring economic and civil rights disparities of North and South, and the well-known philosophical differences of East and West.

Sesame Street illustrated the more passive, technical approach to education that was poised to dominate the curriculum field in the 1970s, and it served as evidence of the growing belief that students of all ages were empty vessels who could be filled with the appropriate content through passive instructional strategies. However, while the flamboyant, experimental trends of the 1960s were rapidly deflating as the seventies began, the liberal ideals were not so easily dismissed in the new decade. The Sixties' emphasis on morality and justice brought to light major critical works that would profoundly impact curriculum scholarship for years to come, including the English translation of Portuguese writer Paulo Freire's *Pedagogy of the Oppressed*, which criticized the banking approach to education that portrayed students as empty, dehumanized vessels, as well as Norman Overly's *The Unstudied Curriculum* and Benson Snyder's *The Hidden Curriculum*, both published in 1970, which further developed Philip Jackson's earlier criticism of the unstated academic and social norms that prevent students in schools from thinking independently or creatively. Thus, both within the curriculum field and in society at large, the 1970s became a time of transition between a more liberal, idealistic, "just say yes," period and the approaching neoliberal, "Just Say No," era of the 1980s. Discontent and fear were fueled by economic hardships, resulting from record-breaking unemployment and inflation. The emergence of *Sesame Street* and the increased federal influence on television illustrated some of the conceptual struggles that were dividing the nation — personal liberty vs. public safety, localism vs. globalism, individualism vs. standardization. As *Sesame Street* and other "high culture" features of public television continued to grow in popularity and influence, the idealistic, experimental 1960s turned into the pragmatic, cynical and self-obsessed 1970s.

It was in this historical moment of conflict, just as the hippie movement had finally lost its impetus, that *The Muppet Show* made its mid-decade debut. In that context, *The Muppet Show* might be seen as an effort on Henson's part to recapture and recreate the imaginative and permissive idealism that was quickly falling victim to the status-driven Me Generation. Determined to free his creations from the didactic realm of children's entertainment, Henson, with the financial backing of an English producer as well as the creative support of his most beloved Muppet, Kermit the Frog, developed the concept of a half-hour variety show that would allow teens and adults to enjoy the Muppets without the excuse of younger siblings. As anyone who's ever watched an episode knows, the show was ripe with chaos, lunacy, explosions, and basically absolute madness, a dramatic departure from the edifying, linear format of *Sesame Street*. What is so interesting about the show is that it seems to have been purposely designed to humorously embody every characteristic of the television "wasteland" that Newton Minow had denounced in 1961. First of all, if "formula comedies about totally unbelievable families" were to be condemned, *The Muppet Show* took the cake, since there was nothing really "believable" about the idea that a band of neurotic puppets, who grew into a sort of "family" in their own right, would produce and perform a comedic variety show that parodied many of the formulaic genres of the day. What's more, as Kathleen E. Kennedy notes elsewhere in this collection, the first season of the *Muppet Show* consistently and fearlessly took on the "hoary themes of sex and violence." In fact, the second pilot alone, "The Muppet Show: Sex and Violence," which aired in 1975 and featured a tone more like that of the full series than the first pilot, took care of most of the list. It began with Crazy Donald (later inexplicably renamed Crazy Harry) announcing the end of sex and violence on television just before violently exploding block letters that read "sex and violence." In the scenes that follow, games, violence, mayhem, sadism, screaming, cajoling and offending ensue with intermittent games of Chess and Scrabble, a ballroom scene with

"Laugh-In" like jokes, the wild beast Animal in a dungeon, a wrestling match cheered on by a crowd that the announcer proudly deems "a fantastic bunch of sadists," a psychedelic rock performance by the "very violent" band, "Dr. Teeth & the Electric Mayhem," a bird-mating jaunt, a monster-clubbing session, the Seven Deadly Sins Pageant, and the Swedish Chef violently shooting down a flying submarine sandwich. The first few episodes nearly complete Minow's wasteland wish list with a "live" Muppet audience, a sketch where the "Western good men" and "Western bad men" are played by Fozzie and Rowlf, and a group of monster villains who sing while clubbing each other and dodging bullets, arrows and explosions. It is no secret that Henson sought to diversify the audience for his puppetry with *The Muppet Show* because he felt that his creations could appeal to both children and adults. However, one could argue that Henson made efforts to decisively distance the show from its government-approved predecessor. Indeed, if, as Morrow has observed, *Sesame Street* was a "new bloom on the wasteland" (47), then *The Muppet Show* seemed to be the epitome of "waste," at least as it had been cynically interpreted by Minow, and it's hard not to see a purposeful connection between the condemnation of commercial television and the typical *Muppet Show* sketches. It is even harder to ignore the blunt jokes, which suggested early on that Henson did not endorse the government-sanctioned "edutainment" model. First, in the "Sex and Violence" pilot episode, Kermit implies his potential exodus from *Sesame Street* when he tells his female dancing partner that he might be able to get her "a job on an educational show for kids." Later, in the same pilot, Statler and Waldorf, the hilarious old curmudgeons who heckled the show each night from the balcony, seemed to compare the government's concern for the "younger generation" to the Kaiser Wilhelm II's campaign to win the minds of Germany's youth through the *Volksschule*, "the school of the masses" (Retallack). When Statler states that he's been thinking about the younger generation because he doesn't know where they're going, Waldorf replies, "Neither did the Kaiser!" Finally, at the end of the second episode, Statler and Waldorf specifically criticize the educational value of the show, in what would be the last overt reference to "school" until Alice Cooper's appearance:

>   STATLER: You think this show is educational?
>   WALDORF: Yes, it will drive people to read books.

As Statler and Waldorf observe, *The Muppet Show* was not promoted as being educational. Yet, in spite of the lack of additional direct educational references in the episodes that followed, there were a few memorable sketches that provide further insight into the pedagogical messages the show has to offer. In the Juliet Prowse episode, Kermit takes on the authoritative responsibility of conducting the Muppet Glee Club, an interesting collection of frogs, chickens, and pigs. After introducing the group, Kermit waves his baton, expecting a typical response, but no one sings. Kermit reminds the group of the Glee Club's purpose and explains that they are to sing when the baton is waved. On his second attempt, the Glee Club follows his instructions to sing when the baton is waved, but they all break out into spontaneous song, each singing his or her own tune. As the apparent "leader" of the group," Kermit is clearly frustrated by the choir's inability to anticipate his expectations, and he attempts to find a song they all know. They eagerly agree that they would all like to sing "Temptation," and Kermit assigns Miss Piggy the solo. This time, when the baton is waved, the Glee Club performs a pretty impressive *a cappella* introduction. The music begins just before Piggy performs her solo, during which Piggy pushes through the singers to cozy up to Kermit. She proclaims her love for him, embracing him with a kiss, while Kermit attempts to conduct around her.

The Glee Club sketch is one example of Kermit taking on what might be interpreted as a traditional pedagogical role. Acting as the director of a Glee Club, a chorus typically associated with universities, he is the "teacher," and the choir members are the "students," who are expected to perform in the role in which they are being directed. However, several factors collide to transform an otherwise "orderly" teacher-student relationship into a "disorderly" moment of harmonious creativity. Kermit, who has obviously taken on the director role somewhat unexpectedly, considering that they have no idea what a Glee Club is supposed to do, is using a widely-recognized directive, the baton, to elicit a pretty typical response, a song. However, the Glee Club members fail to respond to his cues, and it is only when he finds something that is relevant to their own interests and desires, a song that comes from the "students," rather than the "teacher," that a meaningful response is achieved. Like students in the classroom, who are uninspired by didactic, knowledge-centered curricula that fails to appeal to their own interests, the Glee Club reminds us that they can sing beautifully together when the song is one *they* choose.

Another pedagogical message is found in persona of Sam the Eagle, who feels it is his responsibility to promote wholesome American morals and values, and it is out of this sense of responsibility that he serves as a self-appointed censor as well as an advocate of acts that he deems appropriately cultural and educational. Sam works diligently to promote acts that Newton Minow might have approved of, leading one to consider that Sam might represent the increasing censorship of both television and education. One such act is the singing duo of Wayne and Wanda, who perform during the first season. Sam approves of their "wholesome, uplifting, and decent" act, but is continually perturbed by their failure to get past the first verse of any song. Sam also participates in the ostensibly serious, but always disastrous, "Panel

Discussions," which are Muppet attempts at civilized conversation on a number of "academic" topics, such as "Is conversation a dying art?" and "What is the meaning of life"? Beginning in the second season, Sam occasionally delivers editorials on the state of the country and the world, harshly condemning "weirdos" and "namby-pamby conservationists." However, nearly every sketch involving Sam results in some kind of an embarrassing, "foot-in-mouth" conclusion. Most notably, in the Nancy Walker episode, he rails against nudity, only to suddenly become aware that he himself is naked beneath his feathers. Sam the Eagle serves as a potent reminder of *The Muppet Show* perspective on the steadily increasing government influence on education and entertainment.

Taken together, the subtle pedagogical messages and the obvious embrace of all the wasteland qualities *Sesame Street* was created to counteract, along with the blatant juxtaposition to its predecessor, reveal that *The Muppet Show* was created to entertain, not to educate. This brings us back to the question of pedagogical messages. What can a show that is, as I have demonstrated here, decidedly "un-educational" tell us about pedadogy? It would be relatively easy to ponder the educational insight of the show if it had been created to deliver some kind of a moral or even a cohesive message, but as Statler and Waldorf often remind us, there really isn't a point to *The Muppet Show*. Unlike the rigid behavioral objectives and rigid, scripted lesson plans that were developing in the wake of *Sputnik*, the "weird, sick show," as Sam the Eagle likes to call it, has no agenda, other than variety, chaos, and a whole lot of crazy fun. In a drastic departure from the linear, themed educational tactics of *Sesame Street,* there's no plot connecting shotgun-wielding Swedish chefs to piano-playing chickens, or dancing sharks to "Pigs in Space," other than pure merry madness.

In spite of its lack of educative intent, *The Muppet Show* does offer an alternative to the teacher as the human conduit for the transmission of subject matter in Kermit the Frog, who, as the "producer" and host, is the glue that patches together the bits and pieces of silliness into a half-hour variety show. Kermit's job is not an easy one, as he is charged with keeping the show moving along in spite of bizarre and unexpected Muppet stunts, as well as keeping all of his guests and Muppet actors happy. In spite of all the chaos, Kermit only rarely expresses his annoyance, generally maintaining a calm composure and the same kind of enduring optimism that characterized his creator. Although Kermit is presumably "in charge" at the Muppet Theater, he is never really in control of what goes on there, and we are constantly reminded of the autonomy of each of the characters, who see Kermit less as a boss and more as a friend. This facilitator role that Kermit plays is not unlike what Dewey envisioned the teacher becoming in the progressive paradigm. As he maintains, "Only by being true to the full growth of the individuals who make it up, can society by any chance be true to itself" (7). For Dewey, promoting the full growth of individuals meant respecting their unique interests, needs, and desires and responding to them accordingly, rather than organizing instruction around a teacher and/or subject-matter-driven agenda.

Aside from the effective lack of hierarchical authority structure, there is another characteristic of the Muppet characters that transcends the chaos of the variety show sketches. In spite of the gratuitous explosions and excessive nonsense, there is a certain nostalgic sweetness about the Muppets, an implicit compassion that seems to undergird the chaos. As Henson himself observed, "There is a sense of our characters caring for each other. A positive feeling, a positive view of life. That's the key to everything we do" (Henson 41). This particular quality of *The Muppet Show* brings to light the Dewey-influenced work of Nel Noddings, who challenges us to adopt care-centered curricula and suggests that the post–*Sputnik* organization of school studies around the academic disciplines is unfair to students because they receive schooling for the head but little for the heart and soul. Perhaps if "a sense of caring" and "positive feelings" were the focus of our educational experiences, the learning process might be a more meaningful and valuable life experience, and, just maybe, we could enjoy a little madness along the way.

Perhaps, then, in the unassuming and optimistic style of Jim Henson, *The Muppet Show* is the most inconspicuous form of critical pedagogy, a non-linear, anti-didactic way of thinking and teaching that extends far beyond our initial impressions. For me, *The Muppet Show* predated and stood in stark contrast to my early formal school experiences in the 1980s, which consisted mostly of tedious worksheets and obsessive rule-following. Having been born just weeks after the first episode aired on American television, I probably recognized the Muppet characters long before I could say their names, and every time I hear Kermit singing "The Rainbow Connection," I am transported back to one of my earliest memories of seeing *The Muppet Movie* at age three. Back then, I was too young to question the sheer lunacy of the sketches. In fact, I probably would never have described them as being chaotic or nonsensical until my school experiences taught me to appreciate linearity. Looking back, I think perhaps that one of the reasons that *The Muppet Show* has had such a profound influence on my generation is that the unpredictable, fictional variety show is actually more like "real life" than the typical classroom. The moment that the curtain opens on an episode of *The Muppet Show*, we are immediately transported into a realm where nothing and everything makes sense all at once, and like the real world, there is little certainty and few things that really make sense, but it is up to us to find a way to achieve our goals in spite of our vast and sometimes inexplicable differences. Moreover, in spite of the purposeful pointlessness the show embodies, there is one message that can't be overlooked, expressed by one characteristic that was required of producer and performers: a vivid imagination, a quality that was quickly disappearing from the increasingly technical, textbook-driven classrooms that were developing in the 1970s. Here, the intense joy of lunacy reminds me of the endless creative possibilities that are lost when we view education merely as the transmission of subject matter, a perspective fueled more intensely now than ever by the pressures of high-stakes standardized testing. However, *The Muppet Show* is the antithesis to the passive technical "banking" method that Freire criticizes, a method that embraces and depends on order, linearity, rule-following, and a contrived sense of "normalcy." Rather, it represents a kind of educative thinking advocated by Maxine Greene: "thinking that refuses mere compliance, that looks down roads not yet taken to the shapes of more fulfilling social order, to more vibrant ways of being in the world" (5).

In spite of *The Muppet Show's* enduring popularity, the series itself was relatively short-lived. The last of 120 episodes aired in 1981, and although reruns were later aired in syndication on TNT from 1988 to 1992, and again on Nickelodeon from 1994 to 1995, Henson's decision to move on to other projects in the 1980s might be interpreted as a gentle acquiescence to the changing times. The progressive educational ideals that had once flourished in the experimental era of the 1960s were a distant memory as the nation's focused shifted toward global economic superiority. Not long after the last episode aired, Reagan's National Commission on Excellence in Education released the infamous report *A Nation at Risk*, which sparked an unprecedented surge of pessimism over the seemingly miserable failure of American education. As a result, capitalism, consumerism, and computerization merged to meet the nation's need for a workforce to fuel the global economy, which left little room in the curriculum for creativity, compassion, or difference.

This decade of pessimism, fear, and mindless consumption was the context in which my government-mandated public education began to compete with popular culture for my attention, and it's been an ongoing struggle ever since. Although most of us spend countless years in some type of formal public education, it seems that all too often, it is our cultural schooling that most impacts our identities, which in turn influences the way that we come to perceive the roles we take on life. As a teacher-educator, what I have learned from Jim Henson's contribution to the "television wasteland" that has dominated my leisure time for as long as I can remember is that, like Henson, I always have been, and always will be, a dreamer. Like Maxine Greene, I believe that imagination is the only way to find "more vibrant ways" of being, doing, and teaching. In light of the crippling frustrations, pressures, and obstacles we face as educators, it's difficult sometimes to maintain the kind of enduring optimism that Kermit exemplifies. And yet, as Kermit taught us through his experiences on the variety show, it may not be easy being green, or different, or an optimist awash in a sea of pessimism, but when it's all there is to be, it just has to be fine. If we can, like Kermit, just "be" whatever it is that we are, whether or not it makes sense, and learn to appreciate ourselves and others in spite of our differences, and, if we can, like Dewey, be "true to the full growth of the individuals who make it up," perhaps then we can see education become the meaningful, personal, life-long journey that it should be. If there were such a thing as Muppet pedagogy, it would be best described by Henson himself, who believed that "we create our own reality, and that everything works out for the best. I know I drive some people crazy with what seems to be ridiculous optimism, but it has always worked out for me. I believe in taking a positive attitude toward the world, toward people, and toward my work" (9). If we could embrace that same positive attitude toward our own work as teachers and students, and realize as educators that sometimes we just need to stop worrying about rules and norms and expectations and just have fun, perhaps we could find the sense of peace that Kermit, and Henson himself, embodied.

Works Cited

Baughman, James L. *Television's Guardians: The FCC and the Politics of Programming, 1958–1967*. Knoxville: University of Tennessee Press, 1985.
Daspit, Toby, and John A. Weaver. *Popular Culture and Critical Pedagogy: Reading, Constructing, Connecting*. New York: Routledge, 1999.
Dewey, John. *The School and Society*. Chicago: The University of Chicago Press, 1900.
Finch, Christopher. *Jim Henson, The Works: The Art, the Magic, the Imagination*. New York: Random House, 1993.
Freire, Paulo. *Pedagogy of the Oppressed*. New York: Herder and Herder, 1970.
Greene, Maxine. *Releasing the Imagination: Essay; on Education, the Arts, and Social Change*. San Francisco: Jossey-Bass Publishers, 1995.
Henson, Jim. *It's Not Easy Being Green and Other Things to Consider*. New York: Barnes and Noble, 2007.
Jackson, Philip. *Life in Classrooms*. New York: Holt, Rinehart and Winston, 1968.
Lesser, Gerald S. *Children and Television: Lessons from "Sesame Street."* New York: Vintage, 1975.
Marshall, J. Dan, James T. Sears, and William H. Schubert. *Turning Points in Curriculum: A Contemporary American Memoir*. Upper Saddle River, NJ: Merrill, 2000.
Morrow, Robert. W. *Sesame Street and the Reform of Children's Television*. Baltimore: John Hopkins University Press, 2006.
Noddings, Nel. *The Challenge to Care in Schools: An Alternative Approach to Education*. New York: Teachers College Press, 1992.
Retallack, James. *Germany in the Age of Kaiser Wilhelm II*. New York: Macmillan, 1996.
Shor, I. *Empowering Education: Critical Teaching for Social Change*. Portsmouth, NH: Heinemann, 1992.
Snyder, Benson. *The Hidden Curriculum*. New York: Alfred A. Knopf, 1970.
Spring, Joel. *The American School: 1642–2004*. 6th ed. Boston: McGraw Hill, 2005.

The Uniquely Strong but Feminine Miss Piggy
Maryanne Fisher and *Anthony Cox*

It is impossible to view an episode of *The Muppet Show* without noticing the feminine, yet domineering and demanding character of Miss Piggy. Frank Oz, the puppeteer behind Miss Piggy, has created a dynamic and complex Muppet who challenges our assumptions about gender and the stereotypes we associate with womanhood. While satisfying many of our expectations for a female character, with respect to her outfits, cosmetic use, and employment, she also displays an atypical independence, aggressiveness, and physicality that we more frequently associate with male characters. For example, although her voice is feminine, she is neither subtle nor demure. When she does not get her own way, she yells or insults others, and sometimes, bullies, hits, or fights with them. She does all of this while wearing extremely feminine clothing that routinely includes skirts, pink feather boas, elbow-length gloves, and outrageous feather-topped hats. In this chapter, we are going to examine this complex character who, ahead of her time, managed to show that women could be strong and in control of their lives, acting almost masculine, but without sacrificing their femininity.

While Miss Piggy can be examined in many different ways and from many perspectives, we suggest that the contrasts she exhibits are responsible for her appeal and are her most interesting aspect. For example, during *The Muppets Take Manhattan,* Miss Piggy repeatedly demonstrates her strong love for Kermit. Her performance displays emotional warmth, but at the same time, she shows aggressiveness when she violently throws him across the room after he insults her. She does not abandon her femininity to increase her masculinity, but instead, she is a balance of the two in unity, leading to a fully developed and interesting character with profound depth. We believe that this balance allows viewers of all gender backgrounds to find some aspect of Miss Piggy with which they can relate and identify.

Regardless of her specific role, Miss Piggy is true to her personality and consistently displays her dichotomous feminine and masculine traits. As a fully developed woman, she engages in romantic relationships, and in these relationships, Kermit the Frog traditionally serves as the target of her affection and aggression. For example, in *The Muppet Christmas Carol*, she plays Emily Cratchit, the wife of Bob Cratchit, played by Kermit. She performs the traditional activities of cooking the Christmas feast and mothering their children, yet she is very vocal and aggressive in her dislike for Cratchit's boss, Ebenezer Scrooge. In *Muppet Treasure Island*, she plays Benjamina Gunn, a woman stranded on an island and who, by remarkable coincidence, is the long lost lover of Captain Smollet, who again is played by Kermit. In this role, she indicates her femininity as the jewelry laden queen of the island, by demanding commitment from Smollet and by professing her love for him. However, she also uses her signature karate chop to send Smollet flying into a gong and violently beats up some rogue pirates who have tried to kill them.

Over time, Miss Piggy has changed very little and her character in the various movies, starting with *The Muppet Movie* (1979), is in line with that of the original television show. In a uniform manner, she demonstrates romantic feelings towards Kermit, enjoys her extensive wardrobe, and has the same mannerisms of moving her hair with the back of her hand gently out of her face. In *The Great Muppet Caper* (1981), the storyline is consistent when thinking about the show. In this movie, the characters are furthered developed, with Miss Piggy playing a role that is central to the plot. *The Muppets Take Manhattan* (1984) continues in this line and also uses Miss Piggy, again as Kermit's love interest, to add to the depth of their interactions. These three movies were widely considered the high-point of Jim Henson's career (Finch 139). Two themed movies were then released, in which it is obvious that the Muppets are themselves acting: *The Muppet Christmas Carol* (1992) and *Muppet Treasure Island* (1996). Even though they are acting, they still interact as though they know each other and have relationship histories; this is expanded upon in other contributions in this volume. All of these movies were films released first in theaters and later sold for home viewing. They were also written by Jerry Juhl, who had been the primary writer for *The Muppet Show* since the second season, thus explaining the consistent and uniform behavior that Miss Piggy exhibits.

A real departure occurs, however, with the more contemporary movies, as the Muppets seem to lose the strength that resulted from their collective personality and history. The start of this departure occurs in *Muppets from Space* (1999), where the Muppets live together in a colorful house as roommates. There is no mention of the romantic relationship between Miss Piggy and Kermit, and instead they appear to be good friends. In contrast to the prior movies, there is not as much reliance on the history of the characters' interpersonal relationships, possibly because it is the first movie to have been released that features the Muppets as themselves in 15 years and thus, the writers may have been concerned that modern audiences would be unfamiliar with the Muppet's past history. However, much of Miss Piggy's personality remains intact, possibly because Jerry Juhl assisted with the writing of this production. Interestingly, this was the first movie to be made after the death of the Muppets' creator, Jim Henson, and the last movie where Miss Piggy was played by Frank Oz. In many ways, this movie represents a significant transition in Muppet history.

The original and most persistent persona of Miss Piggy is clearly a product of writer Jerry Juhl, puppeteer Frank Oz, and Muppet creator Jim Henson. When their involvement decreased, understandable changes began to appear in the Muppet productions. As a consequence of the loss of their contributions and the subsequent interpretation by new writers and puppeteers, we limit our analysis to cover *The Muppet Show* and the movies up to and including *Muppets from Space.*

In this chapter, we examine in detail the complexity of Miss Piggy's feminine and masculine sides. We propose that she challenges conventional stereotypes of femininity by behaving, at times, in masculine ways. Simultaneously, her physical characteristics and occupation choices are highly feminine, as is as her professed love for a male character. We will investigate the dichotomy of Miss Piggy and the impact that her depiction may have had on audiences. To provide sufficient context, we next examine the concept of gender, and the ability of television to influence societal perceptions of gender norms and stereotypes before we explore the unique and opposing aspects of Miss Piggy.

Understanding Gender and Miss Piggy

In order to make a television show funny, dramatic, or in some other way attention grabbing, those working in the industry may choose to use exaggerated behaviors. Gender stereotypes offer many opportunities for exaggeration. A gender stereotype is a belief about the psychological characteristics of women and men, as well as the activities that are appropriate for each gender to perform; it is a belief and attitude about femininity and masculinity (e.g., Smith 75). However, such beliefs are not rigid or fixed since television possesses the power to change how we construct and understand gender in real life (Inness 162). That is, watching an actor portray a character, even a non-serious and humorous one, has the power to alter our perceptions on important issues such as gender. Thus, producers, directors, screenwriters, and actors, who reside in a particular culture and era and who have certain beliefs or values, can change the beliefs and values of others. They might decide to create a skit for a show because it would be funny, the audience then views it and laughs because it is funny, and the skit is considered successful for having met its goal. However, the skit may also have challenged our expectations and possibly, as they are continuously challenged, cause us to reassess or change them. The last element of this paradigm, understanding precisely what is being challenged, is left for academics to unravel.

The way that women and men have been portrayed on television, and in other media, has long been the focus of attention for psychologists, educators, and media watchers. One particular aspect of concern is the lack of strong female characters in mainstream media, and in fact, the lack of female representation more generally. For example, Mary Desjardins, in her report for the Museum of Broadcast Communications, reports that women are less likely than men to appear in leading roles, particularly as intelligent "experts" on news shows, at least in North America. This phenomena has been termed "symbolic annihilation" (Gerbner 46, Rhode 687). Additionally, in cartoons but presumably elsewhere too, females are often shown as emotionally warmer and friendlier, but simultaneously less competent than males (Thompson and Zerbinos 659, 662). These portrayals have long term consequences given that television influences and reinforces our beliefs. When women are rarely shown as one of the central characters of a television show and are continually portrayed to be emotionally warm and irrational, then viewers might come to believe that these are the features associated with all women. Therefore, when one encounters a female character who does not match the prototypical woman, this character is worthy of examination. Miss Piggy is an example of a female figure who is central to the *Muppet Show*, has remained a primary character in all the Muppet movies, and yet is not particularly warm, kind, or compassionate, nor, like many of the Muppets, rational and clear-thinking. She is unique in that she is incongruent with the stereotypical portrayal of women in mainstream media.

There are numerous ways to define femininity and masculinity, and these definitions change over time as society evolves. In the crudest sense, femininity is essentially a description of the stereotypes people have about women; for example, if the stereotype is that women are kind, nurturing, compassionate and passive, then femininity reflects these characteristics. The same is true for masculinity; if the stereotype is that men are assertive, authoritarian, physically active, and strong, then masculinity is composed of these characteristics. In this way, stereotypes and social constructions of gender are intimately intertwined and change over time in synchrony. Unfortunately, there is no single universally accepted and "correct" method for defining femininity and masculinity. So, for our analysis of Miss Piggy, we use the well-known work of psychologist Sandra Bem, who asked college students to assess adjectives based on whether they were typical of women or men, and then used these adjectives to construct a measure of femininity and masculinity (157). Thus, while other perspectives are possible, we rely upon the social constructionist concept of gender as it strongly reflects stereotypes about femininity and masculinity. The benefit of this definition is that it enables us to study a wide variety of characteristics and to apply stereotypes as a source of information about gender and an element of humor.

We note that this benefit does have an associated cost. Although useful from the standpoint of diagnosing someone's adherence to gender roles (i.e., whether they are mostly feminine, masculine, both or neither), Bem's model is not perfect. One criticism of her findings is that she did not investigate examples of femininity and masculinity that would be considered positive versus negative in value (Ricciardelli and Williams 638). Ricciardelli and Williams found that femininity was composed of positive traits such as patience, sensitivity, devotion, responsibility and appreciation, and negative traits such as timidity, weakness, need for approval, dependence, and nervousness (644–45). Masculinity was composed of positive values such as strength, confidence, firmness, forcefulness, and feeling carefree, and negative values like aggressiveness, bossiness, sarcasm, rudeness, and feeling superior (Ricciardelli and Williams 644–45). We leave it to others to determine the positive and negative values associated with Miss Piggy's traits, as well as the implications these values might have for audiences.

When it comes to Miss Piggy, then, we are using the word "feminine" to reflect characteristics such as those isolated by Ricciardelli and Williams and Bem: shy, loyal, compassionate, and understanding, as well as physical traits such as dressing in a "girlie" way and wearing, for example, pink, lace-trimmed skirts and dresses. When we use the word "masculine," again we are doing so with reference to Ricciardelli and Williams and Bem, and thus it means independent, athletic, analytical, and aggressive, as well as the adopting a "manly" style of dress. Of course, there are other attributes of femininity and masculinity that we have not mentioned, but these few attributes should provide sufficient context for understanding their construction.

Obviously, gender is a concept that varies across cultures; what is considered feminine in one culture would not necessarily be so in another. Therefore, the observations about Miss Piggy also inform us about the evolving and changing stereotypes within a particular culture; in this case, American culture starting in the mid–1970s with the *Muppet Show* and ending with the 2005 release of *The Muppets' Wizard of Oz*. Thus, we begin our analysis of Miss Piggy by examining her history so that readers can consider her behavior with respect to the social and cultural trends in which she was born and lived.

The History of Miss Piggy

The first puppet ever to resemble Miss Piggy was collaboratively designed by Michael Frith and Don Sahlins (Finch 84) and constructed by Bonnie Erickson (née Lewis), the same designer for other Muppets including Statler and Waldorf ("Bonnie Erickson"). In this form, she was blonde with small beady eyes and was at this time unnamed. This "Proto Piggy" was created for the "Return to Beneath the Planet of the Pigs" sketch in *The Muppet Show: Sex and Violence* television pilot that was ordered by ABC in 1973 and aired in 1975. Fran Brill was the voice for the pig in this sketch. After this appearance, Miss Piggy's next appearance was in 1974 on *Herb Alpert and the Tijuana Brass Special*, where Jerry Nelson performed her as a hopeful singer. The Muppet segments for Herb Alpert were taped in 1974 ("Miss Piggy").

In the special, a smooth-talking pig agent, Hoggie Marsh, provides Herb with the opportunity to work with his latest discovery, a shy singer named Miss Piggy. This is Miss Piggy's first television appearance, and her name is mentioned for the first time ("Miss Piggy"). Her personality is a precursor to the one she would later develop on *The Muppet Show*, with many of her personality traits in place, such as her undisguised pursuit of men and her strong need for attention. She was also much more similar in appearance to the Miss Piggy who appeared in the first (1976) season of *The Muppet Show*. In the first season, she had long hair, large blue eyes and her signature desire for Kermit, who was the love of her life. She was, however, a character with a relatively small role, but gained status as Nurse Piggy on the recurring skit, "Veterinarians' Hospital" (Finch 101).

Miss Piggy's character dramatically changed one day when Frank Oz had her behave differently than expected. The script called for Miss Piggy to slap Kermit, but instead, he stuck out Miss Piggy's chest, drew back her shoulders, assumed a look of offended rage, and carried out a karate chop, accompanied by a loud yell (Finch 101). Immediately, the personality of Miss Piggy was altered. During this second season, Frank Oz was given the chance to increase her prominence, with one effect being that she became more glamorous looking. Carolyn Wilcox oversaw many of the modifications to Miss Piggy's appearance, with particular attention to improving the shape of her head for mechanical operation and maintenance and for attractiveness (Finch 101). Throughout the remainder of her portrayal on both *The Muppet Show* and in the various Muppet movies, her appearance is constantly evolving, as her eyes, hair length and style, snout (nose) length, tongue color, and facial shape all vary over time. Karen Falk, the Henson Archivist, has suggested that Miss Piggy was originally conceived in the early 1970s by her designer, Bonnie Erickson, as a parody of the singer Peggy Lee ("Miss Piggy"). However, the name Piggy Lee was short-lived and is no longer associated with Miss Piggy.

In the debut of *The Muppet Show*, Miss Piggy first appears in the "At the Dance" sketch, performed by Richard Hunt. Compared to her depiction in the movies and later seasons of the show, her voice is much lower and smoother, and her appearance is not nearly as glamorous. In this initial episode, she has a pastier complexion, her hair is straight, very dull, and ruddy blonde, she wears less makeup, her eyes and ears are smaller, with the left one bent over, and her mouth, when opened, resembles a pig's mouth. In the "Glee Club" sketch (also in the first episode), Frank Oz performs her speaking voice and Richard Hunt performs her singing voice. After Season One, Frank Oz becomes the sole voice and puppeteer for Miss Piggy, until his busy schedule permitted him to perform only the voice for *Muppet Treasure Island*, with Kevin Clash as the puppeteer, and *Muppets from Space*, where Peter Linz performed the puppetry. In 2001, Eric Jacobson replaced Frank Oz and now serves as the principal puppeteer for Miss Piggy.

It is during the Episode One (Season One) "Glee Club" sketch that the viewer sees two behaviors occur that will become trademarks of Miss Piggy. First, she seeks stardom. Second, the viewer sees a clear display of her affection for Kermit; she calls Kermit "my love" in response to him telling her ("Piggy honey") to take the solo. Miss Piggy sings "Temptation" as her solo; she comes to the front of the singers and starts to overtake Kermit (who is conducting) to make it look as though she is singing it to him. He tries to keep the baton moving until Miss Piggy eventually lunges at him. Although this sort of relationship dynamic is consistent, whereby Kermit acknowledges the mutual affection shared between him and Miss Piggy, Miss Piggy is uniformly the aggressive suitor. The portrayal of their relationship is highly varied in terms of how this dynamic is acted out in the various episodes and movies and can be considered as reaching its climax with their wedding in *The Muppets Take Manhattan*. It should be noted that the wedding could be construed as artificial, given that it occurs as part of the play in which they are performing, and there are no references later to their marriage. An earlier attempt on behalf of Miss Piggy to marry Kermit had failed (Season Three, "Marisa Berenson"), when, at the last minute, Kermit introduced the next act rather than saying, "I do."

While Miss Piggy plays a wide variety of roles and appears in the majority of *The Muppet Show* episodes, her two main recurring roles are as a nurse in the "Veterinarians' Hospital" sketches, and as the first mate on the "Swine Trek" on the "Pigs in Space" sketches. According to Frank Oz, Miss Piggy is one of the few Muppets to be fully realized in three dimensions ("Miss Piggy"), thus suggesting that she is one of the more fully developed and important of all the Muppets.

Femininity and Masculinity Within Miss Piggy

She is, perhaps as a consequence of being a pig, rather chubby and voluptuous, which is ironic given that a constant theme throughout the Muppets is that she is a model, and even participates in beauty contests, such as the one in which Kermit first sees her in *The Muppet Movie*. On the one hand, this facet shows that beauty comes in many forms, including those that are not slender. On the other hand, a pig is too far removed from a human to make such portrayals realistic. In fact, in *The Muppet Movie*, the other contestants in the beauty pageant are all human women who are slender. Thus, by virtue of her species, a pig and an animal not typically associated with the ideals of femininity, Miss Piggy violates the traditional North American association between thinness and female beauty.

One way that masculinity and femininity is expressed is through attire. Miss Piggy tends to be overly, and perhaps excessively, feminine in this regard. She almost always wears gloves, often with rings on top of her gloved fingers, and tends to wear dresses and skirts rather than pants. However, there are notable exceptions, such in *The Great Muppet Caper*, where she rides a motorcycle out of a moving truck while dressed completely in biker leather, which is stereotypically considered as tough and masculine (Inness 57). In an earlier scene, she performs as a swimwear model, in appropriate feminine swimwear, during a fashion show and an imagined synchronized swimming scene. Thus, while dressing in a highly feminine style for most of her appearances, she will sometimes wear masculine attire when performing in a highly masculine manner.

A recurrent theme that is often observed is that Miss Piggy abides with feminine stereotypes, whilst simultaneously going against them. Inness, when discussing tough girls, proposes "a tough woman ... must be model-beautiful and slender" (55). Miss Piggy breaks this assertion, as she is chubby, but she does have many characteristics that are stereotypically associated with beauty (e.g., long blonde hair, large blue eyes, highly feminine attire).

Another key indicator of one's gender is his or her employment. However, as with all elements of gender, one must consider the stereotypes that existed during this era with respect to "appropriate" professions for women. In the past, television often showed women in conventional, feminine occupations such as nursing, such that from 1950 to 1980 television nurses were 99 percent female, whereas physicians were 95 percent male (Kalisch and Kalisch 533). One of Miss Piggy's recurrent appearances on the show is as a nurse in "Veterinarians' Hospital," where she, Janet, and Rowlf (who is "Dr. Bob") are thought to be performing surgery or diagnosing a patient's illness, but instead use the situation to be humorous. Miss Piggy and Janet are shown to be feminine, with their long blonde hair down, and as "sidekicks" or assistants to Dr. Bob, a role traditionally filled by nurses. Before Dr. Bob enters the room, they behave in ways that are overtly feminine and unprofessional; for example, Miss Piggy checks her appearance in the shiny back of a stethoscope (Season One, "Juliet Prowse"). As Kalisch and Kalisch argue, women are well accepted as "nurses," at least on television, as this occupation fits well with other feminine stereotypes, such as being nurturing, care giving, and compassionate (511).

In Miss Piggy's other recurrent role, she plays the "second in command" during the "Pigs in Space" skits for which there were 31 skits over four seasons. Women were not accepted as astronauts in the 1970s, when this profession was entirely dominated by men. In fact, the only female space-farer (Valentina Tereshkova) is considered to have been a participant in a Soviet propagandistic publicity stunt (Hartford 179). Thus, the viewer is presented with an unlikely scenario where a female character is centrally involved in space exploration. This said, her role shows her as weak and heavily reflects feminine stereotypes. In many of the skits she is incompetent at controlling the space ship, at navigating, or at operating any of the critical controls. The captain, Link Hogthrob, encourages her to do laundry and ironing (Season Two, "Edgar Bergen") saying that she is specially trained for the challenges that they present. In another episode (Season Two, "Madeline Kahn"), the viewer learns that the controls that are in front of her will only operate unimportant systems, such as the air conditioning. In the Teresa Brewer episode, the "Swine Trek" is out of swill. Consequently Link orders, "Miss Piggy, go cook us some swill," again applying a strongly feminine stereotype that women are specially able to cook. Thus, as an astronaut, Miss Piggy is defying convention, but while doing so she is not presented in a way that is admirable and is treated poorly by her male companions. Hence, Miss Piggy again displays dichotomous, and yet often humorous, behavior. In an unusual parallel, other women in 1970s science fiction television (e.g., Lieutenant Uhura on *Star Trek*) were also relegated to supporting roles, suggesting that this type of portrayal speaks loudly of the culture of television women in the 1970s.

To determine contemporary perspectives on Miss Piggy, we asked 57 students at Saint Mary's University in Halifax (Nova Scotia, Canada) to briefly describe Miss Piggy on an index card. These students had successfully identified at least five of six *Muppet Show* characters, thus indicating that they had some familiarity with the show and its characters. A simple frequency analysis of the adjectives used in the descriptions reveals that the top ten adjectives (or adjective phrases) are: loud (19 occurrences), loving of Kermit (15), feminine (9), girlie (8), confident (7), glamorous (6), annoying (6), outgoing (6), demanding (5), and humorous/funny (5). It should be noted that we normalized the data with respect to spelling, tense, word suffixes, and in the case of phrases, by minor rewriting (e.g., "loves Kermit" and "in love with the frog" to "loving of Kermit"). Again, we see an unusual dichotomy in that she is considered as either feminine or 'girlie,' but that she displays the distinctly unfeminine trait of being loud, perhaps to the extent of being annoying. She is considered as glamorous, a feminine trait, but is also confident, outgoing, and demanding, traits associated with masculinity, as suggested by Bem. In the next section we examine Miss Piggy's romantic association with Kermit, which yields evidence of additional contrasts in the feminine and masculine nature of Miss Piggy.

Miss Piggy and Kermit in Love

One of the more entertaining aspects of the Muppets, in our opinion, is the relationship between Miss Piggy and Kermit. While other Muppets have displayed romantic interest, such as Gonzo and Camilla the chicken, the relationship between Miss Piggy and Kermit is the one that is clearly the most significantly developed in *The Muppet Show*. As in the other areas of Miss Piggy's character, her love affair with Kermit is dichotomous in nature and breaks several gender-based stereotypes, thus making their relationship more interesting. Much of their relationship must be inferred from their actions, or vocalizations, as the viewer rarely sees them in any sort of embrace, and certainly they are not shown in any sort of sexually intimate manner. While other aspects of their relationship are unique, such as its cross-species aspect, we ignore these aspects as they violate non-gender stereotypes and hence, remove us from the focus of this chapter.

While the audience is led to believe that Kermit and Miss Piggy are in love, the relationship appears to be one-sided. Miss Piggy is portrayed as adoring Kermit, calling him 'her love,' which consequently leads her to appear very feminine in her warmth and affection (unless, of course, he does something to challenge or embarrass her, in which case she shows him anger). In contrast, Kermit rarely calls her by any affectionate terms, tries to spurn her advances, and even denies that they are romantically involved (e.g., in the interview in the Special Features on the DVD release of Season Two).

In their relationship, she is the active pursuer, while Kermit plays a passive role. For example, in the Season Two episode with George Burns, Miss Piggy and Kermit have a skit together where he is refusing to dance with her, and she is continually trying different ways to get him to do so. When she tries to show affection, snuggling him or touching him, Kermit resists and says, "Awwwww Piggy!" In the John Cleese episode in Season Two, Miss Piggy's only performance is as a pregnant bride in her wedding dress. The song she sings is about her unfortunate situation, where she goes to a church to be married to the father of the baby, except that his current wife will not let him marry someone new. Kermit makes an appearance in a tuxedo, presumably as the man in the song. At the end of the skit, Miss Piggy suggests that they could get married, but he states that he has no intention to marry. Then he instructs her, in an uncharacteristically demanding way, to remove "that pillow from under her dress" and leaves. She yells after him that she likes the pillow, allowing the viewer to infer that she would like to be married and pregnant.

Kermit considers Miss Piggy to be highly aggressive, perhaps as a result of her actively seeking a relationship with him. His belief is evidenced in a skit during the Zero Mostel episode in Season Two where Kermit needs to find two "lady wrestlers" that the theater owner, Scooter's uncle, wants to see on the show in exchange for providing the payroll. At the end of the episode, Kermit says, "Where in the world am I going to find another heavy weight aggressive tough female with a killer's instinct?" and just then, Miss Piggy shows up in a satin, pastel colored ball gown with long evening gloves to match, pearls, and a large ring. She has her long blonde hair down, and after she pushes it gently and femininely off of her face, she cooingly inquires as to what Kermit, "her wonderfulness," is doing. He says that he was just thinking about her, and then states, "This is a spot that requires an actress with tremendous strength, versatility, and someone who is all female." A brief conversation ensues; "What is it, Joan of Arc?" "Ah, no" "Naughty Marietta?" "No" "Lady Macbeth?" and then Kermit confesses, "It's more like a lady wrestler." On hearing this comment, Miss Piggy pauses, looks astounded, then is visibly upset and begins to chase Kermit around the theater yelling, "Lady Wrestler?!" In the next scene, Kermit is dressed in a wig, body suit, cape, and mask so that he can impersonate a female and wrestle with the "Granny Wrestler" to satisfy the theater owner. In their match, Kermit loses and is flung into the audience. Miss Piggy, on seeing this, jumps up and asks what the granny has done to "her poor Kermit" and then screams "hiya" and tosses the granny to the ground. Thus, we can see that, although feminine, Miss Piggy has well-known masculine qualities of aggression, assertiveness, and athleticism.

While scenes such as the one just described show that Kermit acknowledges Miss Piggy's aggressiveness, he also tries to de-escalate Miss Piggy's temper and anger at times. For example, in *The Muppet Christmas Carol*, she is angry towards Kermit's boss, Ebenezer Scrooge (played by Michael Caine). In response, Kermit attempts to dissipate her anger and reminds her to be thankful for what they have, which prompts Tiny Tim (played by Kermit's Muppet nephew Robin) to toast Scrooge. One might speculate that he is trying to make her more feminine by encouraging her be kinder and more compassionate. It is highly intriguing that Miss Piggy and Kermit do not necessarily follow the norm whereby the heroine is more attractive than her love interests (Downs and Harrison 17). In our student survey, only three respondents, all female, stated that she was attractive or beautiful, indicating that she is not generally known for her attractiveness. In fact, comments on Internet "blog" sites discussing the attractiveness of actresses often reveal comparisons of unattractive actresses to Miss Piggy or associate her name with actresses who are considered obese. Moreover, Miss Piggy is far larger than Kermit, which goes against the stereotype that women should be smaller than their mates.

Kermit's perspectives on Miss Piggy's appearance are no less confusing than his attitude towards her personality. In *The Muppet Movie*, he is awed by the sight of her during a beauty contest. However, in *The Muppet Show*, he insults her body size and calls her fat (Season Two, "Teresa Brewer"). In this episode, Kermit tells Scooter that he has to cut Miss Piggy's ballet number in the next week's show because she is too fat and the episode focuses on this concept. For example, at one point Miss Piggy decides to go on a diet after overhearing remarks about her weight and later in the show, Miss Piggy visits the guest star, the slim blonde singer Teresa Brewer, to ask her advice. During this encounter, Miss Piggy comments that she had always thought that Teresa was one of "us skinny people" but maybe she had learned something, anything, from her "fat friends." Teresa, after suggesting that she might be able to help, asks Miss Piggy to join her for lunch, which includes a decadent looking cake. During this lunch Kermit walks in and chastises Miss Piggy for going off her diet. In response, and in her typical aggressive and assertive manner, Miss Piggy shoves his face in a cake and leaves. Later in the same episode, she privately works out to an exercise video. Thus, while Miss Piggy often flaunts gender norms, she is also highly concerned with gender stereotypes regarding attractiveness.

Although often atypical, Miss Piggy and Kermit do, at times, follow convention in their relationship. For example, Miss Piggy is the affectionate one in the dyad. During an "interview," (Season Two, Bonus Features) she talks about her marriage to Kermit and states that they throw parties and live a seemingly enjoyable life, while Kermit denies dating or being married to her. This denial does not mean that Kermit does not care for Miss Piggy; in fact, quite the opposite is true. In *A Muppet Family Christmas*, Kermit is the only character who is concerned that Miss Piggy is trying to make her way to the farm house in a snowstorm. She is late because of a modeling shoot and her last minute Christmas shopping (which was primarily to buy Kermit a gift of flipper slippers). In *The Muppets Take Manhattan*, they have a highly traditional church wedding, with her in a white, long dress and him in a tuxedo, and in *The Muppet Christmas Carol*, Miss Piggy and Kermit are married with children and show a couple's usual affection towards each other.

Although Miss Piggy unequivocally adores Kermit, her love for Kermit does not prohibit her from hitting on other men. When ballet dancer Rudolf Nureyev is the guest star of the show in Season Two, they do a skit together in a steam room wearing just towels. He is obviously very uncomfortable with being undressed and in a small room with Miss Piggy. Miss Piggy behaves boorishly, hitting on him while admiring his athletic body and trying to remove his towel. They then sing "Baby, It's Cold Outside" with Miss Piggy coercing him to stay with her. He eventually loses his towel but grabs his robe in time, such that his nudity is never revealed, and dashes out of the steam room. In general, it is believed that men tend to have a stronger sex drive and desire greater numbers of sexual partners than do women (Schmitt et al 85). Thus, it should be Kermit, and not Miss Piggy, who is seeking to form relationships with the guest stars. This scene provides yet another example of Miss Piggy displaying a masculine characteristic.

These examples signify that, while pursuing a traditional heterosexual relationship, Miss Piggy does so in an unconventional and atypical manner. She continuously violates gender stereotypes for women, and instead, often satisfies those of typical men. In the next section, we examine Miss Piggy with respect to other, similar female characters, to better place her in context.

Miss Piggy in Context

The lack of positive role models for girls and women was partly addressed by another character in the mid 1970s when *The Muppet Show* first aired (1976): Princess Leia from *Star Wars* (1977). Although she is played by a real person (Carrie Fisher) rather than being a puppet, Princess Leia is another example of a dichotomous character who encompasses both feminine and masculine stereotypes. Some aspects of her appearance are feminine: she has long hair, wears cosmetics, and during the infamous "Jabba's Palace Scene," wears a revealing and skimpy gold bikini. At other points in the movies, she is dressed for combat in green fatigues with a weapon on her thigh. She is a princess, a very feminine stereotype that companies such as Walt Disney have exploited (Wachutka 22), yet she is fiercely independent and behaves with a high level of responsibility to the Rebel Alliance, which she helps to lead. Her behavior also reflects this balance of feminine and masculine. When she meets the Ewoks, an indigenous species of small furry animals from the planet Endor, she behaves in a very stereotypical feminine manner by talking softly to them and telling them not to be afraid. However, moments before meeting them she is riding a "speeder" dangerously through a semi-dense forest trying to shoot down an enemy.

Like Miss Piggy's relationship with Kermit, Leia's relationship with the rogue Han Solo is equally complex. Han seems to appreciate Leia because she is independent and strong-willed, and yet she is distraught when he is captured and made into a "carbonite statue" to hang in Jabba the Hutt's palace. Later she asserts her masculinity by dressing as a bounty hunter and sneaking into Hutt's palace to rescue Han. After she has released him, she then asserts her femininity by taking her bounty hunter facemask and helmet off, freeing her long hair to flow around her and Han while she comforts him in a soothing voice and tells him that she loves him. Thus, we see several strong parallels between Princess Leia and Miss Piggy, as both are the sole female characters in all male casts and must use male characteristics in order to be perceived as equal to the surrounding males. Yet, in both cases, neither character is forced to abandon her primary gender role. Hirschman and Stern have suggested that Princess Leia provides one of the earliest examples of a "positive" liberated woman who has not sacrificed her femininity to become liberated (170). Thus, by virtue of their similarity, it can be suggested that Miss Piggy is also a positive example of a liberated woman. This similarity led to a natural portrayal of Miss Piggy as Princess Leia in Season Four's episode with Mark Hamill during a "Pigs in Space" skit. Miss Piggy also portrays Princess Leia on the cover of the summer 1983 issue of *Muppet Magazine* and in a parody segment on *Muppet Babies.*

According to some scholars (e.g., Inness 138), Wonder Woman is the precursor to many of the female comic book heroines of recent years. We contend that she is the precursor to Miss Piggy, as well. Created by psychologist William Marston, with her first appearance in *All-Star Comics* in 1941, Wonder Woman was constructed to be a role model for young women who were otherwise neglected by the comic industry (Marston 42). Wonder Woman was a successful character, presumably because she blended stereotypes of femininity with masculinity in an exciting and interesting way. She was strong, autonomous, and independent and did not rely on any male character, yet she, at least in later years, upheld the stereotypes surrounding feminine appearance. Miss Piggy echoes this complexity thirty years later. Like Wonder Woman, she is fiercely independent, does not rely on anyone, is physically aggressive, and yet generally abides by feminine stereotypes for her occupational role and appearance. Miss Piggy has a high level of self-efficacy and independence, traits that are associated with masculinity. Interestingly, Lynda Carter, the actress who portrayed Wonder Woman on television from 1975 to 1979, was the guest star of an episode in Season Four, during which Miss Piggy played the role of Wonder Pig.

Although the *Muppet Show* was presumably watched by a wide audience that included children, compared to female protagonists in other shows enjoyed by children, such as Smurfette, Strawberry Shortcake, Snow White, or Jasmine (in Disney's *Aladdin*), Miss Piggy is far more tough, masculine, and challenging of female stereotypes. This lack of similarity with heroines in children's media is not necessarily unexpected, as her portrayal in *The Muppets Take Manhattan* has been described as aimed at adults, not children, and she herself as "power-hungry, [and] sex-driven" (Kelleher 521). Furthermore, the first words on the screen in the first *Muppet Show* pilot episode, "Sex and Violence" provide additional evidence that the show, and hence Miss Piggy, is meant to appeal to an adult audience.

We are not suggesting that Miss Piggy is exceptionally violent, although, interestingly, other female protagonists have recently been cast in this way. *Xena: Warrior Princess*, a television show released in 1995, centered around a nearly six-foot tall woman dressed in a leather outfit with well-developed sword-fighting skills (Inness 160). Xena does not rely on a man to save her when she gets into unsafe situations, but instead, uses her physical talents to save herself. The theme of the show is in fact her physical fights, from which she always emerges as the victor (Inness 162). Miss Piggy is fundamentally different from Xena in that she is not a warrior, but merely a woman who will resort to violence when pushed to do so. That is, Miss Piggy does not necessarily aspire to fulfill a traditionally masculine role, and does so out of necessity, not by choice. However, there are still similarities, as evidenced by Miss Piggy's mugging in *The Muppets Take Manhattan*. In an era where there is widespread concern about women's safety when they are alone, Miss Piggy's actions showed that women do not always have to be passive victims. Thus, when she is mugged, she borrows some roller skates and chases the thief down (and it is a considerable chase). Just as one knows that Xena would be safe if she walked through a park late at night (Inness 8), one knows that Miss Piggy also has the ability to defend and protect herself. Like Xena, Miss Piggy does not need to be rescued by a man, which is a recurring theme that is raised for other strong heroines. For example, Belle in Disney's animated movie, *Beauty and the Beast*, saves the male Beast from death. Another example is Disney's Mulan, in the movie of the same name, who steps in and takes her father's place in the army to save China from the Huns, or the aforementioned Leia saving the frozen Han in *Star Wars*.

One can also compare Miss Piggy with other female protagonists who challenge stereotypes of femininity and masculinity. In her book, *The Unruly Woman*, Kathleen Rowe indirectly compares Miss Piggy to Roseanne Barr, who plays herself, and Murphy Brown, played by Candice Bergen; Rowe suggests that Miss Piggy, like Arnold and Brown, is an unruly woman. An unruly woman is one who fails to conform to feminine stereotypes and instead is excessive and outrageous, which questions the boundary between femaleness and maleness. She proposes that unruly women are often disliked because they do not portray conventional femininity, particularly because of their independence and power-seeking behaviors. Although we agree with Rowe's analysis, we contend that what is interesting about Miss Piggy's toughness, and that of Roseanne or Murphy Brown, is that the viewer does not sense that this behavior is a performance, or that she's trying to "act" tough. Instead, toughness seems to be a trait that is inherent to her personality and oddly, the reverse often happens, where she seems to purposely be "acting" nice, often to get her own way.

Inness has argued that toughness in women is portrayed as the female character's ability to assume masculine traits (5). The reason that a female is considered tough, she argues, is because she possesses the characteristics that are stereotypical of men while not being overly concerned with appearing feminine. James Beggan and Scott Allison comment upon Inness' work and suggest that she has identified four key elements of a "tough girl": body, attitude, actions, and authority (799). Body is the physical correlate of toughness, such as athleticism or highly-defined muscularity, imposing form (e.g., large, taller or more muscular) or of typically masculine clothing. Attitude refers to the expression of competitiveness, risk acceptance, competence, control, independence, lack of fear and a low tolerance for authority figures. Action is centered around the ability to act in a thoughtful and intelligent manner, acting when necessary without fear. Authority is the individual's ability to take on a position of authority and leadership with assurance and confidence.

Using this framework allows us to explore Miss Piggy's toughness from an assortment of viewpoints. Miss Piggy does not demonstrate all the physical traits of a tough "body" in that she is far from muscular. She is also one of the largest Muppets among the primary group (e.g., she is larger than Kermit, Gonzo, and Scooter, and approximately the same height when compared to the Swedish Chef or Fozzie Bear), and one of the few Muppets to physically fight with human characters, such as the secret agents in *Muppets from Space*. However, all adult pigs are stereotypically considered as large, so it may be that her size is more congruent with the portrayal of her species rather than her personality. She is strong, as her ability to toss other characters around proves, and she displays athleticism. For example, she is able to gracefully ride a horse in the television special, *John Denver and the Muppets: Rocky Mountain Holiday* (1982), and roller-skate fast enough to catch a purse-snatcher in *The Muppets Take Manhattan*.

Miss Piggy's attitude displays strong tendencies for competitive and aggressive behavior towards others. When she is placed in a position that is demeaning, she reacts with harsh words, verbally attacking the person who has insulted her, and then, often, follows this with a loud "hiya!" and a karate chop. She is competitive around other women who might spark a romantic interest in Kermit or who steal the limelight from her, such as her impromptu duet of "I'm a Woman" with guest star Raquel Welch — a female beauty icon of the era. She is also exceedingly competitive when she wants something someone else has, such as being a television news anchorwoman. When given her big break in *Muppets from Space*, she is allowed to act as an anchorwoman temporarily to conduct an interview with Gonzo at a local television station. When the original anchorwoman, played by Andie MacDowell, finds Miss Piggy has taken her job, the result is a display of verbal aggression followed by a physical fight.

Regarding the third element of Inness' tough girl model, Miss Piggy also challenges the way someone might expect a female to be with respect to action. She thinks for herself and reaches decisions that are ultimately best for her. For example, although there was a snowstorm brewing and she might miss Christmas with her Muppet friends, Miss Piggy still chose to carry out a modeling shoot and then take a taxi to the farmhouse in *Muppet Family Christmas*. This decision was in spite of Kermit's protests, and she assured him that she would be fine and would arrive in time for Christmas. Miss Piggy is also quite capable of performing the necessary actions to get the information she desires. In *The Muppets Take Manhattan*, when she thinks that Kermit might be cheating on her and falling in love with Jenny, a waitress at a diner, she dons a trench coat and starts to spy on the two of them. At no time does Miss Piggy portray a character who is immobilized by fear, who cannot reach a decision, or who can not respond immediately and aggressively when threatened.

The last element, authority, is weakly displayed when compared to the other characteristics, primarily because of the role Miss Piggy has on *The Muppet Show* and in the various movies. In *The Muppet Show*, Kermit is ultimately in charge, looks after scheduling, ensures employees are paid, and so on. In the movies, this position of power remains stable; in *The Muppet Movie*, Kermit is the one who collects the various Muppets to travel with him to Hollywood. Miss Piggy is therefore a supporting character, rather than one who displays leadership and authority. This does not imply that Miss Piggy is without influence, but rather she relies on fear and intimidation to achieve her wishes. In the Season Two episode with George Burns, Kermit says that he has to let Miss Piggy do her song because if he does not, she will break both of his arms, thus using threats of violence and not leadership ability to manipulate others. When Kermit is missing in *The Muppets Take Manhattan*, Miss Piggy leaves it to others to organize the search and instead plays a supporting role.

Inness believes that one way to reduce the toughness of a female character is to soften her portrayal with images that are associated with femininity (56). This may allow the female character to be more palatable to audiences. From this perspective, Miss Piggy is tough, but her toughness is kept in balance with her long blond hair, dark eyelashes, her shiny and gaudy jewelry, her long satin mauve or pink dresses, and her almost ubiquitous long gloves. It is amusing to see a character in a satin dress and evening gloves be verbally assertive and even physically aggressive because it is unexpected and contradicts stereotypes of femininity.

However, Miss Piggy is not truly a "tough girl," as she does not fully display the leadership, and only shows some of the necessary physical attributes suggested by Inness. Furthermore, she does not disregard her femininity in order to be tough. Her appearance is very important to her, as she wishes to remain feminine to be a model or pursue other glamorous feminine career choices. Thus, we can view Miss Piggy as a woman who will use masculine traits of toughness, decisiveness, and aggression to look after her own welfare. However, she is not fully masculine in that she does not display the leadership and analytical properties that Bem has found are associated with masculinity.

It would be incorrect to think that this juxtaposition of toughness with feminine appearance is merely a fabrication to keep television audiences engaged. Women in other venues of entertainment express the same dichotomy. For example, Beggan and Allison examined *Playboy* centerfolds and noticed that some of these models described themselves in ways that would be considered tough (e.g., fighters, dislike for feeling inferior, enjoying a good argument, independent, committed to their careers) yet posed in the nude and in ways that embody Western ideals of femininity (811). Although *Playboy* models are hardly typical of women in the "real" world, and they are involved in an industry that is aimed at men's entertainment, it leads one to wonder if the mixture of masculine and feminine is actually an accurate rather than a fabricated view of women's behavior. It seems, then, that some women really do possess this toughness and blend it with exterior conformity (i.e., making their appearance conform) to feminine stereotypes.

Interestingly, Beggan and Allison proposed that, in order for cultural representations of "tough women" to be accepted and developed further, two groups must come to agree with this identity (814). First, it is girls and women who will come to occupy the tough girl image and display it freely in society. Second, it is men, who remain the culturally dominant figure in Western society, who must embrace and accept women who subscribe to this image. In order for the tough girl image to succeed, they argue that men must be willing to accept alternative views of femininity.

Given that these authors were discussing a type of entertainment that was primarily aimed at men, their conclusions are sensible. We go further, though, and suggest that for a "tough" female character such as Miss Piggy to be accepted by audiences, regardless of the viewers' gender, she had to look feminine and simultaneously represent a dynamic complexity of feminine and masculine personality features and physical characteristics. Her dichotomous use of masculinity and femininity allows her to be far more challenging to gender stereotypes than a more conformist character would be, and presumably, allows her to be markedly more humorous. Humor can flaunt this juxtaposition: how often do we see glamorous looking women become physically aggressive when they are insulted? Do we ever see these women wearing roller skates and chasing down a purse-snatcher? Would these women push back when they were told that they were specially capable of cooking or ironing, as Miss Piggy is told by Link in "Pigs in Space?" To make these comparisons even more outrageous, Miss Piggy is a loud, assertive pig, who is in love with a gentle frog who is much smaller than herself. This dichotomy of feminine and masculine is the very heart of Miss Piggy, and we propose that it is precisely what has allowed her to have such an enduring presence with the Muppets.

Among a highly varied cast of characters that includes, among other things, a frog, a bear, and Gonzo, who is not of any earthly species, Miss Piggy is the only female, primary character. She was an integral part of *The Muppet Show* from its inaugural pilot episode to *Muppets in Space*. She is even included in the most recent Muppet release, *The Muppets' Wizard of Oz*, a movie that is discussed elsewhere in this volume. She appears in all of the Muppet movies, except for Kermit's solo movie, *Kermit's Swamp Years*, and has a pivotal role in many of them. Perhaps she is a prevalent character not just because she is complex and interesting, but also because the production staff of the Muppets wanted to ensure that there was at least one visible female character. This possibility is supported in that Jim Henson recognized that there was a lack of strong female characters aside from Miss Piggy and sought to rectify this issue in the *Muppet Babies* television show by creating Skeeter, Scooter's twin sister (Finch 206).

This said, it has to be more than an issue of convenience that allowed Miss Piggy to have longevity with the Muppets. It is unlikely that a shallow, undeveloped character would have had her lasting prominence. As we have discussed, we believe that the key to understanding the complexity and humor of Miss Piggy is to examine her from the social perspective of gender. Using this approach, we have shown that she satisfies both feminine and masculine stereotypes, without having to sacrifice the key elements of one to satisfy the other. That is, while being a strongly feminine character, she can also display stereotypical male characteristics without losing her femininity. While dressing in pink satin evening gowns, she is fully capable of acting aggressively and athletically, thus acting like a male while still being female.

Miss Piggy's unique blend of traits, both physical and non-physical, has captured the interest of the general population and continues to do so. She has "authored" four books, including the highly popular *Miss Piggy's Guide to Life* (1981) that was on the *New York Times* bestseller list for 29 weeks, reaching the fourth position on July 5th 1981 and has appeared in a music video, various recent television shows, and was on the cover of *Life* magazine in August 1980 with the banner "Miss Piggy for President." She released her own perfume, Moi, in 1998, and in 2005 she appeared on postage stamps in the United States and in Belgium. As a popular and successful element of the Muppets, it is clear that her violation of some female stereotypes is in some way acceptable and has not harmed her appeal. We suggest that since her non-traditional behavior is tolerated, Miss Piggy, the Muppets, and television have successfully challenged our gender stereotypes using humor. It is possible that Miss Piggy has influenced viewers to challenge their own views on gender, perhaps empowering them to act without as much concern as they might have otherwise for social expectations. An underlying theme to our discussion has been that the dichotomy of Miss Piggy's character is precisely what makes her appealing, in that she displays qualities with which both women and men can associate. Given that she directly challenges gender stereotypes and presents to viewers society's notions of femininity and masculinity, there is always some action, characteristic or behavior to which viewers can respond. Such responses need not be positive; all that matters is that there is a response, as this signals that viewers are, at some level, considering their adherence to gender stereotypes.

Furthermore, this response might be aimed at one or more of the various levels of Miss Piggy; one might be concerned with her words, provided by the script writers, or the way she says a statement, as provided by the voice performers. Viewers might be concerned with her movements, as provided by the puppeteers, or with the fact that she actually exists at all and has stayed with the Muppets since the beginning. Regardless of the level of interaction, Miss Piggy, through her performance, displays and challenges society's attitudes and acceptance of what it means to be feminine and masculine. She may be "just a Muppet," but she is also showing us what it means to be human, to be feminine, to be masculine, and she helps us to understand one another a little better. This is an incredibly large influence for one make-believe character, but would one actually expect any less from the wonderful, uniquely strong, but feminine, Miss Piggy?

Works Cited

Beard, Henry. *Miss Piggy's Guide to Life*. New York: Alfred Knopf, 1981.
Beggan, James, and Scott T. Allison. "Tough Women in the Unlikeliest of Places: The Unexpected Toughness of the Playboy Playmate." *Journal of Popular Culture* 38 (2005): 796–818.
Bem, Sandra. "The Measurement of Psychological Androgyny." *Journal of Consulting and Clinical Psychology* 42 (1974): 155–62.
Bisset, Alex, ed. *Compact Oxford Canadian Dictionary*. New York: Oxford University Press, 2002.

"Bonnie Erickson." Muppet Wiki. 31 December 2007 <http://muppet.wikia.com/wiki/Bonnie_Erickson>
Desjardins, Mary. "Gender and Television." The Museum of Broadcast Communications. 12 December 2008. <http://www.museum.tv/archives/etv/G/htmlG/genderandte/genderandte.htm>
Downs, Chris, and Sheila Harrison. "Embarrassing Age Spots or Just Plain Ugly? Physical Attractiveness Stereotyping as an Instrument of Sexism on American Television Commercials." *Sex Roles*, 12 (1985): 9–18.
Finch, Christopher. *Jim Henson, The Works: The Art, the Magic, the Imagination*. New York: Random House, 1993.
Firth, Michael, and Henry Beard, eds. *Miss Piggy's Treasury of Art Masterpieces from the Kermitage Collection*. New York: Henry Holt, 1984.
Gerbner, George. "Violence in Television Drama: Trends and Symbolic Functions." *Television and Social Behavior: Media Content and Control*. Eds. George Comstock and Eli Rubinstein. Washington, DC: 1972, 28–187.
Hartford, James. *Korolev: How One Man Masterminded the Soviet Drive to Beat America to the Moon*. New York: John Wiley & Sons, 1997.
Hirschman, Elizabeth, and Barbara Stern. "Representations of Women's Identities and Goals: The Past Fifty Years in Film and Television." *The Why of Consumption: Contemporary Perspectives on Consumer Motives, Goals, and Desires*. Eds. S. Ratneshwar, David Glen Mick, and Cynthia Huffman. New York: Routledge, 2000. 164–176.
Inness, Sherrie A. *Tough Girls: Women Warriors and Wonder Women in Popular Culture*. Philadelphia: University of Pennsylvania Press, 1999.
Kalisch, Philip, and Beatrice Kalisch. "Sex-role Stereotyping of Nurses and Physicians on Prime-Time Television: A Dichotomy of Occupational Portrayals." *Sex Roles* 10 (1984): 533–53.
Kelleher, Wendy. "The Canning Season" [review]. *Journal of Adolescent and Adult Literacy* 47 (2004): 521–22.
Lewis, Jim. *In the Kitchen with Miss Piggy: Fabulous Recipes from My Famous Celebrity Friends*. New York: Time-Life, 1996.
_____, and Lousie Gikow. *Miss Piggy's Rules: Swine-Tested Secrets for Catching Mr. Right, Keeping Him and Throwing Him Back When You've Had Enough*. Philadelphia: Running Press Book Publishers, 1997.
Marston, William. "Why 100,000,000 Americans Read Comics." *The American Scholar* Winter 1943–44.
"Miss Piggy." Muppet Wiki. 31 December 2007 <http://muppet.wikia.com/wiki/Miss_Piggy>
Rhode, Deborah. "Media Images, Feminist Issues." *Signs: Journal of Women in Culture and Society* 20 (1995): 685–710.
Ricciardelli, Lina, and Robert Williams. "Desirable and Undesirable Gender Traits in Three Behavioral Domains." *Sex Roles* 33 (1995): 637–55.
Rowe, Kathleen. *The Unruly Woman: Gender and the Genres of Laughter*. Austin: University of Texas Press, 1995.
Schmitt, David, and 108 members of the International Sexuality Description Project. "Universal Sex Differences in the Desire for Sexual Variety: Tests from 52 Nations, 6 Continents, and 13 Islands." *Journal of Personality and Social Psychology* 85 (2003): 85–104.
Smith, Barbara. *The Psychology of Sex and Gender*. Toronto: Pearson Education, 2007.
Thompson, Teresa, and Eugenia Zerbinos. "Gender Roles in Animated Cartoons: Has the Picture Changed in 20 Years?" *Sex Roles* 32 (1995): 651–73.
Tuchman, Gaye, Arlene Kaplan Daniels, and James Benet, eds. *Hearth and Home: Images of Women in the Mass Media*. New York: Oxford University Press, 1978.
Wachutka, Ali. "Becoming a Princess: The Transition from Individual to Sex Object." Arizona State University, Department of English. 31 December 2007. <http://www.asu.edu/clas/english/writingprograms/printersdevil/2006/princess.doc>

Muppets and Money
Andrew Leal

"Hello, all you lovers of hot dogs and money!" Thus speaks the cheerful Muppet Skip in a 1966 film produced by Muppets Inc. for Wilson's Meats. One of several such projects designed for business meetings and presentations, this opening gleefully equates lunch meats, advertising, and commerce as the same process: a continual grinding. The rest of the ad, however, looks at that process as filtered through sardonic narration by Jim Henson and vacillates between satirizing market research and spoofing "arty" experimental films (albeit one which experiments itself, via pop art collage and a dancing, stop-motion can of ham). As collaborator Frank Oz recalled, Henson "always knew from the very beginning that commerce and art were a symbiotic duo, that he had to make the money in commercials to do the stuff he wanted to do" (*The World of Jim Henson*). This symbiotic duo is inexorably linked, but Henson managed to find the art in the commerce, though conversely and perhaps inevitably, many of his more purely "artistic" films (such as *Labyrinth*) failed to recoup their expenses.

The career of Jim Henson continually straddled the lines between art and commerce, between advertising and "public service" educational projects, between broad comedy and more expensive, often less than remunerative explorations into fantasy. The continued cultural and economic existence of his Muppet characters has followed much the same path. Henson's adroit juggling of financial considerations with aesthetics is reflected in much of his work, and contradictions abound. These contradictions multiply even further within the projects produced after his death, as the Muppets have been pushed and pulled in several directions by many hands (and not just those occupying the puppets' interiors). The Muppets themselves are multifaceted: fictional characters, physical artifacts (which can be repaired, refurbished, preserved in museums, or sold on E-bay), and commercial property. They are characters within a narrative, yet as in *The Muppet Movie* and elsewhere, they are keenly aware of that narrative. The Muppets are media personalities, appearing as themselves on talk shows to glibly discuss their personal lives, promote projects like any number of Hollywood figures, and to act as pitch-puppets for everything from food to MasterCard or Virgin Atlantic airlines. Kermit in particular has also been used to advocate causes apart from consumerism or self-promotion, such as a series of public service announcements in the late 1980s about conserving energy and saving the planet earth. In 2007, the interests of consumerism and environmentalism merged, as Kermit became the spokesfrog for Ford's new hybrid car.

Thus *The Muppet Show* cast frequently represents the little guy standing up against the ruthless capitalist, yet they've also been used continually as commercial spokescharacters. As a viable financial property, the Muppets have been heavily exploited through merchandise and have also been the subject of multiple financial maneuverings and takeovers, to the point where the Walt Disney Company currently owns not only the characters, but "The Muppet" name, and *Sesame Street* can only use the term by sufferance (and possibly due to its own official non-profit status). As spokescharacters, they engage in hard-sell tactics; as a property, their corporate owners vacillate between making them "edgier" and hipper or marketing them purely as a children's property and a source of nostalgia; and as characters, collectively, they examine a range of traits and approaches to money, and thus, to the larger world.

The Commercials: Violence Sells

Kermit the Frog, as the most recognizable Muppet, is the idealist, yet like Henson himself, he negotiates several roles and situations. In the early days, he frequently appeared in commercials, less as a pitchman than as a perennial victim. The early Muppet commercials, produced for a variety of regional and later national sponsors beginning in 1957, bring new meaning to the word "hard sell," as anyone who failed to buy the sponsor's product would inevitably be devoured, explode, suffer defenestration, or some other grisly fate. Such vague teams as Wilkins and Wontkins, Scoop and Skip, and others performed this task, but Kermit also participated. Usually teamed with the burly Mack, Kermit would be tossed out of a window, stabbed with a fork, or have a bite taken out of him, all in the service of selling Claussen's bread or Onky meats. Rowlf the Dog usually encountered less opposition when promoting Esskay Meats in the presence of the lovely commercial spokeslady Pat. When Henson gradually began marketing his own characters, he used the same tactics. An ad for an early product, Ideal Toy versions of Rowlf and Kermit, features the puppets interrupting Rowlf's salespitch to use hard-sell tactics: "Buy us, oh buy us, oh buy us we beg, and if you don't buy us, we'll bite you in the leg/Buy us at once, we're a bundle of charms, and if you don't buy us, we'll break both your arms." This typifies the Muppet sense of humor and serves as Henson's subtle attempt to simultaneously sell children's toys yet remind adult viewers that the Muppets have yet to lose their edge.

In addition to marketing his own characters and other people's products, Henson produced clever "meeting films." Some accompanied the commercial campaigns and provided a comedic orientation for the company's salesmen, satirizing the behind-the-scenes process, the fame of the Muppets, and the product itself, followed by the commercials. In 1965, a similar series was launched for IBM, commissioned by IBM's head of television and film, David Lazer. Lazer subsequently left the company to join Henson full-time, serving as producer of countless Muppet projects and as a key administrative figure in Henson Associates.

The proceeds of these early commercial campaigns helped fund Henson's efforts not only to create his own stable of characters but to experiment as a filmmaker, resulting in such projects as his 1967 short film, *Time Piece*. *Time Piece* combines Henson's love of cinema, jazz, and images with social satire, much of which deals with consumption and money. The nameless man, played by Henson, works a soul-crushing job, tortured by sexual frustration and the drudgery of stamping papers and literally churning out what appears to be a form of garbage (charred boxes) on an assembly line. The film earned an Academy Award nomination and was subject to earnest academic examination, as in Paul Schreivogel's 1970 *Films in Depth* piece, "Time Piece: A Film Study," which asked such queries as "'What does the reverse motion of the table-setting scene say about our 'instant' society? How is it related to the cooking of the meal?" The satirical commentary on consumption and the workplace is readily apparent, but perhaps best exemplified by a single image. Henson's face appears on a dollar bill, offering a cry of "Help!" which serves as the only dialogue in the film (repeated on many occasions). In 2008, Henson.com added a gallery of *Time Piece* images, including the "man on dollar bill," and the full short was made available for download through iTunes.

P Is for Pitchman: Sesame Street *and the Muppet Image*

In contrast, there is the utopian vision of *Sesame Street*. The show was conceived as an educational venture, and Henson was very concerned about the marketing of the Muppet characters. Within the show itself, economic reality was (and still is) seldom addressed and, despite the presence of several thriving businesses, money seldom if ever changes hands. Money exists as an object, a quarter to illustrate the letter Q, or five pennies to demonstrate a quantity, but otherwise it has no reality. Luis and Maria own a repair shop but only because they enjoy the work and someone has to repair Mr. Snuffleupagus' giant toaster. Bert and Ernie live together in a basement apartment but never work, have no visible parents, and don't pay rent. In the special *Christmas Eve on Sesame Street*, in order to get presents for each other, the pair go to Hooper's Store and engage in a barter system, trading rubber duckies and paper clip collections for goods. Even a recurring character known as "The Salesman" continually tries to sell Ernie such objects as an O for a nickel, but he never receives payment, or else an invisible ice cream cone is paid for in invisible coinage. One of the few occasions when money is specifically addressed in basic economic terms centers on Cookie Monster; this is natural, since Cookie is the only character whose sole purpose is consumption and desire, and the puppet had in fact made his debut in an IBM meeting film, devouring a computer. In a 1976 episode, Cookie Monster collects money from the residents of the street, claiming it's to help save an endangered species. The monster uses the money to buy cookies for himself, astutely claiming that he's the only remaining Cookie Monster in existence (Episode 0849; episode documents, CTW Archives).

The use of the Muppets on *Sesame Street* was itself the result of Henson's careful financial negotiations; though his correspondence exhibits a certain sympathy for the CTW's aims and an eagerness to assist in those, he was all too aware how this would affect the image of Muppets Inc. and anxious to obtain appropriate recompense for himself and his team of designers and puppeteers. Wrangles between CTW executive Ronald L. Weaver and Henson accountant Irving Chesnell over quoted salaries for the construction and performance of the Muppets, with Chesnell denying CTW the option to audit their accounts for the segments, very nearly led to the reduction or even omission of the Muppets for the second season of *Sesame Street*. Henson also arranged for a 70–30 share of the profits from merchandise but in general remained cautious about putting the educational Muppets on consumer products and even more concerned about tainting their image. Well until the 1980s, with the exception of cameo appearances and talk show spots, Henson generally kept his *Sesame Street* family distinct from the other Muppets, a segregation based both on the differences between children's and more adult characters and, more significantly, between non-profit and commercial endeavors. Kermit was the only notable cross-over character, and as such, was the subject of critical concern early on. *Hey Cinderella!*, a Muppet special produced in 1968 and initially appearing in Canada in 1969, made its American debut in 1970. Since *Sesame Street* was already in its first season by then, *New York Times* critic Jack Gould assumed this was an example of Children's Television Workshop going commercial and selling out: "Apparently, the Children's Television Workshop ... is not averse to cashing in when success strikes. Whatever television may be called, public or commercial, sooner or later the compromises start if the ratings are right. *Sesame Street* last night lost a little of its luster as Kermit broke the faith and became one more pitchman."

In an April 20, 1970, letter, Jim Henson refuted this assessment, pointing out that Kermit had been used on network TV and in commercials for years, "as most of my work has historically been adult" (CTW Archives). Due to his work on *Sesame Street* and his own concerns for children's television, he had "become a great deal more selective, and have turned down many lucrative offers that seemed to be trying to capitalize on *Sesame Street*" (CTW Archives). Henson noted that promotion for the special, sponsored by tobacco company R. J. Reynolds, did not make use of Kermit's *Sesame Street* fame, and he offered a reasonably truthful summary of his own practical attitude towards his work: "As for myself, I don't intend to leave commercial television. This is where the Muppets and I have worked for many years, and it is the income from commercial TV that makes my participation in educational TV possible. What I will try to do is what I have tried to do on *Sesame Street* this season, that is to work with a degree of integrity and responsibility to the children of the country" (CTW Archives). As Stefan Kanfer reported in *Time* magazine, "When it was given a network airing, the frog was compromised. Or so Henson decided. Like Jim Thorpe, Kermit played for money, and now must relinquish his amateur standing. He is being phased out of the show. He will be replaced by such Muppets as Lecturer Herbert Birdsfoot and Sherlock Hemlock, a bumbling sleuth." This actually occurred during the second season, but after a time, Kermit's popularity and icon status led to a return, while Herbert Birdsfoot receded into the background and the more popular Sherlock Hemlock filled a different function. To avoid further problems, in 1971, producer Dave Connell raised the possibility of buying exclusive rights to Kermit for the duration of *Sesame Street* (CTW Production memo. February 1, 1971). This never happened, and in 1976, in fact, then CTW president Bill Whaley expressed concern and negotiated for a new merchandising percentage agreement with Henson, in particular feeling that Kermit's exposure on a non-commercial series laid the foundations for the frog's future success, and that as such CTW deserved a percentage (Whaley suggested 40 percent) of all Kermit related merchandise sales (even those not tied to *Sesame Street*). Thus, from being branded a sell-out, Kermit (or at least Jim Henson and Muppets Inc.) was now perceived as a hold-out. Though Whaley and Henson lawyer Al Gottesman eventually came to terms, the incident demonstrates the fact that by 1976, Kermit and the Muppets had gone from a novelty act, occasional commercial pitchmen, and educators to international superstars.

Struggles of Management: Muppet Show and Beyond

Following the success of *Sesame Street*, Henson had increased his profile but also struggled to market the Muppets as suitable entertainment for adults. Two pilots for what would eventually become *The Muppet Show* aired in 1974 and 1975, but neither was picked up by U.S. networks: *The Muppet Valentines Show* and *The Muppet Show: Sex and Violence*. The latter title did not necessarily reflect the content but was built ironically on the perceived sales value of both items on network television, and featured a "Seven Deadly Sins Pageant" (Avarice was a living cash register, obsessed with "money, money, money.") To supplement his income in the meantime, and based on the success of the earlier meeting films for Wilson's Meats and IBM, Henson launched a new series of "Muppet Meeting Films," no longer built around a specific product or corporation but sold and rented to any company, for use as icebreakers and during coffee breaks or to satirize specific concerns, fears, and changes in industry and salesmanship. The first batch was produced concurrently with *The Muppet Show: Sex and Violence*. The 1975 meeting films thus marked early appearances by future *Muppet Show* regulars Sam the Eagle, Janice, Waldorf (as P. Fenton Cosgrove), and Gonzo, alongside the more familiar Kermit. However, the real star of the Muppet Meeting Films, introduced that same year, was Leo, a manic salesman. Leo's defining moment was in the aptly titled "Sell, Sell, Sell!" Leo delivers a corporate pep talk that begins sedately and grows increasingly feverish, tying salesmanship to American heritage and stressing the importance of earning an "honest buck." Reaching a hysterical crescendo, Leo says that one must sell for the sake of children, motherhood, and apple pie and for puppy dogs, among others (with slides appearing behind him). Henson simultaneously kids and reinforces the idea that free enterprise capitalism is inseparable from America, since after all, the "American dream" is largely tied to financial prosperity.

"Sell, Sell, Sell!" also inspired the pitch reel for *The Muppet Show*. Leo reprised his role, again growing increasingly frantic, and noting that if they sell the show, "We'll all be famous and temperamental and hard to work with," and noting that there are fortunes to be made, crescendoing to imply that God himself will bless the network with a 40 percent share of the ratings (and since the radio era, ratings equaled increased advertising revenue and thus, more money). When the series finally reached fruition, however, it represented a throw back, a run-down vaudeville theater, which suffered continually from its own economic problems. At one point, the performances are held at a train station while the theater is fumigated.

On *The Muppet Show*, Kermit, as manager of the motley troupe and producer, is the one faced with the day to day financial problems. Though this reality only sporadically intruded on *The Muppet Show*, when it did, it did so with great force. The primary embodiment of this was J. P. Grosse, the oft-mentioned and only occasionally seen owner of the theater, a gruff capitalist mogul with no interest in either mass entertainment or high art, only the bottom dollar. His name intentionally calls to mind the financier John Pierpont Morgan, and the surname "Grosse" is an apt description, since gross he is in manner and taste, and financial gross is his great love. In his first on-screen appearance, he appraises the theater only as property and orders nephew Scooter to consider taking a lien out "on the frog." Grosse is concerned only with the condition of the theater and its potential as far as profit is concerned. In other episodes, J. P. sells the mineral rights to the theater to a group of Arabs, represents a debt collection agency, and tellingly tries to directly affect the show's acts, mimicking the power that sponsors historically yielded in the radio and early television era by promising to fill the payroll only if Kermit books lady wrestling. Thus Grosse serves as a composite caricature of the landlord, the sponsor, the cruel employer, and the cigar-smoking big business capitalist. In the closest thing to a sentimental moment for the character, in his second appearance along with the homophonic guest star Jaye P. Morgan, Grosse attempts to steal the spotlight to sing an atonal song about money, which he dedicates to "the boys" at his debt collection agency. He rules through bullying, nepotism, and bribery. Writer Jerry Juhl described J. P. Grosse as "a good concept so long as we didn't see him, but when we introduced him in person, he was just too harsh. You didn't want to have him around" (Finch 166). He forces Kermit to sacrifice his artistic integrity for money, although in the series, in contrast to the subsequent idealism of *The Muppet Movie*, that integrity was itself questionable, in a world in which acts included prancing poultry, invisible hamburgers, and the various oddities of Gonzo. One could potentially read this as a criticism of the rigors of the commercial entertainment system, yet Jim Henson worked within the system.

The success of *The Muppet Show* caused Henson and his Muppets to seek further fortune on the big-screen with *The Muppet Movie*. Directed by Henson, this $8 million production brought Kermit and company into the real world, brought in a range of celebrity cameos, and elaborated on the "let's put on a show" concept. The movie is also presented as a film made by the Muppets, as they arrive to attend the screening, and the plot focuses on Kermit, an idealistic dreamer who's encouraged to go to Hollywood in order to "make millions of people happy," gathering friends along the way, and finally receiving a standard "rich and famous" contract from Lew Lorde (played by Orson Welles, who knew something about the pitfalls of Hollywood that the movie naturally ignored). *The Muppet Movie* grossed over $76 million at the domestic box office, spawning more movies and even heavier merchandising, without adversely affecting the public perception of either Kermit or creator Henson as idealistic dreamers but clearly proving that entertainment and moneymaking are, of course, hardly at odds. The script itself, as if to heighten Kermit's status and portray his goals as the basic pursuit of the American dream (and thus admirable), presents a contrast in the form of the vicious, purely mercurial Doc Hopper. Hopper, like Grosse, is another stock capitalist antagonist (although with slightly more complexity), and he literally wants to put a lien on Kermit's legs. A loose parody of such fast food magnates as Colonel Sanders, the character is the ambitious owner of a chain of fried frog leg restaurants. When Hopper's flunky discovers Kermit, Doc feels he's found the perfect spokesfrog. While Grosse is blunt, tactless, and utterly crude, Hopper is outwardly charming and gracious, flattering Kermit, who makes "a wonderful frog," and offering him financial compensation. Kermit is appalled, however, by the idea that he could promote the consumption of his own species. Doc's means of production does more than exploit the masses: it fries their limbs and serves them with chili and barbecue sauce. While Doc sees expansion and a better public image, Kermit sees only visions of "frogs on crutches," representing the "little people" who are trampled on in the course of business. Hopper becomes increasingly obsessed, and increasingly less scrupulous, in his attempts to obtain Kermit. He hires a crackpot German scientist to brainwash Kermit to do his bidding and later gathers a professional frog killer and a gang of general hoodlums, finally deciding that he wants him dead or alive.

In a final stand off, Hopper reveals that his obsession is rooted in his dream of some day owning a thousand frog leg restaurants. Kermit points out that Doc's dream has effectively destroyed his scruples and even his humanity, revealing that he has no friends. In contrast, the entire film has been built around Kermit's own dream of going to Hollywood. Again demonstrating the gray area surrounding money, however, this dream is still described in terms of becoming "rich and famous," and Kermit achieves this goal. In differentiating the two, the movie does so in Hollywood terms and recalls the work of Frank Capra and Preston Sturges. Unlike Hopper, Kermit's dream is valorized because, like Joel McCrea at the end of Sturges' *Sullivan's Travels*, he feels that making people happy on the screen is his calling, and in the process, he accrues a band of friends whom he helps. The trappings of being "rich and famous" are in fact absent, except in the fact that the Muppets have made their movie. In a sense, Kermit's is a Horatio Alger story, while Doc Hopper is a slanted version of Henry Ford, Harlan Sanders, and any capitalist in an agit-prop drama, or for that matter, a Capra movie. In fact, Charles Durning bears a passing resemblance to Edward Arnold, who played plutocrat J. Anthony Kirby in Capra's *You Can't Take It With You*. Yet unlike Arnold's Kirby, Hopper remains unrepentant. Kermit's speech gives him pause, but after scratching his head and with only slight reluctance, he gives the order to kill Kermit (planning to use his stuffed carcass for the commercials instead). Only a *deus-ex*-muppeta in the form of a giant Animal dispels Hopper, perhaps acknowledging the fact that in real life, the powerful capitalist is not so easily set aside.

As *The Muppet Show* continued to gain popularity, Miss Piggy became the show's breakout star, glamour icon, and the focal point of a merchandise blitz which encompassed calendars, dolls, magazine covers, and in particular, the book *Miss Piggy's Guide to Life*. While Kermit is the idealist and straight man and figures such as Grosse and Hopper are greedy villains, Miss Piggy occupies the middle ground, representing the desire for wealth and fame, embodying its allure (without always possessing its trappings), and showing the pitfalls. In *The Muppet Movie*, Kermit and company are assigned the "standard rich and famous contract," and that's that. On *The Muppet Show*, and in other specials, movies, and merchandise, Piggy's blind ambition carries her through a variety of personal and professional pitfalls. On *The Muppet Show*, she bribes audiences to increase her popularity, rankles when guest stars steal her spotlight, tries (and fails) to suck up to J. P. Grosse, and maintains constant contact with her agent (usually Bernie). Fashion, food, and living high on the hog (ahem) are her goals, and unlike Kermit, she displays a certain pragmatism to what she must do on the way. *Miss Piggy's Guide to Life*, allegedly penned by Piggy herself, expounds on this philosophy and gleefully exploits her materialism, though her own financial management is such that she has to borrow five dollars from Kermit. The book itself became a bestseller, remaining on the *New York Times* list for nearly thirty weeks. Decades later, when Piggy's star was slightly dimmed, she and Kermit the Frog appeared in a Denny's commercial as celebrity spokes characters. Piggy gleefully expresses her hunger for a Denny's Grand Slam, complete with sausage and bacon. When pressed on the subject, Piggy denies the cannibalism accusations by claiming, "Moi is 100 percent botox." Coincidentally, soon after, Denny's fired its advertising agency. This spot completely contradicted the earlier message of *The Muppet Movie* and was representative of how the Muppets' characterization and purpose often became muddled under hands other than those of their creator.

Under New Management

Following Jim Henson's sudden death in 1990, the Muppets faced their own battle for survival and ownership, as Michael Eisner and the Disney Company grappled with the Henson family. The Muppet characters themselves, in fact, when trying to figure out who Jim Henson was in the special *The Muppets Celebrate Jim Henson*, discover his name on their paychecks and naturally assume that he was an accountant. In 1992, following the first aborted deal with Disney, the studio still distributed *The Muppet Christmas Carol* as the first theatrical feature for the Muppets "under new management," so to speak. The film was the first to feature the Muppets' enacting a classic literary tale instead of an original story, but the basic conflict is a very familiar one. Ebenezer Scrooge, simultaneously protagonist and antagonist, represents a Victorian era capitalist, a money lender who sees Christmas as "the foreclosure season." He's also a tenement landlord who "charges folks a fortune for his dark and drafty houses," and when faced with well-meaning charity collectors in the form of Bunsen and Beaker, he responds that the homeless must go to the prisons and workhouses, and "if they'd rather die, they'd better do it, and decrease the surplus population" (*The Muppet Christmas Carol*). Though in Dickens' original text Scrooge has only Cratchit as a clerk, the Muppet version supplies the miser with a bevy of scurrying rats as bookkeepers.

By expanding his staff, Scrooge becomes more explicitly a Victorian, industrial age exploiter, oppressing his employees in a manner not unlike the factory workers in Dickens' own *Hard Times*. The lack of coal, low wages, constant harassment, and even the reluctance to provide holidays all suggest that Scrooge and Marley would be all too ripe for unionization in a later time. The fact that the rats and the timid frog Cratchit are infinitely more human than Scrooge at the outset provides a studied contrast; in Scrooge's favor, it does suggest a sort of early affirmative action, hiring employees of all species and abusing everyone regardless of creed, color, foam, felt, or feathers.

The creation of a Muppet London, with Scrooge and his family and fiancée as the only notable human interlopers, presents an almost ideological casting of types. As noted, all of Scrooge's clerks are rats, nature's scavengers and bottom feeders, yet they're all portrayed sympathetically. Penguins appear as a group of merry, financially secure revelers who are able to host a skating party, but their presumed wealth is not an obstacle to goodness, since they use it in "the Christmas spirit." Scrooge's fellow businessmen, by contrast, are a cadre of pigs, complacent figures in waistcoats and top hats. While the group chuckles at Scrooge's demise in the future, they're scarcely better than he is, snorting happily about lunch while surrounded, just as Scrooge is, by poverty and want, including a family of hungry mice (mice, after all, are cuter than rats, and so they appear sporadically as representatives of a poor but good family, mirroring the Cratchits). Finally, Old Joe, the fence who cackles over the proceeds raided from Scrooge's abode, is a large spider, seated in the center of a dingy room, but with long arms which reach out. He spins a web of theft and profits from the rag-picking of his three equally dubious associates (a bird, an insect, and a slimy creature who resembles a cross between a toad and a potato). With Scrooge's redemption, however, all of the above characters join together for the finale, a joyous feast which seemingly erases all class and economic distinctions for the sake of the happy ending. *The Muppet Christmas Carol* remains the best critically received and most financially successful of the handful of feature-length Muppet vehicles which followed Henson's death; though budgeted at $12 million, the domestic gross was a respectable and encouraging $27 million.

From that promising start, however, subsequent attempts at film and TV comebacks were more sporadic, and the question of audience remained: in 1996, Kermit found himself headlining sing-along videos about cars and planes at the same time as *Muppets Tonight*, a prime-time return, tried to position the troupe as hip and edgy with guest stars like Coolio and Michelle Pfeiffer. The Muppets continued to be the subject of a fierce bidding war, and at one point were owned by the German conglomerate EMTV. At the 2001 MuppetFest event, Miss Piggy appeared briefly on a video monitor and complained that Kermit sold the company, and all she got was a t-shirt emblazoned with the slogan "Somebody in Munich Loves Me" (Horn 44). The joke reflected both the lack of a clear ownership identity and the fact that, hardcore Muppet fans aside, the troupe's profile was fading fast in the U.S., with *Muppets from Space* doing little to revive their fortunes. Yet in several European nations, the Muppets remained beloved. This too hearkened to the time when the Muppets were seen in countless nations and languages and essentially served as cultural ambassadors, even going behind the Iron Curtain.

Communism: No Bears on Park Avenue

From commercialism and capitalism, one finally comes to Communism. Henson jokingly referred to it as far back as 1958, in fact, in a Wilkins Coffee spot. A Russian coffee shop, complete with a hammer and sickle overhead, sells "Party Line Coffee"; Wontkins, in a change of pace, recommends Wilkins, only to be chewed out by Wilkins as a traitor for promoting "capitalist coffee." Naturally, he then whispers an order for two pounds to be delivered to his back door. Decades later, the Muppets would interact with Communist powers and people on a more direct level.

As proof that differing socioeconomic systems do not deter the Muppets, in 1983, Big Bird starred in the first co-production between a U.S. television network and the People's Republic of China. *Big Bird in China*, which aired in both countries, had the bird functioning as a goodwill ambassador, learning about China. The special tends to avoid commerce, instead presenting a wide array of citizens dancing, to the extent that dance appears to be China's principal industry. However, Big Bird also gazes in passing at Mao's Tomb, and, in a telling scene, the camera spotlights a group of Red Army members, smiling and pointing. No malice is attached, as the group is merely amused by the Capitalist Muppet who has innocently blundered into their nation. In the greater tradition of innocents, fools, and clowns, Big Bird does not carry with him any scent of imperialism, of capitalist exploitation, or any other concerns. In fact, so beloved would Big Bird become as a result that in 2003, when China launched its own *Sesame Street* co-production, the Chinese producers were surprised and even affronted when Sesame Workshop suggested they design a Chinese counterpart to Big Bird. This is a common practice, precisely to avoid imperialistic accusations and to tailor the character to match the culture and desires of the specific nation. China, however, wanted Big Bird, so they received "Da Niao," the literal translation of the character's name. Caroll Spinney trained the Chinese performer, and Sesame Workshop, in press materials, officially explained that Da Niao is Big Bird's cousin, identical in both appearance and personality.

A year after *Big Bird in China*, Jim Henson made the first of many visits to the Soviet Union, performing Kermit and meeting with noted Russian puppeteer Sergei Obratzov. Henson continued to make periodic goodwill trips to Russia, culminating in the Muppet involvement in the first joint-coproduction between the Soviet Union and the United States. This project was the 1988 special *Free to Be ... a Family*, broadcast in both countries through a satellite hook-up and hosted and produced by Marlo Thomas. The purpose of the special was to emphasize the fact that kids in the U.S. and Russia are much the same and can relate to one another, in hopes of bringing peace between the nations. Coincidentally or otherwise, the Berlin Wall collapsed the following year, and the Cold War officially ended. A variety of U.S. and Russian entertainers are featured, with the former represented by Jon Bon Jovi, Robin Williams, Penn and Teller, and naturally, the Muppets. The special was produced and co-written by *Sesame Street*/Muppet songwriter Christopher Cerf and other Henson vets. In satiric sketches, Kermit and Miss Piggy visit Moscow and encounter the Russian puppet star Khriusha the pig. At one point, the puppets exchange films criticizing the other side. While Kermit narrates the sad tale of a Russian puppet elephant, unable to join his ballerina lover in America, Khriusha presents a stinging attack on American inequity, focusing on an unemployed Muppet bear, living in a cardboard shack on the streets of New York City. Park Avenue stoutly refuses to house bears (with signs proclaiming such), and this particular bruin suffered an astonishing reversal, when a new Wall Street job (on the floor of the exchange, as a doormat) promptly evaporated. His "typical plutocrat" bosses (played by Marlo Thomas and Whoopi Goldberg) arrive at work with wads of cash hidden under their hats and sleeves and in their arms. A sudden sneeze by Thomas sends the cash into the street, to be taken by passersby, so they blamed the media and fired the bear. Kermit and his fellow Muppets are somewhat taken aback, one remarking, "Not much to say to that." While tongue-in-cheek, the willingness of both Henson and the Russian producers to spoof the stereotyped images of their respective socioeconomic systems is refreshing and laid the groundwork for further Muppet inroads in the waning years of the Soviet Union.

The success of the special and of Henson's goodwill tours led to an experiment: a test broadcast of *Fraggle Rock* over Soviet television in April 1989. The broadcast achieved unprecedented ratings and mail from 3,500 viewers, persuading the governing body to broadcast that program and *The Muppet Show*. Soviet entrepreneurs contacted Henson about merchandising rights as well. Henson thus had the distinction of producing the first Western television series to air in Russia, for though the Soviet Union's control was waning and would officially dissolve in 1991, state control of programming remained strong. The fact that Muppets were first in Moscow is a testament to their international appeal, to Henson's own skills as a negotiator and ambassador (just as he'd deployed them in commercials and in securing funding), and to the continuing enigma of the Muppets. The inroads Henson made in Russian television served simultaneously to further Western communication via pop culture and his own dreams of bringing peace to the world; they also opened up a new market. U.S. television producers were now better able to export their products to Russia, even before the so-called "Fall of Communism" was officially declared.

Despite the commercialism and merchandising, despite their slightly reduced status in the States, weathering Pepe's Long John Silver's ads and Piggy's predilection for pork, the Muppets themselves continue to survive. A new movie is currently in the works, and despite Disney's continual delays, *The Muppet Show*'s second and third season DVD sales have proven profitable. In late 2006, Disney inked a deal with French channel TF3 to produce an all new *Muppet Show* specifically for French audiences. While Mickey Mouse is now seen primarily as a symbol of either big business or cultural imperialism, Kermit and company are still protected by their roles as sage jesters; just as they were free to blow each other up without tainting their image, they survive Denny's and Disney Channel specials as back-up to Hannah Montana. Individual Muppets have become casualties (you won't see any Scooter dolls), but on the whole, they continue to transcend socioeconomic boundaries and somehow survive the financial setbacks; as Gonzo and Rizzo noted in *The Muppet Treasure Island* DVD commentary, "Don't you just love capitalism?"

As of 2008, the Muppets, along with the global economy, have undergone many changes and struggles. In 1978, John Skow of *Time* Magazine could express his firm confidence in the soundness of Muppets: "What is small and green, and surrounded by confusion, and is applauded each week by more people than there are in the entire U.S.? No, not the wobbling dollar, but a more cheerful and indeed more bankable asset: Kermit the Frog." Today, the dollar still weaves and falls, but Kermit himself has not always been securely perched. As a character, he's mostly comfortable on the arms of Steve Whitmire, but as an asset, icon, and media celebrity, the ownership shifts and round robin buy and sell have left the Muppet assets divided. The DVD releases of *Emmet Otter's Jug-Band Christmas* and *The Christmas Toy*, specials still owned by the Henson Company and originally bookended by the frog, have simply excised his scenes rather than come to terms with Disney. However, the world of "new media," online and downloadable, has helped to reacquaint audiences and consumers with the frog and friends. Sesame Workshop has limited Kermit clips on the show, but via their 2008 website relaunch with a vast video archive, most of his clips are now easily found (he's listed as a "special guest star" in the cast/character bios). New viral Muppet clips and the portal on Disney's website have helped with the revival, showcasing not only the charms of Kermit but also the musical talents of Beaker and the incoherence of the Swedish Chef.

Today, nearly twenty years after his death, the popular image of Jim Henson is that of a dreamy, gentle hippie with a beard who worked with puppets and wanted to bring peace to the world. The Henson Company and family, since selling the Muppets to Disney, has fostered that image through the use of Henson's "doodles" in merchandise and through assorted books (such as *It's Not Easy Being Green* and *Doodle Dreams*) that further that interpretation. While there's a certain amount of truth to that, these books tend to gloss over or utterly ignore Henson's commercial work or his own way of negotiating that world. As manager Bernie Brillstein recalls, the actual Jim Henson in essence "had two careers: one public and successful, the other personal and noncommercial. They fed each other." By 1989, in truth, Henson had indeed agreed to sell the Muppets to Disney (excluding the *Sesame Street* Muppets, so as to once again protect their role as commercial-free educators). Yet the deal would also have included the purchase of Henson's personal creativity and expertise, and thus allowed Jim Henson to retain creative control over his characters while delegating the sales and merchandising and business aspects completely to other hands. Henson's death and the loss of that personal creativity scuppered the deal. The latest Muppet TV special, *Letters to Santa*, debuted on December 17th on NBC with impressive ratings, but only two out of 17 puppeteers had actually worked significantly with Jim Henson. The name Henson is completely absent from the credits, in fact, and the Muppets themselves are now maintained not by the Muppet Workshop but by an independent company called Puppet Heap (formed by *Bear in the Big Blue House* designer Paul Andrejco, with a few *Sesame* or Henson company veterans). Still, the Muppets have proven time and again that they can transcend socioeconomic borders, so one can only hope that they can weather the continued struggles to place them in today's market. After all, the time is ripe once again for Kermit and Fozzie to help calculate the national debt.

Works Cited

Beard, Henry. *Miss Piggy's Guide to Life*. New York: Muppet Press, Alfred A. Knopf. 1981.
Brillstein, Bernie. *Where Did I Go Right? You're No One in Hollywood Unless Someone Wants You Dead*. New York: Little, Brown, 1999.
CTW Archives. Boxes 35, 37, and others. Internal correspondence, episode records, and other documents.
Finch, Christopher. *Of Muppets and Men: The Making of the Muppet Show*. New York: Muppet Press/Alfred A. Knopf. 1981.
Free to Be ... a Family. Dir. Gary Halvorson. 1988. Videocassette. Family Home Entertainment.
Gould, Jack. "Cinderella as ABC Classic." *The New York Times*. April 11, 1970.
Great Performances. *The World of Jim Henson*. Dir. Sarah Lukinson.
Horn, Danny. *Muppetfest Memories*. December 8–9, 2001. Fanzine.
Kanfer, Stefan. "Who's Afraid of Big Bad TV?" *Time*. 23 Nov. 1970.
The Muppet Christmas Carol. Dir. Brian Henson. Screenplay by Jerry Juhl. Perf. Michael Caine, Dave Goelz, Steve Whitmire, Jerry Nelson, and Frank Oz. 1992. DVD. Disney, 2005.
Skow, John. "Those Marvelous Muppets." *Time*. 25 Dec. 1978.

Appendix: The Muppet Show

Season by Season

Episodes are listed as they appear on the DVD collection or as they were originally aired in the case of unreleased seasons as of publication of this text (Seasons 4 and 5).

GUEST STARS, SEASON ONE / SERIES ONE

1.1	Juliet Prowse — South African–born dancer, singer, and actress
1.2	Connie Stevens — American actress and singer
1.3	Joel Grey — American actor, singer, and dancer
1.4	Ruth Buzzi — American comedienne and actress
1.5	Rita Moreno — American singer and actress
1.6	Jim Nabors — American actor and singer
1.7	Florence Henderson — American actress
1.8	Paul Williams — American actor, singer, and songwriter
1.9	Charles Aznavour — French actor, singer, and songwriter
1.10	Harvey Korman — American comedic actor
1.11	Lena Horne — American actress and singer
1.12	Peter Ustinov — British actor, author and raconteur
1.13	Bruce Forsyth — British game show host and entertainer
1.14	Sandy Duncan — American actress and singer
1.15	Candice Bergen — American television actress, daughter of Edgar Bergen, famed ventriloquist
1.16	Avery Schreiber — American comedian, writer, director, and actor
1.17	Ben Vereen — American singer, dancer, and actor
1.18	Phyllis Diller — American comedienne and actress
1.19	Vincent Price — American author, gourmet, art aficionado, and actor
1.20	Valerie Harper — American actress and writer
1.21	Twiggy — British model, singer, and actress
1.22	Ethel Merman — American actress and Broadway singer

1.23 Kaye Ballard — American actress and Broadway singer
1.24 Mummenschanz — Swiss experimental performance art group

Guest Stars, Season Two / Series Two

2.1 Don Knotts — American comedic actor
2.2 Zero Mostel — American comedian, actor, and singer
2.3 Milton Berle — American comedic actor ("Mr. Television")
2.4 Rich Little — American comedian and impersonator
2.5 Judy Collins — American folk singer and songwriter
2.6 Nancy Walker — American comedienne and actress
2.7 Edgar Bergen — American ventriloquist
2.8 Steve Martin — American actor, comedian, and writer
2.9 Madeline Kahn — American actress, comedienne, and singer
2.10 George Burns — American actor, comedian, and singer
2.11 Dom DeLuise — American comedic actor
2.12 Bernadette Peters — American actress and Broadway singer
2.13 Rudolf Nureyev — Russian-born ballet dancer and actor
2.14 Elton John — British singer, pianist, and songwriter
2.15 Lou Rawls — American rhythm and blues singer and actor
2.16 Cleo Laine — British jazz singer
2.17 Julie Andrews — British actress and Broadway singer
2.18 Jaye P. Morgan — American actress and singer
2.19 Peter Sellers — British comedic actor
2.20 Petula Clark — British actress and pop singer
2.21 Bob Hope — American comedian and actor
2.22 Teresa Brewer — American pop singer, songwriter, and author
2.23 John Cleese — British comedic actor and writer
2.24 Cloris Leachman — American comedic actress

Guest Stars, Season Three / Series Three

3.1 Kris Kristofferson and Rita Coolidge — American actor and country/western singer and songwriter (Kristofferson); American country/western singer (Coolidge)
3.2 Leo Sayer — British pop singer
3.3 Roy Clark — American country/western singer and banjo player
3.4 Gilda Radner — American comedic actress
3.5 Pearl Bailey — American singer, songwriter, and actress
3.6 Jean Stapleton — American comedic actress
3.7 Alice Cooper — American shock singer and songwriter
3.8 Loretta Lynn — American country/western singer and songwriter
3.9 Liberace — America concert pianist
3.10 Marisa Berenson — American model and actress

3.11   Raquel Welch — American actress
3.12   James Coco — American comedic actor
3.13   Helen Reddy — Australian singer and actress
3.14   Harry Belafonte — American singer and actor
3.15   Lesley Ann Warren — American actress and singer
3.16   Danny Kaye — American comedic actor, singer, dancer and gourmand
3.17   Spike Milligan — Indian-born British comedic actor and writer
3.18   Leslie Uggams — American singer and actress
3.19   Elke Sommer — German actress
3.20   Sylvester Stallone — American actor
3.21   Roger Miller — American folk/country singer and songwriter
3.22   Roy Rogers and Dale Evans — American actor and actress famous for their singing Westerns (King and Queen of the Cowboys)
3.23   Lynn Redgrave — British actress
3.24   Cheryl Ladd — American model and actress

Guest Stars, Season Four / Series Four

4.1   John Denver — American country/folk singer and songwriter and actor
4.2   Crystal Gayle — American country singer
4.3   Shields & Yarnell — American mime duo
4.4   Dyan Cannon — American actress
4.5   Victor Borge — American comedic actor, classical pianist, conductor and composer
4.6   Linda Lavin — American actress
4.7   Dudley Moore — British comedian, pianist, and actor
4.8   Arlo Guthrie — American folk singer and songwriter
4.9   Beverly Sills — American soprano opera singer
4.10   Kenny Rogers — American country/western singer and songwriter
4.11   Lola Falana — American singer, dancer, and actress
4.12   Phyllis George — American actress and former Miss America
4.13   Dizzy Gillespie — American jazz trumpet player
4.14   Liza Minnelli — American actress and Broadway performer
4.15   Anne Murray — Canadian pop singer and songwriter
4.16   Jonathan Winters — American comedian and actor
4.17   *Star Wars* — Appearances by Mark Hamill (American actor) as himself and Luke Skywalker, C-3PO (Anthony Daniels — British actor), R2-D2, and Chewbacca (Peter Mayhew — British actor)
4.18   Christopher Reeve — American actor
4.19   Lynda Carter — American actress
4.20   Alan Arkin — American actor, author, singer, and composer
4.21   Doug Henning — Canadian-born magician
4.22   Andy Williams — American singer
4.23   Carol Channing — American actress and Broadway performer
4.24   Diana Ross — American singer

Guest Stars, Season Five / Series Five

- 5.1 Gene Kelly — American actor, singer, and dancer
- 5.2 Loretta Swit — American actress
- 5.3 Joan Baez — American folk singer and songwriter
- 5.4 Shirley Bassey — Welsh-born cabaret and jazz singer
- 5.5 James Coburn — American actor
- 5.6 Brooke Shields — American actress and model
- 5.7 Glenda Jackson — British actress and politician
- 5.8 Señor Wences — Spanish ventriloquist
- 5.9 Debbie Harry — American singer (lead singer for the rock group Blondie)
- 5.10 Jean-Pierre Rampal — French flautist
- 5.11 Paul Simon — American singer and songwriter
- 5.12 Melissa Manchester — American singer and songwriter
- 5.13 Tony Randall — American actor
- 5.14 Mac Davis — American singer
- 5.15 Carol Burnett — American comedienne and actress
- 5.16 Gladys Knight — American rhythm and blues singer
- 5.17 Hal Linden — American actor
- 5.18 Marty Feldman — British comedic actor
- 5.19 Chris Langham — British actor, comedian, and writer
- 5.20 Wally Boag — American actor, comedian, and balloon artist
- 5.21 Johnny Cash — American country/western singer and songwriter
- 5.22 Buddy Rich — American jazz percussionist and bandleader
- 5.23 Linda Ronstadt — American singer and actress
- 5.24 Roger Moore — British actor

The Cast and Their Original and Current Performers

Kermit the Frog (Jim Henson; other characters performed by Henson include Doctor Teeth and Link Hogthrob) [Kermit performed by Steve Whitmire since 1990.]

Fozzie Bear (Frank Oz) [Fozzie performed by Eric Jacobson since 2002.]

Miss Piggy (Frank Oz, although other puppeteers provided her movements and voice in some early episodes) [Piggy performed by Eric Jacobson since 2001.]

Gonzo the Great (Dave Goelz; other characters performed by Goelz include Bunsen Honeydew and Zoot)

Scooter (performed by Richard Hunt; others performed by Hunt include Sweetums and Janice) [Scooter performed since 1992 by multiple Muppet performers including Brian Henson and Adam Hunt.]

Waldorf (Jim Henson) [Waldorf performed by Dave Goelz since 1992.]

Statler (Richard Hunt) [Statler performed by Jerry Nelson (1992–2001) and Steve Whitmire (2002–Present).]

Sam the Eagle (Frank Oz) [Sam the Eagle performed alternately by Kevin Clash (2002, 2003), Eric Jacobson (2005, 2008) and Drew Massey (2005–06).]

Rowlf (Jim Henson) [Rowlf performed by Bill Barretta since 1996.]
Beaker (Richard Hunt) [Beaker performed by Steve Whitmire since 1992.]
The Swedish Chef (Jim Henson — voice and Frank Oz — hands) [The Swedish Chef has had several performers in the years since Henson's death; Bill Barretta has primarily performed the role since 1996.]
Animal (Frank Oz) [Animal performed by Eric Jacobson since 2002.]

Other TV Series Featuring The Muppet Show *Cast*

Muppet Babies (animated series) aired from 1984 to 1991 (CBS)
The Jim Henson Hour (featured "MuppeTelevision" sketches which attempted to update *The Muppet Show*) The first nine episodes aired on NBC from April to July 1989, episodes ten and eleven appeared on Nickelodeon in 1992 and 1993, and episode twelve, which never aired in the U.S., appeared on UK television in 1990.
Muppets Tonight aired on ABC in 1996 and on The Disney Channel in 1997 (Gonzo is the most prominent player of the original cast in this series.)

Muppet Television Specials

The following television specials feature the original cast of The Muppet Show as their stars.

The Muppets Valentine Special (1974)
John Denver and the Muppets: A Christmas Together (1979)
The Muppets Go to the Movies (1981)
The Fantastic Miss Piggy Show (1982)
Rocky Mountain Holiday with John Denver and the Muppets (1982)
The Muppets: A Celebration of 30 Years (1986)
A Muppet Family Christmas (1987)
Kermit's Swamp Years (2002)
It's a Very Merry Muppet Christmas Movie (2002)
The Muppets' Wizard of Oz (2005)
Studio DC: Almost Live Hosted by Dylan and Cole Sprouse (2008)
Studio DC: Almost Live Hosted by Selena Gomez (2008)
A Muppets Christmas: Letters to Santa (2008)

Muppets on Film

The Muppet Movie (1979)
The Great Muppet Caper (1981)
The Muppets Take Manhattan (1984)

The Muppet Christmas Carol (1992)
Muppet Treasure Island (1996)
Muppets from Space (1999)

Muppets on the Web

The following websites are a sampling of sites that contain interesting or helpful information for fans and scholars of *The Muppet Show* cast.

Muppet Central: www.muppetcentral.com
Disney.com|The Muppets: http://disney.go.com/dxd/index.html?channel=102451#/disneygroups/themuppets/
MuppetWiki: http://muppet.wikia.com/wiki/Muppet_Wiki

About the Contributors

Alissa Burger is a doctoral candidate in American culture studies at Bowling Green State University, where she focuses on film, literature, gender studies, and innovative transformations, such as that achieved by *The Muppets' Wizard of Oz*. Alissa's research interests include critical film theory; representations of gender, power, and magic; and the role of music in popular culture. Her favorite Muppets are the "Mahna Mahna" Snowths.

Anthony Cox is a co-director of the Centre for Psychology and Computing, which unfortunately is not as prestigious as Muppet Labs. He has a Ph.D. in computer science from the University of Waterloo and credits his success to the sound advice of Fozzie Bear, his favorite Muppet. When not publishing on the Muppets, he performs research in evolutionary psychology, human-computer interaction, and software engineering. As an independent consultant, he travels extensively and as often as he can with his spouse Maryanne Fisher.

Hugh H. Davis, instructor of English at Saint Mary's School in Raleigh, North Carolina, received his B.A. from the University of North Carolina and M.A. from the University of Tennessee. Currently president of the Popular Culture Association in the South, as an avid devotee of the study of popular culture, Davis integrates it into his teaching, often considering literary adaptations as transformations of texts. Among his publications is the first academic study of the Muppets, "A Weirdo, a Rat, and a Humbug: The Literary Qualities of *A Muppet Christmas Carol*," which appeared in *Studies in Popular Culture*. His favorite Muppet is Rowlf.

Rayna Denison, lecturer in film and television studies, University of East Anglia, UK, researches and writes on animation and transnational film cultures, particularly Asian and American film. She has published one other Muppets related article in *Intensities Journal* titled, "*The Muppet Show: Sex and Violence*: Investigating the Complexity of the Television Body." She is currently currently working on two book projects, *Film Genres: Anime* and *Viewing Ang Lee: Authorship and Adaptation*. Her favorite Muppet is Gonzo the Great.

Maryanne Fisher received her doctoral degree in experimental psychology in 2004, and her research interests primarily focus on the evolutionary basis of behavior, and sex/gender issues. She's an assistant professor at St. Mary's University in Halifax, Nova Scotia, where she's a member of the Department of Psychology, and the Women and Gender Studies program. She's also the co-director for the Center for Psychology and Computing. One day she hopes to create a Muppet-based personality inventory. She would love to be like Kermit or Dr. Teeth, but in reality, she's probably more like Miss Piggy. In her spare time, she likes to drive around town talking like Bobo and singing *Muppet Show* songs with her spouse, Anthony Cox.

Jennifer C. Garlen teaches English at the University of Alabama in Huntsville. A graduate of Agnes Scott College, Georgia Southern University, and Auburn University, she earned her doctoral degree in eighteenth-century British literature but now spends most of her academic energy teaching and studying popular literature, culture and film. She is a lifelong devotee of the Great Gonzo.

Anissa M. Graham teaches composition and literature as an instructor of English at the University of North Alabama. After receiving degrees from Georgia Southern University (B.A.) and Auburn University (M.A.), Anissa has gone on to pursue research interests in 18th and 19th century British fiction as well as popular culture topics, such as comic books, film, and music. Her favorite Muppet is Rowlf.

Gideon Haberkorn studied history and philosophy, as well as British and American literature and culture, at Gutenberg Universität Mainz, Germany. He is working on completing a Ph.D. in English, in order to find fame if not fortune in academia, and on completing his training as a teacher of English and philosophy, in order to find financial and vocational security in the real world. His research interests include realism, popular culture (although he hates the term), narratology, and the philosophy of mind. His favorite Muppet is the Great Gonzo.

Kathleen E. Kennedy is a mild-mannered medievalist by day, who moonlights as a Muppet critic. She is an assistant professor at Penn State–Brandywine. While Kennedy strives to emulate Grover's helpfulness, many might argue she resembles Gonzo more in being, as Kermit hedges, "distinct."

Andrew Leal received his M.A. in English literature from the University of Syracuse. He has contributed to the books *Animation Art* and *The Animated Movie Guide* and liner notes to the World War II–themed DVD *Cartoons for Victory*. Since 2006, he has been an administrator and key contributor to the online encyclopedia Muppet Wiki. Unlike Sam the Eagle, he does not consider Beethoven to be his favorite playwright.

Julie G. Maudlin is an assistant professor of early childhood education at Georgia Southern University, where she teaches undergraduate and graduate courses in teacher education and explores the connections between culture and curriculum. She is proud to ascribe to the Miss Piggy school of femininity, although she generally abstains from karate-chopping, which is greatly appreciated by her husband.

Tara K. Parmiter received her B.A. in English from Cornell and her Ph.D. from New York University, where she teaches in the Expository Writing Program. Her areas of interest include turn-of-the-twentieth century American women's fiction, literature and the environment, children's literature, and travel and captivity narratives. Tara has always been partial to Janice's laid-back, hippie vibe, though she's not quite ready to live on a beach and walk around naked.

Lynne D. Schneider earned her B.A. from the University of Michigan, Honors College, and an M.A. from Binghamton University, and is finishing work on a Ph.D. in early modern English literature. Her favorite Muppet is, of course, two Muppets, Waldorf and Statler, beloved for their dialogue of charming and vivacious wit.

Ginger Stelle has a B.A. in English from Southern Illinois University–Carbondale, an M.A. in English from Hardin-Simmons University in Abilene, Texas, and an M.A. in English from Baylor University in Waco, Texas. She is currently pursuing her Ph.D. in English at the University of St. Andrews in St. Andrews, Scotland, with a specialization in 19th century literature and a secondary interest in literature and film. She is particularly interested in the way various texts (both in literature and film) participate in ongoing conversations with one another. Perhaps this accounts for her interest in the Muppets, because with every project the Muppet team undertakes, the conversation grows. Furthermore, she considers *The Muppets Christmas Carol* to be the greatest film adaptation of Dickens's classic novella ever made. Having grown up watching the Muppets, she has always appreciated the Muppets' uniquely self-reflexive style of humor and their ability to walk perfectly the line between genuine homage and brilliant parody.

Jennifer Stoessner has a doctoral degree in theatre history, literature, and criticism from Ohio State University. Her research focuses on contemporary performance and American puppetry and her dissertation is entitled "Building American Puppetry on the Jim Henson Foundation." She is a professional puppeteer and is currently the education programs associate at La Jolla Playhouse in California. Though she has a Kermit tattoo, her heart belongs to Gonzo the Great.

Ben Underwood is a Ph.D. student in English at the University of Illinois at Chicago, where he focuses on twentieth-century/contemporary literature and critical theory. He is currently assistant director of the First-Year Writing Program at UIC, and associate editor of ebr: electronic book review <www.electronicbookreview.com>. After a stint in the Muppet All-Star Cover Band, Underwood has modeled his life after Kermit the Frog.

Index

Advertising 202–216
American ideals 136–137
Angel (television series) 65–66
Animal 9, 13, 98–99
Art 25, 38, 40, 116–126
Ashanti 111
Astor, William Waldorf 43–44
"At the Dance" (sketch) 50
Authorship 155–168
Avenue Q 78

Backstage 18–19, 20–21, 29
Barr, Roseanne 195–196
Beaker 96–97
Beauregard 75–76
"Bein' Green" (song) 65–66
Big Bird 212
Big Bird in China 212–213
Bradshaw, Richard 73
Brooks, Garth 88–89
Brown, Murphy 195–196

Capitalism 10–11
Carnival 27–28, 40
A Christmas Carol 94–101
"Classical Chicken" (video) 125
Cleese, John 149–150
Cookie Monster 82–83, 205
Coolio 89
Cooper, Alice 58, 60, 61–63, 67, 170
Culture 116–126, 172
Curriculum theory 170–180

The Dark Crystal 77
DeLuise, Dom 148–149
Dr. Teeth 150–151
Dreams 9–22
Duncan, Sandy 144–145
DVD 164–167

The Ed Sullivan Show 55, 142–143
Education 170–180

The Electric Mayhem 98–99
Ellsworth, Milton Statler 44
Elmo 83
European tour 132–133

F Troop 57
Fairy tales 103, 113–115
Family 9, 14, 140
"Fever" (song) 146
Forsyth, Bruce 160
Fourth wall 20, 23
Fozzie 21, 23, 49, 52, 58, 76–77, 97, 98, 129–130, 133, 138
Free to Be … a Family 213–214
Freud, Sigmund 51

Gale, Dorothy 110–113
Gender 30–32, 36, 110–113, 181–200
Generation X 125–6
Genre 15, 17–21
Gibson, Mel 83–84
Goelz, Dave 16, 34
Gold, Louise 162–163
Gonzo 32–33, 34, 58, 62, 77, 86, 89, 95–96, 116–126, 150
Gorgon Heap 59
Grade, Lord Lew 13, 161–162
Great Britain 154–168
The Great Muppet Caper 23, 93, 132–134, 182, 187
Grosse, J.P. 208

Hamlet 83–84
The Happiness Hotel 136–137
Harper, Valerie 18–19, 50
Henson, Jim 11–12, 71–73, 74, 77–79, 162, 202–216, 174–175, 180
Herb Alpert and the Tijuana Brass Band Special 186
Hogthrob, Link 148
Honeydew, Bunsen 96–97
Hopper, Doc 9–22, 140, 209

Index

Identity 10, 14, 25–27, 31, 33–37, 64, 135
It's a Very Merry Muppet Christmas 125
"I've Grown Accustomed to Your Face" (song) 143

Jim Henson Foundation 77–78
Jim Henson Presents: The World of Puppetry 78
The Jimmy Dean Show 84
Juhl, Jerry 182, 183

Kermit, Prince of Denmark 89–90
Kermit the Frog 9–22, 20, 55–56, 59–60, 61, 65, 66, 75–76, 96, 97–98, 110, 129–130, 131–136, 140, 143, 175–176, 177, 179–180, 182, 187, 190–193, 205–206, 209

Leo 207
Lombardo, Guy 59

Martin, Steve 23
Merman, Ethel 19, 56–57
Miss Piggy 31–32, 56, 62, 76, 88, 106, 133–134, 146, 150, 181–200, 210
Money 202–216
"Monsterpiece Theater" 82–83
Moreno, Rita 145–147, 152
Morgan, Jaye P. 148, 152
"Movin' Right Along" 129–130
Muppephone, Marvin Suggs and the Amazing 151
Muppet Babies 199
The Muppet Christmas Carol 94–101, 124–125, 182, 191, 192, 211–212
A Muppet Family Christmas 192, 197
"Muppet Morsels" 165–166
The Muppet Movie 9–11, 13, 19–22, 93, 129–132, 135–136, 139–140, 182, 188, 197, 208
The Muppet Show see individual characters, guest stars, and sketches
Muppet Treasure Island 182
Muppets from Space 33, 182, 197
The Muppets Take Manhattan 13–14, 93, 134–135, 181, 187, 192, 195, 197
Muppets Tonight! 88
The Muppets Wizard of Oz 103–115
Myth 104–105, 114–115

National identity 154–68
New York 138–139
Nureyev, Rudolf 123, 193

Oz, Frank 31–32, 161, 186

"Panel Discussion" (sketch) 145–146, 176–177
Parody 4, 114
Performance Art 117
Performativity 107–110
The Phantom of the Muppet Show see Uncle Deadly
"Pigs in Space" (sketch) 189
Pinocchio 75
Playboy 198
Price, Vincent 57–60, 63, 67
Princess Leia 193–194
Proscenium arch 45–47, 49
Prowse, Juliet 48
Punch and Judy 75–76
Puppeteers of America 72
Puppetry 3, 71–79

Queen Victoria 120

Rats (Muppets) 98
Reality television 106–107
Reeve, Christopher 87
Richard III 119–120
Rizzo 95–96
Road film 131
Rowlf 84, 138, 157–159

Sam and Friends 16–17, 71, 84
Sam the American Eagle 62–63, 87, 99, 121–124, 176–177
Schwartz, Bruce 73–74
Scooter 21
Sellers, Peter 86, 119–120, 148, 159
Sesame Street 81–84, 171–174, 177, 204–206
Sex 142–152
Shakespeare, William 47, 81–90, 120, 123
"Sherlock Holmes and the Case of the Disappearing Clues" 158
Sills Beverly 124
Sketches see individual titles
Solo, Han 194
Stallone, Sylvester 150
Stapleton, Jean 149
Statler and Waldorf 21–22, 40–53, 88, 97, 100–101, 175
Stevens, Connie 45
The Swedish Chef 76–77

"Talk Spot" (sketch) 146
Tarantino, Quentin 109–110
Thompson, Hunter S. 121

Time Piece 204
Travel narratives 130–140
Twiggy 159

Uncle Deadly 85
Ustinov, Peter 159–160

Variety show 3
Vaudeville 15–17, 20–21
The Very Best of the Muppet Show 165
"Veterinarian's Hospital" (sketch) 85–86, 188–189
Violence 142–152

Waldorf *see* Statler and Waldorf
Warren, Lesley Ann 150–152

Wayne and Wanda 50, 122
Welch, Raquel 88
Wences, Señor 74
Whatnot Muppets 34
Whedon, Joss 65–66
The Wizard of Oz 103–115, 136
Wonder Woman 194

Xena: Warrior Princess 195

Yorick (Muppet) 55–56, 84
YouTube 125

Zealand, Lew 90

www.ingramcontent.com/pod-product-compliance
Ingram Content Group UK Ltd.
Pitfield, Milton Keynes, MK11 3LW, UK
UKHW041948140426
5217IPUK00014B/704